ALSO BY MIKE BYNUM

High Tide, A Story of Class and Courage
Bryant—The Man, the Myth
Never Say Quit
Aggie Pride
We Believe
Bound for Glory
Bear Bryant's Boys of Autumn
Knute Rockne: His Life and Legend
Vince Lombardi: Memories of a Special Time

MANY AUTUMNS AGO

THE FRANK LEAHY ERA AT BOSTON COLLEGE AND NOTRE DAME

MANY AUTUMNS AGO

THE FRANK LEAHY ERA AT
BOSTON COLLEGE AND NOTRE DAME

*Edited
by*
MIKE BYNUM

October Football Corp.

Portions of this book have been previously published. Listed below is their original source of publication:

The game stories in Chapter 1 and Chapters 3-6 first appeared in the *Boston Globe*.

The game stories in Chapter 2 and 19 first appeared in *The New York Times*.

The game stories in Chapters 7-18 and 20-40 first appeared in the *Chicago Tribune*.

Arch Ward's story on Frank Leahy in his book, "Frank Leahy and The Fighting Irish." Copyright © 1944 by Arch Ward. Reprinted by permission of the estate of Arch Ward.

Jacket Cover Artwork: Dennis Luzak, Greenwich, CT
Jacket Cover Design: David Hirsch Design Group, Chicago, IL
Book Design: O'Rourke Graphics, Chicago, IL
Book Lithograph: R.R. Donnelley & Sons Company, Chicago, IL

ISBN: 0-945718-01-2
Library of Congress Catalog Card Number: 88-62020
Copyright © 1988 by October Football Corp.
ALL RIGHTS RESERVED UNDER INTERNATIONAL AND
PAN AMERICAN COPYRIGHT CONVENTIONS
PRINTED IN THE UNITED STATES OF AMERICA
FIRST EDITION

FOR MONSIGNIOR GEORGE KERR, FREDDIE MILLER
AND ZIGGIE CZAROBSKI —
THREE WHO GAVE THEIR ALL FOR ALMA MATER.

Contents

FOREWORD / i

A TIME FOR GREATNESS / 3
    by David Condon

THE BOSTON COLLEGE YEARS / 27

FATE BRINGS A DATE WITH DESTINY / 63
    by Arch Ward

THE NOTRE DAME YEARS / 77

AFTERWORD / 229

APPENDIX / 233

MANY AUTUMNS AGO

THE FRANK LEAHY ERA AT BOSTON COLLEGE AND NOTRE DAME

Foreword

It was late in the evening of September 12, 1981, and the flicker of the candles' light had reached full glow. With each hour that passed in the Monogram Room in the Athletic & Convocation Center on the campus of the University of Notre Dame, the toasts, the laughter and the old football stories all seemed to grow a bit larger. Once again, Frank Leahy's boys had returned to Camelot for another of their always-memorable reunions.

They were gathered here to commemorate the 40th anniversary of Leahy's first Notre Dame team in 1941, and the 35th anniversary of the 1946 national championship team. They had all travelled from faraway places for this formal affair. The Monogram Room was packed full to its seams.

Annually, Leahy's boys make this trek to Notre Dame to celebrate the many successes that they once enjoyed. There was, of course, a lot to celebrate. Their eleven-year era was the most colorful and, perhaps, the greatest in the history of college football.

After building a powerhouse squad at Boston College in 1939 and 1940, which included a 20-2 record and that cherished victory over Tennessee in the 1941 Sugar Bowl, Leahy took over the head-coaching reins from Four Horseman Elmer Layden in February 1941 and quickly reestablished Notre Dame's place among the elite of the college football world. It was a lofty status which they were to dominate until the end of the 1953 season when illness forced Leahy to retire. But what a memorable stretch run. Four national championships, four Heisman Trophy winners, 22 all-America and a 87-11-9 record. Nobody did it better than Leahy's teams.

In the 1940s and the 1950s, America was still in search of its heroes. And they packed the big stadiums in New York, Cleveland, New Orleans, Baltimore, Los Angeles and South Bend, to view these great gridiron contests involving their team — Notre Dame. Wherever the Fighting Irish were playing, you were sure to have a clan meeting of the great newspaper sportswriters.

As the revelry in the Monogram Room began to hit high gear, one of Leahy's players recounted to me that on a train ride en route to play Penn in 1952, he remembered waking up as the train slowed down while passing through a small town. "It was early morning, and there standing on the station platform were 25 to 30 children with a few nuns who were waving at us. They were all holding a big banner which read: 'Go Fighting Irish, Beat Penn.' It was a sight which made all of us proud. Very proud."

Now, some 35 years after Leahy's boys had played their last game, it is time to take a look back at their greatness once again. *Many Autumns Ago* is the first volume of a two-volume series which will hopefully rekindle memories of this special time.

Volume I attempts to recount the great history which Leahy's boys created. Countless hours were spent in libraries across the country in an attempt to find those game stories that America's best newspaper sportswriters had penned. The two sections, *A Time for Greatness* and *A Date With Destiny*, were written by David Condon and Arch Ward, respectively. These two great sportswriters from the *Chicago Tribune* knew Leahy and his teams best.

The second volume to *Many Autumns Ago* will attempt to bring to life the wonderful story of Charlie O'Rourke, Ziggie Czarobski, Angelo Bertelli, Johnny Lujack, George Connor, Jerry Groom, Dan Shannon and the others who made the Frank Leahy era so unique.

I'm sure that in the pages that follow you will enjoy this sentimental journey to yesteryear.

Mike Bynum
Birmingham, Alabama
August 8, 1988

A Time for Greatness
by David Condon

A Time For Greatness

"Show me a hero, and I will write you a tragedy."
—*F. Scott Fitzgerald*

CHICAGO — The Master lives.
The Master became legendary in a lifetime that began in O'Neill, Neb., and concluded 15 years ago today.
Two different natal dates — only days apart — are found. No matter: Coach Francis W. Leahy died in a Portland, Ore., Lutheran hospital only weeks short of his 65th birthday. Yet a decade and one-half after burial on the Congregation of Holy Cross University of Portland campus, a half-continent removed from his beloved Notre Dame, The Master lives in memory, legend and myth.
Biographers have problems sorting fact from a subject's balky memory as well as from myth. The task was only slightly less difficult for the late Wells Twombley, Leahy's official biographer ("Shake Down The Thunder") because Twombley's tape-recorded interviews came during the final weeks; Twombley was at the hospital when Leahy eased into eternity, and spread the report to the media. Twombley interviewed Leahy's wife, Floss, and the Leahy children, as well as other kin, former players and Notre Dame officials. He had access to personal papers and memorabilia. Twombley's major handicap, however, was lack of long acquaintance and intimacy with The Master.
Frank Leahy seemed indestructible when we met at Notre Dame in 1941. As an assistant to Jim Crowley at Fordham, he had forged

the "Seven Blocks of Granite" line (Vince Lombardi, et al.). Frank then took a head-coaching job, quickly turning Boston College into a powerhouse. After two seasons he was summoned to Notre Dame, his alma mater, to succeed Elmer Layden, who, following the 1940 season, was lateraled into the National Football League's commissionership. By mid-autumn of 1941, there was confidence that Leahy was directing the Irish to their first unbeaten gridiron campaign since Knute Rockne's 1930 finale, a national championship campaign that found senior tackle Leahy sidelined with a knee injury but religiously studying Rockne's strategems.

O-o-o-o-o-o, yes, lads, in 1941 Frank Leahy seemed a living Gibraltar. Who envisioned this physical legend succumbing to an accumulation of miseries, including leukemia and heart trouble? Ironically, when the end was near despite Leahy's self-denial, I was the first to sense he had accepted the inevitable appointment in Samarra. Leahy was in Chicago for meetings with his employer and greatest benefactor, Canteen Corporation's Patrick L. O'Malley. One night I picked up Coach at an economy hotel to dine at Sportsman's Park race track. The Master pecked at his meal, half-heartedly made a few $2 bets, and very soon suggested departure. Crimson oozed through his shirt; that afternoon leukemia had dictated another blood transfusion. The Master stood and forlornly asked: "David, would you kindly assist me up those short steps?"

The oh, so physically proud man stared defiantly ahead as we departed. An hour later I told my wife: "Tonight I saw a brave man start to die." Patricia listened, then said: "Remember in 1955 when Coach took us aside at the Eliots' party? You had officially been the *Tribune's* sports columnist just four months. Remember, Coach said, 'Lad, have you suffered sufficiently to accept success? Are you sure you want to pay a horrible price?' "

I remembered. There are so many things to remember about The Master. Not all memories conform to the myths. Yet Leahy never pulled his punches, nor did he ask your punches to be pulled. There was a night I berated The Master for his still smouldering grudge against Terry Brennan. Leahy excused himself brusquely and strode into the lonesome night. Baseball's Charlie O. Finley whispered: "Frank barely could restrain himself from punching you."

Terry Brennan, only 25 when he succeeded a cavalierly dismissed

Leahy, always was a sore subject to introduce in Leahy's presence. Two hours after Brennan had confirmed the *Tribune's* scoop on his firing, Leahy telephoned to say: "David, the wire services have asked for comment on the Brennan dismissal. Listen to my statement:

" 'I appreciate the contributions Terry Brennan made to three of my undefeated teams....' "

"Coach, you can't take a cheap shot at Terry."

A vehement argument ensued. Reluctantly, The Master permitted me to issue a bland statement. If he could not bury, neither would he praise. Leahy compromised more that night than had Rev. Theodore Hesburgh, Notre Dame's president, two years previously. Brennan's 2 and 7 Irish were then at Southern Cal. In Chicago, *Tribune* editor Don Maxwell showed me a wire story quoting Leahy on Notre Dame's lackluster performances. "Get reaction from former coaches, and others," said Maxwell.

First was Hunk Anderson. Hunk wasted no profanity in blasting Leahy. Elmer Layden was as critical but less profane. Reached in Los Angeles, Terry said he would make a blistering retort after the game, but added: "It's vindictiveness. Frank is mad because I will not let Paul Hornung appear on his television show... when he was at Notre Dame he took strong precautions against the players being distracted...." Brennan added many details.

Father Hesburgh was reached and said: "Brennan is not going to make any statement."

"But he already has made it to me, and I feel free to print it after the game."

"Terry will lose his job if he is quoted," said President Hesburgh.

When I quickly reported back to Terry, I said: "... but you have a contract." Terry laughed at my naivete and said, "Dave, who has a firm contract with Notre Dame?"

"Well, give the kid a break, but someday let Father Hesburgh know we run our paper," said Maxwell, who later joined the Hesburgh Fan Club. As an afterthought, the editor added: "Remember when young Father Hesburgh became president? I assigned you to do a flattering story."

Yes, I remembered. Father Hesburgh's secretary laughed as she said: "He even makes his own coffee. Father (John J.) Cavanaugh never made coffee."

Father Hesburgh drove me about campus in his tiny Studebaker. He bought ice cream cones. He showed me where he hoped to build a major laboratory and said he was proud that Notre Dame had never turned out an Alger Hiss. We wound up atop O'Shaughnessy Hall, which was still under construction. Hesburgh gazed afar, then suggested that such a vantage point would "end Leahy's secret practices."

Lads, the end also was coming for The Master. He was berated for his "sucker" shift that pulled opponents offside although we never heard criticism of the coach from whom Leahy copied the maneuver. At the winter clan meeting, Columbia's Lou Little offered a "suppose?" ND returned a kickoff to the Columbia 7, and then suckered Columbia with the shift. What would Leahy say about that action? "If we returned only to Columbia's 7, I'd say, 'My, but Coach Little's defense has improved,' " quipped Leahy.

In 1953, Leahy's "greatest" team twice rallied to tie Iowa 14-14 as Frank Varrichione "fainted" to stop time and prolong ND scoring drives late in each half. The dramatics were old when Mathuselah was a scrub, yet Iowans howled about ND's cheap tactics (a Hawkeye subsequently revealed he was Iowa's "designated fainter"). Veteran *Chicago Tribune* reporter Irv Vaughan never went to locker rooms. Yet Twombley's Leahy biography cites Irv's bathhouse dialogue with Varrichione. The facts: To oldster Irv the tactic was commonplace. He ignored the incidents and quickly wrote his game story. He sped back to Chicago, paused at the *Tribune,* and was faced with wire stories about the "faints." Grumbling much ado about nothing, Vaughan rewrote his account — borrowing a few of Varrichione's wire service quotes.

Then Vaughan again told a tale often heard from his deceased contemporary in our department, University of Chicago's all-time great back, Walter Eckersall. Eckie was a widely-recruited Chicago prep phenom almost 90 years ago. He selected Michigan and entrained for Ann Arbor. But Chicago's Mr. Clean, Amos Alonzo "Grand Old Man" Stagg, boarded the train on Chicago's South Side. He confronted Eckie with proof that Eckersall had played pro baseball under an assumed name. Stagg would divulge the professionalism unless Eckie matriculated at Chicago. Eckie quickly opted for Chicago.

So much for ethics of long ago. Neither Leahy nor Rock invented gridiron chicanery although both tested elasticity of the rules. Years ago an eastern Catholic school always called back a seminarian, whose eligibility was long exhausted, for crucial games. Edward "Slip" Madigan of ND first made California St. Mary's great with transient athletes. Notre Dame might have forgotten both Gipp and The Four Horsemen had it not bounced out (for academics) a freshman who sometimes played professionally as Johnny Blood while using his real name, John McNally, in college, wherever.

When Buddy Parker was preparing his N.F.L. champion Lions for the 1953 College All-Star game, he offered $500 to Bill Daddio — later a Joe Kuharich aide at ND — to spy on the collegians. Daddio refused. Meanwhile, what was on the mind of Georgia Tech's Bobby Dodd, the Collegians' coach? Dodd was begging me to place a spy in Detroit's den. The previous year, when Dodd coached the All-Stars against the pro champion Rams, the collegians' espionage was handled by a big-name, West Coast figure obtained by Red Sanders of U.C.L.A.

ND grad Bud Dudley, as athletic director at Villanova, scheduled Georgia for the "Grocery Bowl." No national TV then, the smaller schools had curtailed scouting expenses. But coaches could exchange a game movie. Bud asked Georgia's Wally Butts for a particular film, and asked what Villanova movie Butts required in return. "Jes' try'n fine one Ah might not already hev," said Butts.

Jack Leahy, my classmate at Notre Dame, spied on a Boston College arch-rival for Uncle Frank and, telephoning his report in freezing weather, declared he was near pneumonia. "Fine, lad," said Leahy. "Now give me their space alignment."

The second year at Boston College, Leahy attempted a win-for-the-Gipper strategem. The father of a BC player had died the previous season while BC was dueling an arch-rival. Now, a season later, the same foe was outside and the fatherless athlete again dressed to do for BC. Leahy somberly wanted his lads to realize that the deceased parent would be spiritually assisting BC, so he rambled something like this: "We shall emerge triumphant because they can use only 11 athletes. But today we have 12 men going for us...."

"We looked at each other quizzically," remembered Bob Jauron, "wondering if maybe Coach had gotten to the ref."

Coach delighted recalling skullduggery at Notre Dame. Like a summer when players could practice informally. Leahy asked Rev. John J. Cavanaugh, then executive vice-president: "May we dig a giant latrine, surrounded by canvas, on Cartier Field? It would save time that the lads waste walking to the fieldhouse."

"A practical idea," agreed Father Cavanaugh.

How practical? Within the enclosure would be The Master, McKeever and other coaches, directing drills through openings in the canvas. "Most embarrassing, though, was sneaking onto the coaching tower at 6 a.m. to direct 'informal' practices, and later learning that my voice was heard by everyone awake at that hour," Leahy related.

Testimony warranting credence demands one give foxy Michigan coach Fritz Crisler an "A" for both effort and candor in seeking first-hand information to prepare his 1942 Wolverines for the first ND–Michigan game since 1909. Crisler had a brainstorm. Just perhaps Leahy might be conducting a practice as informally as Layden sometimes had done. Who dared hallucinate that Fritz Crisler would attend a Notre Dame practice? So Crisler and entourage did approach Cartier Field. Alas, a manager was at the gate. Fritz did not concel his identity. Soon word came that Leahy was not receiving. Would Crisler leave his card?

P.S. Michigan won, 32-20.

Encountering athletes on campus, Leahy always had stock questions for their welfare but seldom let answers penetrate. One day, while meeting Creighton Miller or Johnny Lujack or some similar jester, Leahy asked in usual order:

"How is your health, lad?"

"Horrible, Coach. I'm weak, have the flu, and my heart is bouncing around."

"Very fine, lad. Fine indeed. And your grades?"

"Pretty bad, Coach. Flunking three subjects and in trouble with another."

"Wonderful, lad. How are your fine parents?"

"Well, my father and mother were in a horrible car accident last week. Both critical in the hospital."

"Sensational, lad. See you at practice."

With America at war, ND legend Red Miller ordered his son,

Creighton — the greatest runner on my all-time ND team — to forego football practice and concentrate on studies. The Master reminded Red of the Miller family's great football tradition at Notre Dame. "But I want him to get the grades," declared Red. Leahy responded, "Don't worry, I'll take care of the grades." It was the wrong thing to say to a man as honorable at Red Miller. Fortunately for Notre Dame, Creighton's blood pressure made him ineligible for military service and his all-America running was vital in Leahy's 1943 championship season.

War brought some familiar and, fortunately, most friendly faces, back to ND. One was Hugh Devore, a legend who defied Leahy's massive array of ends to try to block him. The other was Edward "Moose" Krause, whom The One Great Scorer may mark as a greater ND legend than Gipp, Rock, The Horsemen, Ara, or The Master.

Leahy summoned Krause to his suite at a convention early in World War II and offered the Holy Cross aide a football assistant's job at Notre Dame. Moose began weeping and long-distanced his wife: "Mother, we're going home. I'm with Coach Leahy. He's giving me a job...."

Krause's return paid more dividends than ND anticipated. He directed the football team on some occasions of Leahy's illness, claiming to be the only modern-time Irish head coach with a totally undefeated record. One game, Boss Krause wondered why the players did not race onto the field after his fiery, pre-game locker room oratory. Finally, an athlete asked: "Who's going to start?" Emotionally, Krause cried: "We'll all start." Eventually, Krause went to war but returned bigger than ever. He took over the basketball job, which had been passed around after the death of George Keogan in 1943. Moose became assistant athletic director, then athletic director, the perfect Rotarian to salve egos galled by The Master. He jests that his greatest contribution was firing himself as basketball coach. His magnificence, though, was running interference for Leahy.

Now, as it was in the beginning....

It was great to be young, and a Notre Damer, in the Indian Summer of 1941. Campus life was casual. Dining hall meals still were served by white-coated waiters. World War II seemed as remote as the moon, although Notre Dame had introduced a Naval R.O.T.C.

program, and faculty members were split on intervention. Beloved English prof Frank O'Malley and Dr. Francis McMahon were national figures arguing for intervention; Rev. John A. O'Brien was an isolationist running with Montana Senator Burton Wheeler and *Chicago Tribune* publisher Robert R. McCormick. A few students were always departing for the "peace time" draft. On the whole, however, campus life was happy. Hundreds upon hundreds of daily communicants. Imported dates for football games. The Oliver Hotel Coffee Shop with St. Mary's girls or student nurses from St. Joseph Hospital. Best of all, an awareness that our young coach would renew Notre Dame's legend. No matter that Coach had discarded Elmer Layden's wholesale squads and limited participation. The world was every Notre Dame student's oyster. When Rev. J. Hugh O'Donnell, the Notre Dame president, strode cross campus there were shouts: "Who lost the Yale game?" Echoes: "J. HUGH O'DONNELL." There was jesting: "Wait until Leahy's football nut friend (Rev. John J. Cavanaugh) becomes president. We'll have practice fields on the Quadrangle."

Students cheered every backfield shift into the Rockne box as Leahy won five in a row. There was joking that Leahy would be selected all-America quarterback since, under new rules, quarterbacks Harry Wright and Bob Hargrave could alternately bring in plays from the bench. Earl Blaik, new at Army, did force a scoreless duel in the Yankee Stadium mud and mist. The game barely was over when signs on campus appeared: "Still Undefeated." Hundreds of students greeted the athletes' Monday return to South Bend's rail station. One brain posted a bulletin asking who needed to salute a gang of imported professionals. A "lake" dunking was suggested for the radical, whose name was supplied by Steve Juzwik. I'm not certain it came off.

Celebration of an unbeaten season, after the home finale with Southern Cal, was short-lived. We were shocked out of a Sunday casualness by Pearl Harbor. Life at Notre Dame never again would be quite the same. Some students raced to volunteer. More joined military reserves. Others, mostly disappointed, were too young or physically undraftable.

Leahy knew life must go on. He began 1942 spring practice with Angelo Bertelli as quarterback in the T-formation. Leahy was copying from George Halas and Clark Shaughnessy. Sid Luckman, the Bears' T-whiz, was one of Leahy's tutors. And, lads, one fears that Leahy's mania for perfection led him to practice more "diligently" than the college codes permitted. Tradition was that the Irish began spring practice on St. Patrick's Day; generally that brought in the newsreel cameramen. In a few of Leahy's early years, however, there already were numerous cripples by the official St. Patrick's opening date.

The regime took no greater toll than on Leahy. Illness and nervous fatigue hospitalized him temporarily in 1942, as related in this book's season-by-season details. So pass along with only a few 1942 incidents: Leahy was grooming sophomore Luke Higgins as a likely mid-season replacement (ahead of Ziggy Czarobski) for starting right tackle Bob Neff. Early on, Higgins was substituted for Neff and yanked for mediocrity. "What happened, lad?" inquired Leahy. The honest Higgins: "I just felt tired." That was the cardinal sin. No one dared tire on Leahy. Which explains why Higgins was shuffled to mid-deck.

The Irish were hapless in early games but Ziggy Czarobski promised Father O'Brien, at class on game morning, that ND would win big over the potent Iowa Seahawks. Later that Saturday afternoon the score was ND 28, Seahawks 0.

Starting with the 1942 season opener, newspapers kept repeating that injured Dippy Evans would have recovered sufficiently "next" week to be a backfield starter. You read that end Jack Zilly was out for the year with injury. Yet everyone on campus knew that Evans would miss his final year (except for a token appearance against Army). They also knew that Zilly's injuries were in the grade department.

Now figure this: Only 19,567 were in attendance at Notre Dame Stadium for Leahy's first game as coach. The bowl was filled only for the 1941 finale with Southern California, packed only for Michigan in 1942, never jammed again (even during dramatic 1943) until the 1946 Purdue game. After that, even with more seating, Notre Dame home games became almost guaranteed sellouts for endless seasons. Credit Leahy for waking up fans as well as the echoes.

Spring of 1943 found practice in earnest although everyone was gearing for war. Gerard "Perfection" Ford, a brilliant end prospect, overtrained St. Patrick's night and drew a two weeks' suspension in letters from Father John J. Cavanaugh, and from Rev. John Burke, the prefect of discipline.

"I've considered going over Cavanaugh's head," joked Ford. To O'Donnell? "No, to the top. To Leahy." Ford did not earn a monogram in 1943, but seemed a certain post-war success. Alas, 1946 found Gerard in New York with his South Bend wife, Eileen, giving birth to the now world-famous Ford Model Agency.

Students had a long sabbatical in late spring and early summer of 1943 as ND prepared to turn over more facilities to naval units, and to gear for a trimester scholastic year. Some footballers took what might be a last trip home; others, Paul Limont, Johnny Lujack, John Yonakor, Joe Signiago, Jimmy Mello, and a pack more, remained in South Bend. Some worked in war plants between occasional "informal" practice sessions. Mid-summer found me yanked from the *South Bend Tribune* to Fort Bliss, Tex. My draft board apologized for taking such a near-sighted prospective general, but needed to provide bodies: only 27 of 62 called by my board could pass any kind of physical. So I was at Fort Bliss the 1943 Saturday that ND opened with a 41-0 victory at Pitt, and was fiercely reprimanded for staying in my hut to hear the game broadcast instead of standing C.Q. at the press center. I remained in an El Paso liquor store to hear the rally beating the Seahawks by one point. The owner, an absolute Notre Dame fan, was so delighted to meet someone who personally knew Lujack, Leahy, Creighton Miller, and the bunch, that he discovered two bottles of precious bourbon and passed them on gratis. Next week, I was as tearful and speechless as was Notre Dame broadcaster Joe Boland when Great Lakes scored that last minute upset. The winter trimester found me back editing *The Scholastic,* working overtime at the *South Bend Tribune,* and occasionally attending class. Leahy and the great warriors had gone to real battle. It was up to Ed McKeever to build a team from physical rejects and a kiddie corps.

Texas Ed fared well until torpedoed by Navy. This brought up even more potent Army but the Irish were cheered because Frank Szymanski, a hefty center, was back from service and would start. McKeever, who had played a freshman year under Rock, tried psychology in the Yankee Stadium locker room. Ed tearfully told that his father, a dying man, was listening to the broadcast. A Notre Dame victory might save the father's life. With Army leading, 52-0, Szymanski philosophized: "Well, we sure took care of McKeever's old man."

In the early weeks of 1944, I asked several prominent sportswriters to do brief *Scholastic* articles on Notre Dame football. *Chicago Sun* sports editor Warren Brown replied: "Things at Notre Dame now are not as I care to remember them." Jim Costin of the *South Bend Tribune* explained personally: "When Joe Petritz (the Notre Dame sports publicist) entered military service, Leahy had me write press releases for several weeks. Then, he refused to pay, saying I should be honored to work for Our Lady. I asked Frank if he coached for nothing, and got a shrug. Once, I criticized Frank in print and got a letter from his brother, Gene, saying I should be denied the sacraments at death."

What did radio announcer Joe Boland, former Rockne lineman, onetime Layden assistant, and my patron, think about such attitudes? Particularly Warren Brown's?

"Brown knows the score," said Boland. "Look, when Leahy came in, I became an assistant at Purdue and learned the sentiment among Big Ten schools. Most plan to drop ND if Leahy comes back. Remember how Crisler cried after Notre Dame won big at Michigan in 1943? Even before the 1941 season ended, the Big Ten planned to raise a stink about Leahy; then came war, which was more important."

Alumni Secretary Jim Armstrong laughed as he began: "We became a Christian school while you were away. The Navy sent us a black monogram winner — in track. Now, about Leahy...

"I like him. Rock was a diplomat, Frank is not. But Frank certainly has alumni support. They criticize his speech and manner as affectations. Yet when you see/hear his brothers, Gene and Tom, with identical mannerisms, you figure their daddy brought up his kids strictly and properly."

Just now I remember the noblest of them all, Illinois' Ray Eliot. Coach Eliot explained: "Playing Notre Dame is like scheduling three consecutive defeats. You lose the week before because your players are looking ahead to Notre Dame. Then Notre Dame trounces you. Finally, you lose the next game because you're still physically and emotionally drained from Notre Dame."

Ed McKeever — such an ace with the blarney that ND alumnus Bill Fay once observed, "Ed could peddle California oranges in Florida" — became the toast of South Bend in 1944. Ed received thunderous ovations at the ND football banquet. Only perfunctory applause followed Father O'Donnell's announcement that Leahy would return after the war under a long-term (10 years) contract. Afterwards, McKeever quickly accepted the Cornell head-coaching job, where he ran into disgruntled alums because he refused to ask his Catholic players not to pray publicly in the stadium.

Hugh Devore took over for 1945. He tied Navy and probably was robbed out of winning that one. But Devore lost to Army big and blew the season finale, 39-7, because Great Lakes head coach Paul Brown reported such severe injuries and illnesses that the press believed the game would be cancelled. Surprise. All Blue Jackets were as potent as the U.S.S. Missouri when game day came. Friends, though, were proud of Devore for twice standing up to The Master. In 1944, Leahy had requested so many ND-Army tickets "from my allotment" that few were left for McKeever. Early in 1945, Devore let Leahy understand that Hugh had personal plans for a head coach's ticket allotment. War was over and The Master home when ND was preparing to play at Northwestern. Leahy said he might sit on the ND bench. Devore said Leahy would not. End of the story.

But, lads, Leahy would be at the helm in 1946. Or would he? For almost two years there had been cloak-and-dagger maneuvering in pro football. Early in 1944, *Chicago Tribune* sports editor Arch Ward announced formation of the All-America Football Conference for postwar play. Ward would take pro football west, where his pal, Don Ameche, would field the Los Angeles Dons. Buck Shaw would coach the Morabito brothers' San Francisco 49ers. Millionaire trucker John Keeshin had the Chicago Rockets. Taxi Magnate Mickey McBride the Cleveland team. There would be teams in Buffalo and Miami (eventually in Baltimore), with Ray Ryan, an oil tycoon, operating the New York franchise. When Mayor Fiorello La Guardia declared gambler Ryan (later slain by the mob) would be persona non grata in New York, silver-tongued Ward persuaded Dan Topping's New York Yankees to jump from the N.F.L.

Founder Ward counted on Frank Leahy being a big factor in the "All-Ameche" circuit. Ward was a Leahy fanatic. He was, may heaven rest the ghostly typewriter of Charles Bartlett, Leahy's first biographer. Yes, snagging Leahy would be a coup. I was eyewitness as the league developed. As protege of fellow Notre Damer Arch Ward since 1944, I opened his mail, signed his letters, took his calls, saw his office visitors, ghosted magazine articles, and listened like a child while Arch detailed the cheap shots even from his own jealous *Chicago Tribune* contemporaries. On the outside a once great friend, Papa Bear George Halas, had turned against Ward. By early summer of 1944, I was so certain that Leahy was to join such other Notre Damers as Jim Crowley, Joe Petritz, Jimmy Phelan, Buck Shaw, maybe Slip Madigan, and many young ND athletes, in the new venture, that I visited my old boss, *South Bend Tribune* editor Bob Walton. I told Walton to prepare for a story that Leahy would not return to Notre Dame.

Leahy practically was delivered to Mickey McBride in Cleveland. He would be paid $1,000 a month while still in the Navy, then $25,000 to $35,000 annually, plus owning a percentage interest in the ball club, once league play started. But something happened. Leahy backed off Cleveland. So he could sign with Keeshin's Chicago Rockets, which would not uproot his family from their home in Long Beach, Ind.? Keeshin later told me: "I had Leahy. Then Notre Dame got my friend, Bennie Sheil (Chicago auxiliary bishop Bernard J. Sheil), to beg me to let Notre Dame keep Leahy. I also had that great tackle, Ziggy Czarobski, bagged for $25,000 over two years, and Leahy got him to stay at Notre Dame."

Was it the All-America overtures that prompted Father O'Donnell to surprisingly announce that Leahy would return to a long-term contract? Was ND pressuring Leahy; was Leahy pressuring ND? If so, who could have blinked first? The Master could have had better paying college jobs, countless pro positions, but at High Noon his heart was with Notre Dame. More so than Notre Dame's official heart was with The Master in later trying years.

Biographer Twombley quotes Leahy as suggesting Paul Brown as coach for McBride. Memory here is that McBride and Ward thought of Brown, then an even more storied football figure (Massillon High, Ohio State) than the young Master. Whatever, Brown signed an agreement, identical to the offer made Leahy, in my presence in Ward's office. Though the war's end was far off, Brown quickly was signing players, including Otto Graham.

Not taking the conference seriously ("they don't even have a football"), and being Ward's friend, cost Layden his N.F.L. commissioner's job. The N.F.L. fought for keeps. It forfeited Cleveland to McBride by transferring the 1945 N.F.L. champion Rams to Los Angeles to compete with Ameche; the coach who made the Rams 1945 champions was Adam Walsh, the center and captain on ND's Four Horsemen team and, briefly in 1944, a Notre Dame assistant.

Meanwhile, why was I having nasty thoughts that Halas had Leahy in mind as eventual coach of the Chicago Bears?

There were many similarities between the then current kings of college and pro football. Both Leahy and Halas came from low-income groups. Both had labored through college and found an eternal love affair with football. Both outwardly were as sincere as insurance salesmen, yet each always kept check on inner emotions except in their rare trusted relationships.

Could it be that pro football's founding father saw, in Leahy, his own successor as coach of the Chicago Bears?

Perhaps the 1946 scoreless duel between retooled Notre Dame and Army's Black Knights was justice in the eyes of the gods. Yet Blaik had the answer in proclaiming that both were a little chicken and played too close to the vest.

A delegation of New York writers, who had gone to South Bend to watch Irish preparations, returned to NY on the Irish football train. They were scarcely en route before Leahy summoned the NY authors and gave each a precious, priceless pair of tickets. So much for what a coach does with "my allotment."

The season found Notre Dame national college champs, the Bears champions of the National Football League with little heed to the Cleveland Browns first crown in Ward's All-America. Leahy would coach the collegians against Halas' Bears in the 1947 All-Star game in Chicago's Soldier Field. Neither "Gloomy Gus" could see how his team would even score.

Forecasters predicted muggishly torrid weather for All-Star game night. Canny Halas arranged for air hoses, much like those then being used to cool passengers while planes were at the loading ramps, to provide a cooled dressing room. Leahy had such no foresight. His athletes sweltered, some never even entering the dressing room at intermission. Yet the college princes and their king slapped a 16-0 defeat on the royal Bears.

After his unbeaten ND campaign of 1947, Leahy again was chosen to coach the collegians, this time against the Chicago Cardinals (Elmer Angsman, Charlie Trippi, et al.) in the 1948 summer All-Star classic. Jimmy Conzelman coached the Cardinals to a 16-0 victory and Coach Leahy left the stadium without visiting his conquered warriors in their locker room. Leahy was justified in his sadness; he was a victim of circumstances, to wit.

Notre Dame and Michigan were unbeaten '47 powerhouses. The Irish were voted Associated Press national champions as they closed with a 38-7 victory at Southern California. When Michigan whipped the Trojans, 49-0, in the Rose Bowl, a post-season poll named the Wolverines No. 1. No matter that Notre Dame had the trophy; there were hard feelings between the rival squads. And Leahy's 1948 All-Stars were headed by galaxies from both schools. Making it worse, Michigan's athletes were schooled in Crisler's single-wing offense.

Leahy thought he had that figured out. He organized the All-Star squad principally in two offensive units. Michigan men would key the single-wing attack, Notre Dame men the T-formation. Fan interest was keen; seldom if ever had such an array of football greats been assembled on one squad. Leahy announced a public scrimmage that would attract more than 10,000 at a dollar a head. It would basically be the single wing versus the T-formation. Unfortunately, a copywriter preparing a prominent *Chicago Tribune* advertisement for the scrimmage promoted it as a duel between Notre Dame and Michigan. The advertisement ran through the morning's early editions before being killed by screams from Leahy and Arch Ward. The All-Star unit was even more shattered.

Perhaps some All-Stars were taking the game against the Cardinals very casually because they were playing for charity, and could be risking princely future salaries. It may have been a night when one team (the Cardinals) had a hot hand against a luckless foe. The Cardinals did have incentive: it was their first appearance in what then was football's jewel game; the only other N.F.L. championship had been won in the pre-playoff, pre-All-Star era, under the coaching of Notre Dame grad and George Gipp teammate, Norm Barry, who is still hearty as these lines are written.

Leahy's stoic features showed strain as he progressed on into unbeaten campaigns in 1948 and 1949. Yet there was more than just the next football game troubling Leahy as he faced the windup of the 1940s. Notre Dame was cutting his scholarships, covertly de-emphasizing. Leahy wanted to quit with a great record; he would not face a future without advantages enjoyed by other schools and long enjoyed at Notre Dame. He was determined to retire after 1949, and passed the word to some athletes. Big Jerry Groom would captain Notre Dame in 1950. When he heard Leahy's woes late in 1949, Groom said to The Master: "Coach, remember what you promised my parents when I enrolled at Notre Dame — that you would be my coach for all four years? Well, I have another year to go."

"That lad's talk sold me — I had to be true to my players and to myself. I could not quit when the odds became great, I was not a quitter. I had to rebuild before leaving," Leahy told me.

Rounding out the 1940s picture: A disheartened Ed McKeever left Cornell with determination to build a powerhouse at the University of San Francisco. Gypsy players were lured haphazardly. No one was happy unless it was McKeever, who wound up as 1948 coach of the Chicago Rockets, where he would have Ziggy Czarobski. The day of McKeever's appointment, George Halas unveiled not only Johnny Lujack but George Connor as Bears. Meanwhile, there was a cloud over McKeever, who had blown a princely $3,000 down payment on a home in Phoenix to return to coaching. Prior to leaving San Francisco he had compiled a list of all U.S.F.'s football players with suspect credentials. The list found itself into print. McKeever was accused of the leak. He told me:

"Before I left, the president asked for a list of players' backgrounds and eligibility status. I wrote a report on my battered portable. My wife begged me not to go on record, but I assured her only the president would have the evidence. He did not release it, nor did I."

McKeever's 1948 Rockets were horrendous. Coach Leahy and I attended a loss in Soldier Field. All afternoon The Master looked downcast and shook his head sadly. The Notre Dame men on the Rockets were not playing as they had played for him. He expressed sympathy for McKeever.

McKeever later became Gaynell Tinsley's chief recruiter for Louisiana State University. In Chicago, the most storied prep back since Bill De Correvont, was a senior at suburban Oak Park High School named Chuck Hoag, who seemingly was destined to rival Ernest Hemingway and football's Bob Zuppke as Oak Park High celebrities. McKeever came to Chicago and said: "L.S.U. has to get Hoag, and doesn't care how. I'm taking out his parents tonight; get reservations at the Empire Room and Chez Paree. And figure out some way Hoag can be pressured to L.S.U. He's a must."

"Forget Hoag," I said. "He's committed to Kansas. I think his future is in basketball. Greatest in America? Hoag, however, is not the greatest in Oak Park. As a friend, because I don't want to hurt Notre Dame, I advise you keep tabs on a kid named Johnny Lattner, at Fenwick High School in Oak Park. Start working on him now, he could make football forget Gipp. Remember... Lattner, at Catholic Fenwick. Not only great all-around, but the most humble lad you'll meet. He'll know your reputation and will listen. A long shot, but he's a far better bet than Hoag."

Forget it. Hoag indeed went to Kansas, where injury hampered fulfillment of his football potential. You know the John Lattner story. Lattner was a freshman friend of Groom, starred offensively and defensively in 1951-52, then was an ironman when colleges returned to the single platoon in 1953. Our Lady sent Lattner, the best, when Leahy needed help the most.

"Jonathan. Jonathan Lattner. O-o-o-o-o-o-o, you are disgracing Our Lady's school. . . ." Lattner still gets the proper inflection today. He recalls how The Master made him spend a week with a football taped to his hand after fumbling five times in a game. Carrying Leahy's heavy casket to its final resting place, Lattner reminded other storied pallbearers that Coach was not leaving without giving them one final workout. O-o-o-o-o-o-o, yes, lads, the Coach was a disciplinarian, and Leon Hart never tires of telling about The Master ordering him to run fatiguing penalty laps. Finishing dog-tired, Hart was summoned to Leahy and mumbled quietly: "Now what the hell does the Old Man want?" Rabbit Ears Leahy said: "A little more respect, lad. Take another lap."

A 35-0 whipping by Michigan State in 1951 was a recurring nightmare the rest of The Master's life. It was offset by always pleasant memories of the Oklahoma conquests in 1952 and again in 1953. The Master, smiling merrily, liked to recall, however, another 1952 success: The Irish were underdogs in an early season invasion of Texas. Leahy, who left nothing to chance, noticed the Notre Dame bench would be in fierce sunshine, the Texas bench in cool shade. He asked if the ND bench also could be on the shade side, declaring: "Texas is a heavy favorite, and if we're fatigued by heat the thousands who paid to see the game will see only a rout." The Master also arranged for ice and sun visors. With time running out and Notre Dame leading the exhausted Longhorns, 14-3, the puckish Leahy ordered some reserves to run back and forth in front of the Texas bench, pausing occasionally for push-ups. O-o-o-o-o-o-o, The Master enjoyed a joke.

Georgia Tech, not played by the Irish since 1945, was unbeaten in 31 games when the Yellow Jackets arrived at ND with a 1953 record of 5-0. All Dixie awaited ND's comeuppance, though Leahy had taken the precaution of letting the stadium turf grow a little higher in view of Tech's vaunted speed. Tech was set for triumph, but before kickoff *Chicago Tribune* expert Wilfrid Smith (a starter on Norm Barry's 1927 pro champ Cardinals), whispered: "No one in his right mind thinks Tech has a chance." Notre Dame led, 7-0, at the half. After intermission, Charles Chamberlain of the Associated Press called my attention to Leahy's absence from the bench. I rushed around the stadium in time to see an unshaven, moaning Leahy being carried to an ambulance. Word spread that The Master had suffered a major heart attack; no surprise. Dr. Nicholas Johns soon diagnosed the ailment as pancreatitis. The mortality rate in acute hemorrhagic pancreatitis may exceed 50 percent. I did not need to be told; a priest for whom I had served mass died of such an attack.

Soon Leahy was coaching again, via closed circuit TV, from his hospital bed. We were at North Carolina when Notre Dame sports publicist Charles Callahan (also as traditional as The Gipper) announced: "Dick Washington has just become the first black to score a touchdown for Notre Dame." No cheering in the press box. Washington didn't even stay in the team hotel, but had private quarters, which even in immediately future years would be required of northern teams taking black athletes into Dixie climes. (I remember when Michigan State's Willie Thrower was flying home with the Pittsburgh Steelers after a game in Florida. He asked Steeler owner Art Rooney: "Let's not play any more games where Willie Thrower is a second-class citizen.")

I covered Notre Dame's rousing 40-14 finale over Southern Methodist in '53. We knew Leahy would have a difficult time extracting himself from the student mobs after his first unbeaten campaign since 1949. Yet as we awaited in a catacomb adjacent ND's locker room, the time seemed endless. Then Leahy emerged, accompanied by my boss, Arch Ward. I was too dumb to get any hint, and took notes as Leahy raved about "the greatest team I ever coached." Well, it did include Tom Carey (who had to quarterback in Ralph Guglielmi's shadow) and the great end Dan Shannon. Later Leahy would say Carey and Shannon were the two toughest fisticuffers he encountered in all his years of boxing and football.

In the locker room that memorable December 5, 1953, Lattner stood near a sign proclaiming: "Through these portals pass the National Champions of 1953." It was not to be. Notre Dame was No. 2 to Jim Tatum's unbeaten Maryland team, but Lattner consoled: "We have America's greatest coach."

Weeks later, Ward telephoned the *Tribune's* sports department to inquire if there was any late news. Well, De Paul was playing basketball. Ward chuckled. How could we know that Floss and Frank Leahy then were sipping drinks as overnight guests in the Ward's apartment. Next day, Ward wrote the story of Leahy's resignation. He speculated that The Master's successor would come from the staff, and listed Terry Brennan among the top candidates. I was forced to recall Father Hesburgh's visit to the Notre Dame Club of Chicago's annual dinner in March 1953. The Notre Dame president had promised a major announcement. Reporters at the bar begged for info. "He'll announce that Terry Brennan is joining Notre Dame's staff," I said. A big name by-liner snorted "Is that all?" and left without finishing his drink, the upset of the year. Johnny Lujack muttered: "Notre Dame already has a backfield coach." That coach was Lujack.

Not quite ten months later, The Master was telling Notre

Dame's student body: "In Terry Brennan you have a truly all-American coach."

●

On September 25, 1954, for the first time since 1945, Notre Dame opened a football season without Frank Leahy at the helm. During his eight-season post-war job, The Master had given his alma mater five undefeated teams. In the end, though, the prophet found himself without honor in his own country. When Leahy had announced his retirement, the question came: "Did he jump, or was he pushed?"

Conclusions were that he was nudged. Toward the end, even Father John J. Cavanaugh's enthusiasm about The Master had cooled. Leahy's taped account for his biographer: "I left Our Lady because I had to in order to stay alive... I was not fired. Father Hesburgh wanted me to continue."

Those well may be the facts. One would judge, though, that for several reasons Father Hesburgh had few regrets when Leahy tossed in the sponge. Didn't he have Brennan in the wings for the inevitable day when Leahy's health no longer permitted the rigors of coaching? Certainly the Notre Dame president would not debate Leahy's decision. One does not ask a man to die on the job?

Father Hesburgh might have suspected that eventually he and Leahy would be on a collision course and been relieved by The Master's decision to quit. One cannot feel that Brennan was pressing. Ward told me that though Father Hesburgh was fond of Brennan, Notre Dame did debate calling in Buck Shaw until Brennan had more maturity. In Chicago's Blackstone Hotel, Father Hesburgh told me that in talking to Brennan after Leahy quit, he told Terry the job was his but, if Terry did not immediately wish to shoulder such responsibility, the chance would come again. When Brennan accepted the responsibility immediately, Hesburgh said, he advised Terry to surround himself with mature aides — as a youthful Hesburgh had done when appointed president.

If one sensed Father Hesburgh had a feeling of relief when Leahy left, it would have been that Hesburgh felt the alma mater to be bigger than both and that he had been personally entrusted to a long mission to lift Notre Dame to greater glories. Father Hesburgh was that way. He did push Notre Dame to new heights. Once, when I queried Father Hesburgh about a rumored coaching change, he said: "I have just returned from India. When you've seen the poverty and hunger there, you realize there are things more important than football." When soaring with the eagles, however, Father Hesburgh certainly must have concluded football could be important, too, and junked de-emphasis to bring in coaches like Ara Parseghian, Dan Devine, Lou Holtz, even the forgettable Gerry Faust.

Leahy personally was not ready for retirement. He had many fair-weather admirers, but few close personal friends.

Millionaire Fred Miller, the president and C.E.O. of Miller Brewing Co. and Leahy's most intimate confidante, died in a plane crash a year after Leahy's final season. Arch Ward was to die in his sleep early in July 1955. It was more than a dozen years after retirement that The Master found his greatest friend and benefactor, Chicago business leader Patrick L. O'Malley, the ultimate confidante of then Mayor Richard J. Daley. O'Malley gave Leahy a purpose for continuing the struggle, even though many of the final years of struggle would be painful.

It was during those final trying years, while under O'Malley, that Leahy proved to the world he was the man his lads and friends had always known him to be.

There were those who thought "good riddance" when Frank left football. And Frank was lost; football was his life. Searching for friends, he came closer and closer to me. Once, his brother Tom Leahy, delivered to me 10 priceless tickets to the Kentucky Derby, saying: "Frank wants you to have these." He paid me to do radio scripts. Very often, he called or came around just for company. As time passed, and new faces appeared, Frank Leahy was more lonesome. One evening, he recalled the 28-14 loss to Purdue in 1950 that ruined his unbeaten streak: "That Purdue sophomore lad, Dale Samuels, who completed all those passes. A Chicago lad. Remember you begged me to recruit him for Notre Dame. . . ."

"Now that George Connor's a fine lad. Wouldn't surprise me if Halas makes him coach of the Bears. . . ."

After one Christmas I was summoned to Chicago's now Northwestern Memorial Hospital to find The Master with a broken leg. "I was carrying some packages and fell, but you know what people will say. . . ."

"That you're getting clumsy. . . ?"

"O-o-o-o-o-o-o-o, lad. They'll say I'm getting old. But I'm not. I summoned you to report I'm getting back into football. Texas A & M wants me. I'll coach for three years, then continue as athletic director and give the coaching job to Bob McBride. I like Texas A & M because it is like the Notre Dame I remember. Small, in a quiet community, all boys, and well-disciplined. They have made be a fabulous offer. Good salary, two TV programs, and $14,000 cash from alumni each year. A dream job. . . ."

The dream job was not to be. One trustee demanded a physical examination. It proved The Master not a well man. Texas A & M would eventually hire Iowa State head coach Jim Myers to replace a gent named Paul "Bear" Bryant, who had left the Aggie school to go home to his alma mater, Alabama, and rebuild their sagging football fortunes.

A small group was at Gene Powalski's steak house, on Chicago's South Side, holding a pre-wedding pow-wow for Ziggy Czarobski. Who showed up out of nowhere? Coach Leahy. He served as a Sunday night TV commentator after Chicago Bears games and could not conceal his disgust at such hapless football. He often was my unpaid speaker when I presided at the Playboy Club's pro luncheon that featured Bear game highlights. One day, he grabbed my arm while Gale Sayers was making a long run down the sideline. "He's carrying the ball in the wrong hand, lad."

"What makes you say that?"

"Because if he fumbles, he'll fumble onto the field. If he was carrying the ball in his left hand and fumbled, the ball would fall out of bounds."

The Master was in and out of business ventures, often used by schemers. He seemed to trust everyone. He once wrote from Denver, a typed letter touting Hamilton Oil and Gas stock at $1.50 per share. It proved to be a big bust.

"I have long regretted that venture," Leahy later confided. "I was taken in by those people."

I believed him.

They were promoting him to build a Frank Leahy Motel in South

Bend, he revealed one night at Randall's Inn. "Build? You can buy this one, cheap," said Bill Randall. Another time he presented me to people with whom he would invest to film his life story. He had told them I would get $12,500 for the script. Okay? "Frank, let's talk a bit more to these people. Who's promoting the movie?" The men tossed out a name. "One chance in a million," I gasped, "that you would come to deal with a person who knows him well. Frank, years ago Arch Ward had a most sad financial movie experience with that man. I'll show you the evidence in Chicago." One movie out the window.

He briefly flirted with politics, delivering a seconding speech for the 1956 Republican Party nomination of President Eisenhower, with whom he had often golfed.

On one occasion, he excitedly reported he was to be general manager of the Los Angeles Chargers in the American Football League. Bob McBride would be his coach. Bob had misgivings about conditions and showed me the league's contract form. It strictly copied the N.F.L. code, except for a final clause: Void if the A.F.L. did not play. Seemed like the promoters were not over-confident. Frank's job did not last long; one week I talked to him in Los Angeles, the next in a Chicago hospital while being treated for "exhaustion." He claimed to have been torpedoed by an ambitious coach.

No football, and a few years of drifting remained. Then Leahy and Moose Krause came to a dinner party for me. Leahy and Patrick L. O'Malley sat together, a pair of champions. Strangely, O'Malley had been a rising Boston businessman when Leahy was at Boston College. Adopting Chicago, he was a Notre Dame addict. Yet the pair did not meet until my party. O'Malley drove his hero back to downtown Chicago. Leahy related dreams of working with young people; of awakening America to the perils of Communism. "Hold on," said O'Malley. "Would you like to work for me at Canteen and spread that gospel through the country?" Was the Pope a Catholic? A deal was struck.

Soon thereafter, Leahy was to be honored at a Notre Dame banquet. Honored? Yes, with a plaque in the new athletic building (now named for Rev. Edmund P. Joyce, C.S.C.). "No matter," said Leahy. "I've insisted you — no one else — be toastmaster." It was a grand party. Legions of old lads returned. Ed McKeever and Wally

Butts came in. Aging Herb Jones, the former athletic business manager, collected autographs with childish enthusiasm. It was the night The Master was born again. His face glowed at 2 a.m. as Bill Randall grilled steaks for O'Malley, Leahy and me.

Once more, Frank Leahy was set to wake up the echoes in another game he loved. He was on a high crest. Years had fallen from his face, spring was back in his step.

Why did leukemia have to rear its head? Perhaps because Frank Leahy was not happy unless paying a price. Somewhere, today, he is not waking up the echoes, but smiling happily at Our Mother.

Chicago, Illinois
June 21, 1988

The Boston College Years

1

Boston College vs. Lebanon Valley

SEPTEMBER 30, 1939

BOSTON — They took the Boston College 1939 football machine, the first ever assembled by Frank Leahy, out of the garage for the first time yesterday and the huge Maroon and Gold juggernaut promptly ran over little Lebanon Valley, 45-0, before 16,000 innocent bystanders assembled at B.C.'s picturesque Alumni Stadium.

Power was the keynote. Though Leahy constantly diluted his team with second- and third-stringers and though they shortened the last two periods to 10 minutes each, the Eagles smashed their way to seven touchdowns, had four more disallowed by the officials, and all in all showed as much promise as any team to appear at the Heights in several years.

You can't learn the Notre Dame system in a fortnight and there were plenty of rough spots in the Eagle attack. The backs were often caught illegally-in-motion and the linemen offside as the timing was still faulty. But for size and strength, hard running, good tackling and good blocking, this team was well ahead of opening-day specifications, and against the outweighed and outmanned Flying Dutchmen looked a good deal like a mobile cement mixer running through a swarm of cyclists.

Leahy started a second-string backfield behind his regular line and the Eagles were a little slow in getting down to work. But towards the end of the first period, Lou Montgomery, the Brockton,

Mass., colored flash, went 17 dazzling yards on a tackle slant to climax a 60-yard march to the season's opening touchdown.

Bob Jauron, the sophomore speedster from Nashua, Mass., kicked the extra point and when, at the start of the second period, Leahy sent in nine new players, including a backfield quartet of Charlie O'Rourke, Vito Ananis, Pete Cignetti and Hank Toczylowski, the Eagles really got rolling. Three touchdowns, bringing the halftime score to 26-0, quickly developed. First came a seven-play, 75-yard march climaxed by a 40-yard scoring pass from O'Rourke to Ananis. Then came a four-play, 41-yard march ended by Cignetti's five-yard buck, and finally Ananis intercepted a Lebanon pass and returned it 30 yards for still another touchdown.

The subs were in for most of the third period and the only score here resulted from Montgomery's glittering 25-yard runback of a punt and, two plays later, Jauron's 25-yard slash over tackle for a touchdown. The regulars were back again for a few minutes at the start of the final period and marched 75 yards in eight plays, with Cignetti's short-side smashes gaining the most yardage. The scoring was completed by a pass interception followed by a Magowan-to-Cowhig touchdown pass covering some 20 yards.

The Eagles had so much the better of the game that only once were they forced to punt. They gained 462 yards by rushing, completed 5 of nine passes for 89 yards, and completely throttled the visitors' attempts to advance the ball. Lebanon made only one first down, couldn't complete a single one of its 12 passes and never was within 25 yards of the Eagles' goal line.

Many B.C. players turned in good bits. Toczylowski, while he was in there, drove the team well. O'Rourke, who was used very sparingly, fired only two passes. Both were completed, including one for a touchdown. Montgomery, though he looked unsteady handling punts, several times dragged the crowd out of its seats with those dodging runs of his. Jauron showed fine speed though his passing was off. Ananis and Cignetti and Kissell did some powerful line-smashing and sophomore Justin Magowan looked pretty promising.

The B.C. line simply annihilated the enemy. Though offensively the timing was often out of kilter as was to be expected this early in the season, the huge frontier charged savagely on defense, rushed the passer consistently and, in general, acquitted itself very well.

The new uniforms were plenty flashy — gold pants, white shirts and gold helmets... Only trouble is the jerseys don't stay white long ... The officials didn't have an easy time of it, but did a good job ... Duke Lake's whistle was particularly active on account of B.C. frequently being offside... Albie Booth, the Yale immortal, made his local debut as an arbiter... Little Boy Blue has already acquired quite a corporation... The weather was great for the fans, not so great for the players... B.C.'s football setting, against the autumn foliage of Chestnut Hill, with the Reservoir and the Gothic towers for a backdrop, is as nice as anything to be found in academic groves... A new stunt born in the fertile brain of John P. Curley, the B.C. graduate manager, was a flag-raising ceremony before the game... The new program was a pip and the band did its stuff in great style, notably when three gobs left the game early and the boot ensemble broke into "Anchors Aweigh"... John Mackin, Mr. Boston College himself, brought a portable radio with him and went half nuts trying to watch one game and listen to four others simultaneously... Add Notre Dame stuff: Coach Leahy sits on a bench a little advanced from the rest of the B.C. players, with his spare quarterbacks sitting next to him and absorbing strategy... B.C.'s second touchdown came on a typical O'Rourke play; though the pass from center was a little off the mark, he snagged it with one hand, waited coolly behind his fine protection and then hung one on a peg for Ananis, 50 yards down the field. Goodreault, who was in the same territory as part of the "straddle pass," cut down the defensive back, Walk, with a great block to make the rest easy.

2

Boston College vs. Holy Cross

DECEMBER 2, 1939

BOSTON — Aided to some extent by the heavy going which curbed the flashy running of Ronnie Cahill, the stellar Holy Cross back, Boston College today ground out a decisive victory over the favored Crusaders.

Holding the purple warriors completely at bay for most of the time, the Eagles drove to a stunning victory in the final quarter when they registered two touchdowns which gave them the victory, 14-0, and put a temporary end to the domination the Crusaders have had over them in recent years.

A capacity crowd of slightly more than 41,000 persons braved the rain and sat in the chill, damp, semi-darkness at Fenway Park to watch the alert Eagles shatter the Crusaders' dream of a bowl bid.

Chief factors in the triumph, the second since 1929 in this series, were Vito Ananis, the 180-pound right halfback from Cambridge, Mass. and Pete Cignetti, the 185-pound fullback from Malden, Mass.

Serving their alma mater for the last time, these two were aided and abetted by little Charlie O'Rourke, another Malden boy, whose slight weight (155 pounds) was no handicap in his throwing.

Captain Ernie Schwotzer of Waltham, Mass., also added his bit by throwing his 186 pounds on a loose ball in the Crusaders' end zone, but this merely added insult to injury for at the time victory was pretty well signed, sealed and delivered to the high-flying Eagles.

It was in the closing minutes of the third period when Ananis' sensational catch of a deep-thrown forward pass from O'Rourke put the Crusaders on the spot down on their own 7-yard stripe.

There wasn't enough time left to deliver the death-blow in that stanza, but on the first play in the fourth quarter, Mr. Cignetti crashed through the Holy Cross middle.

There were three full yards for him to make on third down when he took the ball and glanced off a wall of frantic Crusaders to score the second touchdown the Holy Cross line has yielded all season, with credit for the other going to Colgate early in the Fall.

It wasn't a great while afterward that Cahill went back to punt from somewhere around his own 15, only to have Captain Schwotzer storm through and block the kick. Caroming off his face, the ball bounced back into the end zone where Schwotzer dived for it and got it away from two frantic Holy Cross men.

There were still seven minutes left to play after Alex Lukachik, who spelled off Dick Harrison at left end, converted his second extra point kick, but it was far from being enough, judging by the way the two teams were playing.

The Crusaders proved their gameness, however, by coming right back to make their biggest advance of the day — a drive that started on their own 12 and went down to the Eagles' 21, where it was brought to a halt by the whistle ending the game.

Long before the contest came to a close, however, the field was stripped of its goal posts — the overjoyed B.C. rooters demolishing one set several minutes before the final whistle blew and taking the other down before Andy Giardi, the Holy Cross fullback at the time, went up in the air to take Alex Nahigian's pass on the Eagles' 21.

In making his touchdown, Cignetti was injured and had to be replaced and, as he went off the field to doff his mud-spattered uniform for the last time, he was the recipient of a demonstration that will ring in his ears for many a day. It was hardly less lusty than the one Captain Schwotzer, another third-year man, got when he went out. The Lions' share of the losers' cheers went to little Ronnie Cahill, who has served Holy Cross well in his three years of service.

The heft of the Boston College line, one of the biggest in the land, kept the Crusaders in the hole all through the first tow periods. At no time during those sessions was the Eagles' goal line threatened, while, on the other hand, they made several drives of their own, getting down almost to the Crusader 20 in the first quarter and barging their way to the 12 in the second.

The Crusaders got as far as the B.C. 33 in the third stanza and then, when they were trailing, 14-0, midway in the fourth, they banged away as far as the Eagles' 21, which is where they stood when the final whistle blew.

The Eagles' superiority was fully borne out by the statistics, which revealed nine B.C. downs against four for the Crusaders and 148 yards rushing as against 40. With their running game stopped by a muddy field and an overpowering line, the Crusaders lofted many a forward pass, firing 23 and completing 10, but for only 59 yards. Boston College completed only 2 out of 11 for 87 yards.

Cahill and Bruno Malinowski, the Holy Cross left-footed booter, had the bulge on O'Rourke in kicking, but otherwise everything favored the Eagles, even the penalties.

The game, one of the year's blue-ribbon events up here, lived up to its advance reputation as being one of the finest-played of the entire year, and it was unfortunate that it had to be contested on a field that failed to provide adequate footing.

The game started as a quick-kicking duel between Malinowski and O'Rourke, with honors slightly in the latter's favor.

The Boston College back proved himself a grand player throughout and tilted the scales in the Eagles' direction at the outset, once by booting more than 60 yards and again by racing around right end for a 21-yard gain and a first down on the Crusaders' 43.

That threat came to naught when Malinowski, the Holy Cross fullback, intercepted an O'Rourke pass. Ananis did the same thing when Cahill attempted to complete one with his side-kick, Joe Osmanski. Before he was downed, Ananis had bolted 39 yards, to the Holy Cross 36. Two penalties for offside put the Crusaders in a deeper hole, but they extricated themselves when Cahill intercepted one of O'Rourke's aerials.

The Eagles made another threat near the end of the period, this time advancing from their own 30 to the Crusader 42, where

O'Rourke sent a long diagonal pass down to the 5, where Cahill intercepted.

There were no serious threats and practically no important operations in the second period until near the close, when the Eagles moved from almost midfield to the Crusader 33, the features being a 15-yard forward pass that Bob Jauron, the sub left half, pitched to Cignetti, and a 13-yard dash through left guard by Lou Montgomery, the fleet Negro back, who was in for Ananis.

That threat appeared ominous for a time, but Silas Titus, the Crusader center, snatched one of O'Rourke's tosses on his own 5 and dashed to the B.C. 42 before he was brought down.

Holy Cross started to put some pressure on the Eagles in the opening stages of the third period, but never succeeded in getting much beyond the B.C. 33, with O'Rourke once saving the situation by intercepting a Cahill pass and then lightened the load still further by quick-kicking deep into Holy Cross territory.

It was shortly after that boot that the Eagles were set in motion for their touchdown. O'Rourke fired the spark with a 15-yard runback of a punt. A few plays later, O'Rourke chucked that beauty to Ananis which set the stage for the B.C. score.

The pass covered 34 yards and Ananis made one of the greatest catches of all time, one that will go down alongside those made by Tris Speaker and others in this same park in another sport.

He and Cahill went up into the air together and the extra inch that Ananis had on his opponent was probably what enabled him to come down to earth with the ball in his arms.

The Crusaders staved off two thrusts, one by Cignetti and the other by Ananis, but as soon as they changed goals Cignetti drove through for what turned out to be all that was needed to win the game.

That touchdown not only fired the Eagles, but had just the reverse effect on the Crusaders, who appeared to become panicky. A pass interception by Henry Toczylowski gave the Eagles the ball at midfield shortly thereafter, and they were constantly heading toward the Holy Cross goal from then on until the period was half over and another touchdown had been scored.

This was No. 36 in the Eagles-Crusaders series, which began in 1896 with a double-header. Up to today's game, Boston College held the edge with seventeen triumphs against sixteen defeats, with the 1926 and 1932 games resulting in scoreless ties.

3

Boston College vs. Clemson

THE COTTON BOWL, JANUARY 1, 1940

DALLAS — Clemson's vigilant Cadets grimly protected a whisper of a lead for 38 thrilling minutes on the burnt-brown carpet of the Cotton Bowl this sunny but sad afternoon and escaped from the hungry talons of the Eagles by the insignificant margin of 6-3.

All the points were registered in the second period of a flaming football game, endorsed by Texans as the best in the comparatively brief history of their post-season extravaganza.

Boston's glamour boys hung up the first points of the day when they settled for a field goal off the talented toe of reserve end Alex Lukachik of Bridgeport, Conn., who toed a darling place-kick 34 yards early in the second chapter.

The capricious Cadets from South Carolina counter-charged almost immediately, raking the second-string B.C. line with reverses and spiking the secondary with a long pass, so that Clemson journeyed 57 yards in nine plays into the end zone to reach intermission with a 6-3 lead.

A powder-keg ballcarrier entitled Charles Timmons, who did most of the damage on the way downfield, scored the winning digits on a power thrust on B.C.'s left flank that sent him catapulting far into the end zone.

In every respect the contest was a colossal disappointment to the gold-shirted Bostonians and their 600 attending undergraduates and alumni, who made the long trek from the winter wonderland of New England to see the mildly warm Texas sunset on a disaster at the flag-bedecked bowl at the nearby fair grounds.

B.C.'s vaunted serial game collapsed in the clutch. And for the first time this season its defense yielded to a sustained scoring advance for Clemson gave our second-string left tackle and end a terrific drubbing en route to the game's only touchdown.

Normally hungry-handed and sure-fisted, the B.C. pass receivers were unable to snare the prodigious passes of Chuckin' Charlie O'Rourke in the presence of considerably less than a capacity audience, with the crowd being estimated as 20,000.

On at least three occasions, O'Rourke's passes were labeled for the winning touchdown, but they broke through and over the clutching hands for which they were intended.

The last of these was a spiraling masterpiece that lean O'Rourke buzzed on an awesome 30-yard flight right into the Clemson end zone, where Dick Harrison arrived after out-running and outmaneuvering two secondary defenders.

But Harrison, wan from his innumerable long chases into deep reception positions all afternoon, simply was unable to pull the ball down. It burst out of his arms to fall harmlessly to the brown turf. With it toppled B.C.'s hopes and aspirations of staging another dramatic last-ditch rally, for that was three plays from the very end of the game.

This was probably as an enticing a game of football as was played in any bowl today, but it unfortunately was viewed by an unreasonably small throng, embraced in which were high school bands from 31 Texas towns, totalling 4,200 members.

Although the long, gangling Banks McFadden, the Clemson tailback, who looks like Huckleberry Finn in a football suit, entered the game as a legitimate all-America, O'Rourke, was the best back on the field both ways.

In fact, McFadden's sole contribution to the contest were his majestic kicks, which skidded across the pale blue sky and settled to earth after such long intervals that considerably more than four or five of his associates were waiting there when it came down.

Naturally, this made it extremely difficult for Boston to engineer runbacks of any length at all.

Actually McFadden ran fourth in this game. O'Rourke was superb, and he had to go most of the way, because the first time he was relieved by Bobby Jauron the latter suffered a twisted leg and O'Rourke had to go almost all the rest of the way alone at left half.

Timmons was the best of the Clemson backs, although nothing much had been said of him before the game. Shad Bryant probably was more spectacular, and doubtless a more dangerous runner, but it was Timmons who had the sheer power and drive to slam the ball ahead at critical junctures in Clemson's scoring advance. A sophomore, this hard running carrier was simply having a field day, dropping in behind Capt. Joe Payne, the blocking back, and rolling over left tackle in waves of power that submerged young Steve Levanitas.

Levanitas was having a hard time of it, getting no assistance from the end on that flank, who forgot his instructions to converge on the play and was simply swept aside in playing a waiting game.

Boston's luck was all bad. Capt. Ernie Schwotzer was hurt in the first scrimmage of the game and never returned. Bobby Jauron, the hottest of the Eagle backs in pregame workouts, was hurt upon the occasion of his bowl debut and that left Boston exactly one deep at left half, and put a big load on the slim but adequate shoulders of O'Rourke.

Clemson had the edge in the statistical warfare, but the Gold Shirts from the Heights had the more and better scoring opportunities. They were in there calling four times and got three points.

On the occasion of Lukachik's field goal, B.C. might have taken seven points and a victory out of the situation. And while in smacks of second-guessing, here, briefly, is what occurred:

On the concluding play of the first period Clemson, pressed to the brink of their goal by the forceful enemy from Boston, needed a kick by Bru Trexler, McFadden's spare, to get 'em out of difficulty. Trexler laced a low, fast kick out of his end zone. O'Rourke, who cast the thinnest shadow of any on the Cotton Bowl carpet, eyed it like a calculating outfielder, then took it about knee-high and on the dead sprint at the Clemson 40.

O'Rourke sprinted wide and fast toward the right or east side of the field, outran three Blue Shirts from Clemson, and finally was bounced off the field of play 13 yards from a touchdown. The officials halted proceedings at this point for the switch to the next period.

B.C.'s second string came pouring into the game to take over.

They looked very inadequate right away. Clemson had countered by inserting its temporarily retired first string and they simply poured through the Eagle line at three points to slap Maznicki for a four-yard loss.

On the second play, obviously intended to reverse Jauron outside end, a horde of Blue Shirts romped at will through the crumbling B.C. reserves and sloughed the carrier in the turf for an eight-yard loss. On the third play, Frank Davis slashed back to the 15-yard line, and on fourth down Lukachik booted a field goal which easily sailed over the bar.

The kick was made on a very slight angle from the right and 34 yards away. Eddie Cowhig held, Dubzinski's pass was on a dime, and Lukachik's effort was good for three points.

Well after the subsequent kickoff, Justin McGowan smacked a wobbly quick-kick for B.C. which McFadden, while fading back in the left defensive wingback zone for Clemson, snared on his fingertips, juggled and finally recovered to run back nine yards to his 43.

From there the boys from Honeysuckle Heaven walloped into the B.C. end zone in nine tries.

Timmons picked off nine yards in two smashes over the B.C. left flank and Bryant dropped a yard trying to reverse around the weak side.

Clemson was running strictly from the single wing, with an unbalanced line, and McFadden and Bryant faking prettily in the deep spots. So the next time Bonny Banks faked to Bryant and faded fast to pass, the B.C. defensive line harassed him dreadfully, so he suddenly swung outside the pack to the right and anteloped for an unpremeditated and mighty important gain of 18 yards to the Eagle 30. Dave White smacked him out of bounds with a lusty tackle.

B.C. coach Frank Leahy fired his first-string backs into the game, along with Harrison and Goodreault, the varsity ends, and right away Goodreault tumbled Bryant for a five-yard loss at his flank.

So McFadden fell back to throw once more. He found a receiver right down the middle this time, an end named "Warhorse" Jackson.

Pete Cignetti had the estimable "Warhorse" covered, but Cignetti was mighty anxious to get the ball himself and slightly underestimated its loft, so that "Warhorse" got it first at the B.C. 18 for a first down for the Cadets.

The rampaging Mr. Timmons was master of ceremonies from there on. He burst out of a big excavation on the far end of the Boston left flank for 11 yards and a first down on the first play. Clemson's country gentlemen mowed a wide swath ahead of him. He drilled right to the lip of the goal through the same sector on the second play, and split his right tackle for a touchdown on the third, ending up deep in the end zone.

Bryant flubbed the attempted point conversion, being wide to the right, and from there on Clemson held on tight and desperately defended those precious three points.

In the second half, B.C. did everything but score. They did all the pressing and they were on the Clemson 7-yard line in the third period and again on the seven in the last, but they just simply couldn't draw a smile from Lady Luck.

On the first occasion, O'Rourke hit Harrison down the center alley with a 21-yard gainer overhead, and Cignetti and Ananis battered ahead for nine yards. B.C. looked hot, but they got fined 15 yards for holding on a first-down plunge, a penalty that hurt plenty.

Two unsuccessful passes by O'Rourke used up the last two downs, the second of which was a dipsy-doodle from Cignetti to Kerr, the guard, to O'Rourke, with Harrison narrowly missing a finger-tip completion 51 yards away in the end zone.

In the last period, Boston's few but vociferous supporters envisioned another late victory when the Northerners barged down to the Clemson 7-yard line and stalled there.

Al Morro, the nose-guard sophomore tackle, instigated the march when he snatched a deflected Clemson pass out of the air and galloped 17 yards to the enemy 34.

B.C. hiked out of its huddle and pulled a lace-pants play, with George Kerr, the guard, ending up as the ballcarrier. He did mighty well, for he chugged to the Clemson 25.

Cignetti carved out a first down at the 22. On this second try, he faked to Kerr and rode straight ahead through the hole left by the guard coming out of line. Clemson hounded Kerr, as expected, and Cignetti raced 9 yards. Timmons saved the bacon with a prayerful tackle.

The durable Cignetti moved the stakes again, bucking to the 16.

O'Rourke and Ananis, being given no blocking assistance, picked up only three yards in a pair of off-tackle runs. B.C. lost the ball when passes to Harrison and Cignetti were unable to penetrate the defensive.

Until O'Rourke skied that breathless pass in the very last moment of the game to Harrison far down over the goal, B.C. was never that close to scoring again. Harrison made a mighty try for it, splitting two defenders to get at the ball, but destiny expelled its breath and the sowskin squirted away from the Malden senior.

It's going to be a long train trek home, fellers.

4

Boston College vs. Tulane

SEPTEMBER 28, 1940

NEW ORLEANS—The typographical terrors of Boston College, the league of nations football team from back North, roared down the gridiron glory road in the sun-smacked Sugar Bowl this afternoon to a monumental 27-7 victory over a titanic, green-clad but thoroughly beaten Tulane team.

Forty-two thousand sho-nuff Dixie football fans sat paralyzed in the sun-soaked stands as the able, vigilant and terrific Bostonians gave the Southeastern Conference champion both barrels in a rousing offensive onslaught.

It took the great unpronounceables less than nine minutes to score their first touchdown, less than 12 minutes to sturdily smack their way to a 14-0 lead, and at halftime they were out front and going away by three touchdowns. Then Dixie hoisted itself out of the stands to vociferously acclaim a great football team as it left for intermission.

It will be a long, long time before the Bayous will recover from this one, the worst defeat Tulane's temporarily-smashed Green Wave has suffered in five seasons.

They were ground down by a hard-hitting, swarming, two-fisted set of B.C. forwards. Their running game broke up against aggressive people entitled Yauckoes and Kerr and Manzo, and the rest. They were haunted, hounded and generally made miserable by an end named Goodreault, who played a spectacular game that virtually clinched all-America acclaim for him on the lush green of this field today.

Against these hardy henchmen of Frank Leahy, Tulane was shut out of the ball game for 59 minutes and 55 seconds. On the very last play of the contest, against a third-string group of Bostonians, they sent a hip-waving, flitter-footed back named James Ely of Shaw, Miss., running over his right tackle for six yards and a you-can't-whitewash-us touchdown.

A super-charged B.C. team won this game by coming out of its corner with both fists folded and swinging from the gong.

The second time it got its hands on the ball it roared 41 yards in four plays and sent young Butch Kissell, the starting fullback, bucking over his right side for three yards and the score.

This was the first of two touchdowns young Kissell of Nashua, N.H., scored. The others were accounted for by Frank "Monk" Maznicki of West Warwick, R.I., and sophomore Mike Holovak of Lansford, Penn., but there was special significance attached to Kissell's.

He was named the starting fullback, but everybody was finger-crossing when it was announced, because Kissell is inexperienced and something of a chronic fumbler. But Kissell didn't fumble the live-long and historic day, and back home in the town tavern they will be hoisting a stein or two to Butch.

That first score was set up by Chucklin' Charlie O'Rourke, whose name this evening is being mentioned along with Davey O'Brien's in the history of great passing in the Sugar Bowl. The chucker, first of all, drove Tulane right back to its three-yard line with a towering 70-yard kick against a stiff breeze out of the no'th, suh. Walter Dubzinski, the B.C. center, beat two of his contemporaries to the ball where he soared over safety Lou Thomas' hat.

Fred Gloden, a fullback from Iowa, punted from behind his goal to O'Rourke, who fielded the kick at midfield and carried to the Green Wave 41.

Then, as the handful of wild-eyed tonsil-strainers across the field yelled a "For Boston" challenge from the stands, the legion of Leahy started to go.

Maznicki rode over Tulane's overpowered right side for six yards.

Kissell bucked straight through the middle for three on a straight power play. Tulane's secondaries crept in. The line tightened and, on the next play, O'Rourke threw one of his inimitable passes.

Henry "the Hammer" Toczylowski received the ball from center when Les Eagles hiked into right formation. He slipped it casually to trim-jawed Joe Zabilski, the running guard, as he moved out of line. Zabilski, in turn, heaved a lateral to O'Rourke.

And here you have the picture of the whole Tulane secondary defense being hoodwinked and shell-gamed, for they all rushed across the field to their left to cover what they suspected was going to be an end sweep. But O'Rourke paused in mid-flight, pegged a beautiful long, diagonal pass to his left to Al Lukachik, the busting left end. Lukachik was out behind defender Bob Glass and all he had to do was catch it. He did, and Glass managed to trail him five yards and haul him down three strides from a score.

Kissell whacked over right tackle for the touchdown and Maznicki bisected the uprights for the seventh point. It took eight minutes to do that. B.C. was almost a point-a-minute wagon to this juncture.

The clock high up on the north end of the flag-bedecked Sugar Bowl Stadium registered just 11 minutes, 14 seconds, when the typographical terrors scored again.

And O'Rourke (that man's in again, maw) again had his finger, or fingers, in the pie.

Gene Goodreault, the end for whom the Dixie scribes are dusting off their superlatives down at the other end of the press coop, hit halfback Thomas a glancing tackle on a short reverse and when Thomas parted company with the ball it was Goodreault who recovered.

That was 40 yards away from the Green pastures. B.C. covered the course in three plays. The first was an in-and-out end run for four yards by O'Rourke. The second was a shakey-driving reverse through the weak-side tackle by Maznicki, who went 23 yards and almost scored. Bodney, an end who came out of nowhere, seemingly, saved a touchdown with a hangnail tackle from the rear. The blocks with which Tulane was nailed on that play rocked the stands.

O'Rourke went in to pitch again. The ball went to Kissell to O'Rourke who faked a throw to the left, then calmly fired far over to the right. Maznicki sneaked out there from wingback in right formation, clear over the goal and 10 yards beyond the Tulane secondary. Maznicki caught the ball standing straight as a statue, and just touched it to the sod for six more points. Lukachik kicked the extra point for a 14-0 B.C. lead.

Both organizations played the second period with their second-string players, and B.C.'s just happened to be superior. They scored halfway down to the end of the half by rallying for a fiery 60-yard, six-play march, and it was Mickey Connolly, the big sophomore left halfback from Norwalk, Conn., who took over O'Rourke's aerial circus role.

A 15-yard penalty pushed the B.C. reserves back to their 40, from which point they took off. On the first play, Connolly spiked the Green Wave with a 50-yard pass which Henry Woronicz of Brockton, Mass., the left end, snagged out of the air. He was covered by a duet of Dixie darlings, but evaded 'em both to catch the ball in two-fisted fashion.

That put it up to the Greenie 26. Teddy Williams, the flying fisherman from Gloucester, then demonstrated why he is considered a great right halfback prospect. Behind crisp, crackling blocks he streaked around left end on a no-shift play. He almost went the distance, but was staggered by a glancing hit and fell on the 11.

Here B.C. was socked by a five-yard assessment for taking excessive time in the huddle, but Connolly sent a center alley pass to Justin McGowan, the blocking back, who caught it on the Greenie 3 and was wrestled to the sod exactly where he stood.

Holovak and Cronin jaw-bucked right to the lip of the goal, and then took it over center for a score. Toczylowski was calling those two plays. Leahy sent him in to make it sure.

That brought B.C. to the intermission with a 21-0 lead, and by the time they were herding their way toward the exit the Dixie fans had recovered sufficiently from the shock to appreciate what they'd seen.

They were probably looking at one of the two Sugar Bowl contestants on next January the first, and so they rose enmasse to give out a roar of approval.

With a back named Bobby Glass of Massilon, Ohio, carving his way through the B.C. line on sheer savagery and individual inspiration, Tulane experienced a flurry of hot ground gaining at the outset of the third period.

But Maznicki shortly put an end to all this nonsense when he came up like a bolt of lightning to smash Glass for a seven-yard loss on an attempted reverse to Monk's side.

Right here and now Tulane made the most fatal of many mistakes this sunny but sad (for them) afternoon. They waited until fourth down to kick from their own 35, breaking one of football's 10 commandments.

They paid dearly for their sin. Gloden was the punter, who stationed himself the normal distance behind center, and waited for the pass. It came, high and majestic, far over his head. When he caught up with it — and he barely beat Goodreault to the ball — he was on his own 3.

Goodreault nailed him right there. It was now B.C.'s ball, and Toczylowski directed the way. He sent Kissell bulling into the line twice and, on the second try, right over right guard for the score.

The play was a fast smash into the line, without the customary backfield shift. It gave B.C. the advantage of beating the enemy's eight-man line to the punch and they just rolled back the Green shirts to let Kissell through.

Those were the last points scored by our heroes in this epochmarking victory for New England football, because Maznicki's kick for the extra point was blocked when a Green shirt leaked through the left side of the B.C. line.

In the fast expiring moments of the fourth and last quarter the Green Waves gratified their pleading cohorts by averting a shutout by means of passes, mostly, but also on account of some very savage running by Ely and James Thibault, a local boy. It was done against mostly third-stringers, but was done with authority. A pass from Ely to Harold Mullin, an end from the town of Bogalusa, La., carried 11 yards to the B.C. 31. Another from the same pitcher into the left flat was snared by Thibault, who ran like the devil right up to the goal where Bob Jauron grappled with him and brought him down.

Jauron merely postponed the inevitable. On the very last play of the game, Ely outran the left side of our line, the secondaries, too, and scored. Thibault, who made it all possible, kicked the extra point.

And right now this quaint, dignified and cordial community is being quietly, but thoroughly, taken apart by a small, but success-stricken band of B.C. rooters. Details of the carnage we'll acquaint you with later.

Very probably this was the greatest single afternoon in the history of New England football since Harvard emerged winner from the 1919 game in the Rose Bowl.

Singularly enough, this Boston College team is one of the best our section of the country has sent out into intersectional competition since the Horweens and Caseys of that long ago day.

Right this minute, Boston College is the selection of the Sugar Bowl committee to play any opponent it can name for New Year's Day. But first, B.C. has to travel on through Temple and Auburn and Holy Cross and all the rest.

And now Francis W. Leahy, the all-America worrier, can start contemplating the future with distrust and concern, for Francis will worry anyway, even with the best football team in the East at his elbow.

5

Boston College vs. Georgetown

NOVEMBER 16, 1940

BOSTON — Under the dynamic supervision of Charles Christopher O'Rourke, whose ominous No. 13 confronted the foe for 60 minutes, Boston College snuffed out the flame of gargantuan Georgetown's 23-game streak by the small but significant margin of one point, 19-18, at Fenway Park yesterday afternoon.

The somber and skinny citizen of Malden, Mass., mailed in his claims to the all-America jury with a barrage of passes that pierced the enemy from start to finish, and he was the difference, a 158-pound difference, between two mighty football teams.

But O'Rourke had a good deal of difficulty reaching the Post Office with his claims, because a large portion of the 41,700 babbling, incoherent congregation stormed upon the field at the finish and insisted on escorting him in a tumultuous parade to the dressing rooms.

Fully confident of the genius of the strawhead from Malden, the indomitable Bostonians bore the real mark of champions at dusk last night, for they faced 0-10 and 13-16 deficits at various stages of this glory game and fought back on top.

They survived one of the very greatest games of football ever played in these precincts because they simply refused to accept defeat in any form. Henry Woronicz, Mike Holovak and Monk Maznicki scored their touchdowns; Maznicki kicked a point, the winning point, it proved.

The hard-hitting Georgetown nearly blew them out of the ball park with a ferocious 10-point assault in the first five minutes of the game. A 42-yard field goal by August Lio, the granite guard, and a one-yard touchdown plunge by Julius Koshlap, which was set up by Hoya tackle Earl Fullilove who had blocked O'Rourke's attempted quick-kick in the close vicinity of the Eagle citadel, dazed the B.C. supporters in the stands.

But these swift and singular feats did not daze the grim young men of Leahy. Behind for the first time in eight straight games, they accepted the ensuing kickoff and raced down the ball park for 72 yards and scored in seven plays.

Henry Woronicz, the hard rock from Brockton, Mass., snipped a deflected pass thrown by, of all people, Lou Montgomery, and stalked five yards to the first touchdown. The play consumed 21 yards from scrimmage.

In the second period, the battling Bostonians moved 90 yards through and over the enemy, a touchdown march which O'Rourke personally instigated with a reeling 30-yard run.

B.C. had to score this touchdown twice, for Maznicki caught a pass from O'Rourke while he was leaping beyond the limits of the field, and it was necessary for Holovak to finally plunge one yard for the points.

The Eagles, in fact, nearly scored three times in this sequence of plays. Immediately after Maznicki fielded a pass out of bounds, O'Rourke sped a bullet over the center to Woronicz in the end zone, but the big Boston end had a half-nelson clamped on him by Hoya halfback Bill McLaughlin and was unable to hold the ball. Georgetown was penalized for the infraction of the interference rule and the ball was moved to their one from their 13. Holovak immediately plunged over.

Thus B.C. led, 13-10, when the combatants stalked off the field for the intermission, turning the premises over to the rival toot ensembles.

Georgetown turned on the offensive heat upon returning to the ring and went 66 yards on some fierce running by James Castigifa, a veritable battering ram, and Koshlap assisted on an aerial dart from Koshlap to Michael Kopcik, the big end.

After McFadden, the blocking back, had gone over to make it 16-13 for Georgetown, Maznicki darted in to deflect Lio's attempted point-after conversion. That was a mightily important defensive play. Nobody thought so at the time, but it was the difference between victory and defeat each way.

At any rate, Boston College took the ensuing kickoff and, virtually ignoring its ground game, swept right into a 19-16 lead on a six-play, 66-yard onslaught which Maznicki turned into a scoring foray when he picked an O'Rourke pass out of the air and raced 24 yards into the end zone.

The Eagles wiped out 43 yards in that one shot. Maznicki ran beautifully after making the catch. He headed directly at Koshlap, faked him, then twisted by, and just outran Louis Ghecas into the end zone.

O'Rourke did not score a point for his side, but at the very end of the game he gave Georgetown an intentional safety and thus scored the final two points of the day — for the other side.

This was considered the very smartest contribution to the ball game. O'Rourke went into deep kicking formation, ran into his end zone upon receiving the ball, then fled back and forth across the field to kill 22 precious seconds before Georgetown became conscious of what was going on and hauled him to the sod.

The seconds consumed by this adroit act subsequently cost the Hoyas two prayer plays, because three plays later the game was all over.

A faint idea of the breathless ebb and flow of this titanic tussle for national recognition can be gained from the period scores. They were: First, Georgetown 10-0, then 10-6; second, Boston College 13-10; third, Georgetown 16-13 and Boston College 19-16; fourth, Boston College 19-18.

The battling birds from the Heights won the statistical contest by a far greater margin than they won the game itself. Boston College led in first downs by 13 to 6, in net yards rushing by 89 to 68, and in passing by a wide difference of 209 yards to 54.

The wide difference is represented by O'Rourke, who cocked back his arm and sped 23 passes against the uncertain aerial defenses of the foe. Fourteen of those target tagging throws were caught, a 15th was grabbed beyond the end of the field and was obliterated from the records, and three others were dropped in a clear field by his associates.

The issue yesterday was between finesse and force, and Georgetown represented force. Behind a tremendously big and competent line, it was loaded with power, but power wasn't enough, because B.C. fielded an adamant set of forwards, too.

Only once did they yield, and that was when Georgetown journied 65 yards to score in the third period, its only sustained advance and, at that, instigated by a local miscue.

The unhappy victim was sophomore fullback Mike Holovak who, like O'Rourke, Woronicz and the two guards, Joe Zabilski and George Kerr, played the whole game without relief. And he entered the fray with a muscle strain.

At the start of the third period, down on Georgetown's 40-yard line, Holovak grabbed a risky enemy pass on the run. He was tackled five yards later and fumbled to an unidentified opportunist foeman. Thus, instead of buckling down to a defensive stand, Georgetown got the ball again and away it went with Castiglia and Koshlap to a touchdown.

Georgetown had the power and occasionally it shed some deception from its advertised spread formation, notably when McFadden scored from the 5-yard line in the third period. This play was a double reverse from Koshlap going to the right, to Ghecas coming back the other way and, finally, to McFadden who cut sharply over his right tackle.

The real strategy involved McFadden's ball carrying, for he is strictly a blocker, and nobody paid a great deal of attention to him while the play was forming.

But Boston College had the finesse. It opened the throttle wide on the offense it had been carefully concealing week after week and game after game. It unveiled a spread formation of its own, operated a flanker that brought about one score, penetrated the Georgetown secondary with cagey pass plays, and the wonder of it is that Boston College did not score more touchdowns than it did.

The statistics bear testimony to the fact that the team on that field yesterday which could travel any length for touchdowns was Boston College. It journeyed 228 yards for its three touchdowns. A field goal, a blocked kick and a safety accounted for 11 of the enemy's 18 points.

The field was not in bad condition, being surprisingly firm after the four-day drench, but it was no race track, either.

Although it was shocked by a five-minute deficit of 10 points at the outset, the figures show that Boston College made 11 first downs and Georgetown none in the first half.

The initial blow of Jack Hagerty's Hoyas caused violent shudders as far south as the press box, and just about then everybody save the gold-trousered Eagles had kissed the ball game goodbye hardly before it had started.

With the sole exception of the Boston University game, the Eagles had all year been striking swiftly at the start, piling up a two-touchdown lead and demoralizing the foe. They had never experienced the anxiety of being behind and nobody was sure just how they'd react.

Georgetown came out of its corner, struck a two-fisted attitude in the center of the arena, and had 10 points without so much as having to work up a sweat to advance it more than 17 yards through the agency of its own offense.

Lio belted the opening kickoff far beyond the limits of the Boston end zone. B.C. put the ball in play at its 20, gained four yards in a smack by Holovak, then got fined 12 yards for holding.

O'Rourke kicked immediately, and Ghecas snaked-hipped back 18 yards. The Hoyas moved it ahead only seven yards in two line bucks and a pass, so August "the Lion" Lio, who was born and bred in East Boston, Mass., eyed the uprights, the slight angle, and declared it was a cinch.

So McFadden held and Lio put the weight of a piano leg behind his kick and sent the ball tumbling 42 yards to and over the cross bar and many yards beyond.

Lio kicked off again. O'Rourke raced it from his goal to the 26, then tried his fatal quick-kick. Fullilove, the able Alabaman at Georgetown's left tackle, burst through without being impeded, blocked the effort squarely and chased the ball until it escaped him out of bounds at the B.C. 10.

The Hoyas scored in three tries from there. The first was a 2-yard left end effort by Ghecas from spread formation. The second was a pass from Koshlap to McFadden. McFadden stepped out of bounds a yard from a touchdown. The third and last was a cutback shot over the B.C. left tackle by Koshlap, and Lio kicked the 10th point.

The Eagles then declared themselves in on the game. Gene Goodreault, who was subsequently carried from the field with a leg injury, received a short kickoff and legged it for 18 yards to his 28. Lou Montgomery, who started at right half, made five yards. O'Rourke faked a throw to Montgomery in a flanking position far to the right, then whipped a pass down the middle to Hank Toczylowski that gained to the Georgetown 45.

A fling to Woronicz put it on the 21 and a third pass scored. It was thrown by Montgomery from the flanker position, which he had been taking eight yards beyond his right end. O'Rourke took the ball from center, whirled, threw over laterally to Montgomery, who in turn, fired a wobbly pass down the field.

It was intended for Woronicz in the first place, but Allen Matuza, the Georgetown center, touched it first, making a basketball leap for the ball and succeeding in tipping it upward. Woronicz was parked directly behind him, made a breadbasket catch and stomped five strides into the end zone.

Maznicki was rushed in for Montgomery for the purpose of kicking the point. He had two tries, because Georgetown was offside on the first, and failed twice.

O'Rourke's 30-yard run through his right tackle and reverse course in the secondary late in the period instigated a 90-yard scoring march. On the last play of the period, O'Rourke chucked one to Maznicki in the right flat for a 32-yard gain, and a toenail tackle by Ghecas, the last Hoya standing en route to the goal line, saved a score then and there.

When the play moved into the second period, O'Rourke tossed another, straight from T-formation without the backfield shift, that Goodreault caught down the middle on the Hoya 18. On fourth down, needing seven yards, O'Rourke cut back inside his right tackle and went clear up to the seven.

Here B.C. practically scored three times to get six points. First, Maznicki caught one off the field of play beyond the end zone. Then Woronicz was virtually blackjacked while in the act of catching another in the end zone, and finally Holovak powered over behind Gladchuk for the score. Maznicki converted the point-after kick.

O'Rourke's rifling right arm accounted for 61 of the 66 yards as the Eagles traveled for their third score in the third period when they were down, 13-16. O'Rourke started this, too. He caught the kickoff following Georgetown's second tally and wriggled to his 34. Two plays later, he faked the Hoyas secondary all out of shape, then found Toczylowski down the center alley with a bulleting pass. Toczylowski planted it on the Georgetown 45. Holovak slugged it ahead, three yards, then O'Rourke did some more artistic faking toward his left before spiraling a pitch to the right which Maznicki snared, then ran 24 yards to the promised land.

Maznicki deliberately ran straight at the Georgetown left defensive wingback, sidestepped him, then beat another defender to the end zone, being spilled over the line by a fine, but fruitless tackle.

And as these inadequate lines are being written, the precincts in and around Kenmore Square are still cluttered up with delirious and delighted citizens who claim, and rightly so, that Charles Christopher O'Rourke of Malden, Mass., and Chester Gladchuk of New Britain, Conn., and Joseph Manzo of Medford, Mass., and everybody on the outfit, but especially O'Rourke, should be on the 1940 all-America team.

It just may be that one of 'em will be — and he's going to be a right-handed passer with skinny shanks, a Buster Keaton poker face, and a Harvard haircut. His name is O'Rourke.

6

Boston College vs. Tennessee

THE SUGAR BOWL, JANUARY 1, 1941

NEW ORLEANS — The incredible Cinderella men of Boston College beat a profusion of bad breaks and the best Tennessee team of all time in the woolliest Sugar Bowl game in a series of seven this humid afternoon.

The score was 19-13, and as the Eagles from the North soared over the ramparts of gridiron glory it was the sleepy-looking thin man, Chuckin' Charlie O'Rourke, who shed a goat's skin in the last five minutes of a fierce and turbulent contest to pass and pedal the Volunteers off the field.

It was O'Rourke whose miscue of a punt set up Tennesse's first touchdown, but it was also O'Rourke who caught on fire in the fading moments, rifled two daring passes into the hungry arms of substitute end Ed Zabilski, then darted through the Volunteer line for 24 yards into the promised land on a run that for sheer inspiration has never been matched in this annual feature.

Never, until that breathless run by the somber Malden, Mass., citizen had Boston College been ahead in this fierce encounter, which kept a record throng of 73,181 clients in a constant uproar from the outset.

The swift Orange-shirted Tennesseeans drew first blood when they received a colossal break — an O'Rourke fumble — in the first four minutes of play, a break which led subsequently to a 46-yard march through and over the Bostonese. Van Thompson of Jackson, Tenn., scored it while riding four yards over B.C.'s right tackle on a power buck behind these blockers.

Robert Foxx converted and, at this point, it looked dreary indeed for the outcharged Eagles. They spent the rest of the half battling for their lives and once generated an offensive march that carried right down to the Tennessee 15, where a pass interception stopped 'em cold.

At intermission the Vols, looking superb and confident and altogether too classy for our side, were up, 7-0. It appeared to be merely a question whether or not B.C. could keep the score down.

But then things commenced to happen. The first time Tennessee attempted to kick in the third period, Henry Woronicz, the B.C. left end, slashed through, blocked Foxx' attempted quick-kick back down the field where Joe Zabilski caught up with it at the Vols' 17.

Two plays later, B.C. was into the checkered end zone. Mickey Connolly, who'd started the half for O'Rourke, swept the Tennessee left flank behind a rousing Toczylowski block to beat the pack into the far right corner of the field.

Little Monk Maznicki calmly hoisted the seventh and tying point through the woodwork; and the throng, or all of it which wasn't strictly for Tennessee, went mad with joy.

The Vols' answer to this was a savage 55-yard touchdown march with the ensuing kickoff. Buist Warren struck hard at a pileup at left tackle, then slid off and across the goal two yards away for the score. Newman picked up a fumble on the place-kick conversion, attempted to circle Don Currivan's end and was slapped down hard and emphatically.

That made it 13-7 against the Cinderella men, but away they went to tie it up again on a 68-yard journey which sophomore Mike Holovak brought to a happy conclusion with a power buck straight over the middle of the lifting B.C. line.

Now here was your tie and here was your ball game if Maznicki could duplicate with a point-after conversion. But on the first try, two eager citizens on the left side of the Tennessee line were offside. So referee Buck Cheves planted the ball one foot from the goal and now Hank Toczylowski, the play picker, reversed his signals, called for a line buck and it failed. Holovak was strangled right on the

Eagles' line of scrimmage.

The score was tied, 13-all.

At the outset of the fourth and final quarter, Tennessee was rolling along down the field. Foxx, a blinding fast carrier, supported by ferocious blocking, had just galloped 19 yards to the Eagle 17. B.C. stopped 'em here, with substitutes Joe Repko and Steve Levanitas powering through with a show of devastating defensive football.

O'Rourke spiraled the ball down the field. Johnny Butler caught it and dashed back 20 yards to his 44, and two long flings from Warren to Cifers and Coleman, his ends, reached the Eagle 12.

B.C. then rallied, grimly, gamely. They forced Tennessee to try a field goal from the Eagle 13-yard line. It failed, because Don Currivan, the sophomore from Mansfield who put B.C. into the Sugar Bowl with a fumble recovery vs. Holy Cross, sliced in to deflect Foxx's try from directly in front of the uprights.

And now the Cinderella men have the ball and they are 80 yards from victory and seven minutes from the finish. Over in the northeast corner of the field their loyal and loud supporters rise in a chant, "Go, Go, Go, Go!"

And the Cinderella men did. O'Rourke, his skinny shanks twinkling, slipped through right tackle carrying all-America Bob Suffridge on his back for five yards. In two blows, Maznicki moved the stakes to a first down at the 30.

Toczylowski then decided to go the whole distance in one try. He called for a cross-over pass to himself, but O'Rourke led him by a full stride as the B.C. blocking back raced down the left sideline all alone.

The next throw was to Maznicki. He, too, was alone and uncovered in the right flat, but O'Rourke's toss fell short and, although Maznicki turned, he was unable to engineer a shoestring catch.

Thus was the Tennessee defense set up for O'Rourke's third and fourth throws, both of 'em covered with glory.

The Vols were covering fast to the outside. So with Maznicki as a decoy, Ed Zabiliski sliced across the secondary from right end and snagged O'Rourke's pass dead over the center and staggered on for a 20-yard gain.

Again O'Rourke pitched and Zabiliski caught. It was the same battery and the same play. This one Zabiliski hugged to his breast grimly, for he was smothered by two Volunteers just as he received

O'Rourke's chin-high shot for a 19-yard gain.

The Vols were withering before O'Rourke's passing barrage. So the thin man fired again. This was into the right flat and Maznicki snagged it on the run, bumbed into two tacklers, but made seven yards to the Vol 24.

Now came the glory play, the lace curtain clincher. O'Rourke took the ball in T-formation, raised his arm in a passing fake to which the enemy defenders committed themselves completely.

But Chuckin' Charlie didn't chuck. He sprinted, instead, through a crevice at his left tackle. Once in the secondary, he turned to his right on almost a direct route behind the line of scrimmage. He ducked past one off-balance linebacker, then cut down the field. Not a hand was laid on him. Out ahead, George Kerr shielded him from a Tennessean who had no chance of ever heading off O'Rourke on his 24-yard race into the right hand corner of the field for the last, most important and winning touchdown of the game.

Maznicki missed the extra point kick, but the point was of no significance because only two minutes were left unexpired.

In the course of those two minutes, Tennessee gave up the ball on downs at its 40, retrieved it on downs, then saw O'Rourke intercept their last dying pass and run it 15 yards before he fell, literally exhausted.

That was the game and 50 seconds later the mad mob from Boston stormed upon the field, tussled with the local constabulary and finally succeeded in setting a Sugar Bowl record, by tearing the goal posts asunder.

This was one of the greatest post-season football games ever played. They've had some scorchers in this particular Bowl, but they unanimously agreed that this was the best of 'em all, played by the two best teams of 'em all.

B.C.'s Cinderella men won it, like they have won many more, because they refused to accept defeat or gruesome breaks or temporary setbacks.

Twice, for instance, Tennessee profited by pass interference penalties, at least one of them dubious in quality and called directly upon the B.C. two-yard line, where Mickey Connolly was charged with blocking off end Ed Cifers of the Vols. This set up Tennessee's second touchdown. In a subsequent Tennessee march, likewise the

Bostonians were slapped hard across the mouth by Fate when Maznicki, jumping to intercept a pass, deflected it to one side and it fell straight into the arms of a Volunteer.

The Cinderella men got no breaks and they asked for none. They scored three touchdowns the hard way.

Of course, Tennessee's opening blast was disconcerting. O'Rourke's fumble of the Vols' first kick, which Capt. Ackermann retrieved at the B.C. 27, upset the Eagles.

They stopped this immediate threat at their 15, with George Kerr and Chet Gladchuk personnally messing up the enemy passing. But O'Rourke's kick was short, after his side had taken over on downs, and the Vols rode home on a 46-yard march, 15 of which was a gift, when O'Rourke was called for pass interference at his 31.

Van Thompson's throw down the middle to Coleman ate up 14 yards. Chuckin' Charlie flattened the receiver with a fierce block. Then Thompson and Nowling simply bucked it across from the 22 behind an orange-shirted line which lifted the B.C. forwards back four and six yards at a lick.

A beautiful run by Gene Goodreault, game leg and all, on the receiving end of an O'Rourke pitch, contributed largely to B.C.'s only serious gesture in the first half. Goodreault gained 28 yards on the play, about half of it on the running end. He might have gone the distance, instead of being forced out at the Vol 31. A blocker out ahead turned to see what was going on and recovered too late to wipe out safety Buist Warren.

Cifers, an end, faded back to intercept a pass after O'Rourke and Maznicki had run the ball to the 20 and that chilled that threat.

In many respects, Mickey Connolly's 12-yard sprint around his right side for the touchdown that made it 7-all in the third period was the best of the conflict.

Woronicz had contributed his punt blocking stint, Joe Zabilski had recovered and Maznicki had chewed off three yards when the cool young customer from Norwalk, Conn., was asked to take the thing over.

He did. The Vols' left end crashed so fast that they didn't even bother to block him. Toczylowski, who was out ahead of Connolly, merely ran past him. Connolly swung deep then cut for the corner. Toczylowski murdered wingback Foxx with a terrific block and

Connolly ran like a race horse to beat two defenders to the right corner of the field.

The Cinderella men should have folded up and conceded the thing after that pass interference had given the Vols the ball two yards from the goal line, and virtually awarded 'em a 13-7 lead.

But they didn't. They came off the ropes swinging, moved 68 yards without a pause. Two determined smashes by Connolly, which was followed by a Connolly pass down the center to substitute end Freddy Naumetz for 17 yards, plus a 15-yard penalty when a Vol substitute talked, were contributing factors.

But in the end it was the B.C. line, infiltered with substitutes like Repko and Naumetz and Currivan and Dubzinski, which lifted the Vols back and back in the grinding march over the last 23 yards.

Maznicki, on a reverse to the left behind cracking blocks, slipped from the Vol 23 to the 15. Connolly drove, headlong and reckless, over right tackle to the Vol 10 for a first down, with goal to go. These were the toughest 10 yards of the game to get.

Holovak hit at right guard and struggled ahead for three yards. Maznicki, who is built low to the ground, and very fast, ducked under a tackler's arms and moved on to the Vol 2. Holovak was called on again, for a smack over left guard, and the Vols stopped him right on the lip of the goal. So it was fourth down, a foot to go. It could have been a yard or two yards or even three, for Holovak rode over the center, literally on the back of giant Chet Gladchuk, and catapulted deep into the end zone for a 13-13 tie.

Thus the stage was set for Chuckin' Charlie. For 55 minutes he was destined to be the goat of the seventh annual Sugar Bowl game. But in the end it was the thin man with the air-rifle arm and the twinkling shanks who spelled the difference between two mighty football teams.

I think the Tennesseeans have no reason to love this man O'Rourke.

Fate Brings a Date with Destiny
by Arch Ward

Fate Brings a
Date with Destiny

CHICAGO — The telephone rang in the hallway off the living room of the house at 820 Chestnut Street in Wabun, Mass. Floss was upstairs tucking Sue and Flossie in. Frankie the Third was in his pajamas, ready for bed after a good night huddle with his dad. The phone bell tinkled again. Probably it was Charlie O'Rourke, or maybe those folks from Norwalk, where he was due to speak at the banquet for Mickey Connolly. He stepped into the hall and picked up the phone.

"Mr. Frank Leahy?" queried an operator in crisp tones.

"Yes, this is Frank Leahy."

"I have a long distance phone call for you," the operator replied, "from Mr. Eddie Dunigan at Palm Beach, Florida. One moment, please. Go ahead, Mr. Dunigan, there's your party."

"Hello, Frank, how are you?"

" Fine, Eddie, fine. 'Bet you haven't any good old northern snow down there in Palm Beach. What do you know?" The receiver shook a trifle in his hands. Why would Eddie Dunigan be calling him from Florida, the same Dunigan who had followed him through his playing career at Notre Dame?

"Well, Frank, I know this much, and so do you — the job of athletic director and head coach at Notre Dame is open, and they want you to take it. Just had a call from there, and they want to know when it will be convenient for you to meet Father Frank Cavanaugh at The DeWitt Clinton Hotel in Albany, N. Y. The athletic board has met and has agreed that you're the man. How about it? Can you make it?"

Hours seemed to pass while the tall, sturdy-built, reddish-haired young man stood there in the hallway. Dunigan finally said, "Hello, Frank, hello — are you still on?"

"Yes, Eddie, I'm still on, but you sort of knocked me out on that last play. Sure, I'll make it. There are a lot of things to be cleared up, of course, but tell Father Frank I'll be there. I'm speaking at a banquet for one of our Boston College boys in Norwalk tomorrow night, but I think I can reach Albany early Wednesday morning. Goodbye, Eddie, and thanks." The receiver clicked and he walked slowly back into the living room. "Who was that, Dad?" asked young Frankie. "An old friend, son," he answered. "Better get up to bed now."

Thus began the homecoming journey of Francis William Leahy back to the University of Notre Dame, the school he had come to as a wide-eyed South Dakota prairie kid less than fourteen years before. In the ten years following his graduation, Leahy had done himself proud as an alumnus of the Indiana college whose athletic background is perennially synonymous with the great American sport of football. Hundreds of brilliant athletes had left the Notre Dame campus to build themselves even more shining careers as coaches and athletic directors. One of them — Knute Kenneth Rockne — never forsook the tree-lined walks and crowded playing fields of the university. He stayed to become the acknowledged master of football strategy and inspiration, welding the nation's greatest elevens year in and year out until death took him from the game in a Kansas airplane crash.

Leahy himself was one of Rockne's last pupils, and one of the great coach's favorites, not because of outstanding native ability, but because of a depth of character that was constantly reflected in his application to the fundamentals of the game, and, above all, his inherent courage and will to win. He had come up the hard way as a boy on the Dakota plains, and his road as a player and coach was no easier. In the decade after his graduation, Frank had served an arduous apprenticeship of eight seasons as an assistant at Georgetown, Michigan State and Fordham before becoming head coach of Boston College's Eagles in 1939. In two seasons, he sent the Eagles soaring to the topmost branch of the national gridiron tree.

Now, not quite thirty-three years of age, he was going home, home to the Dome, to the old Gym where he had first met Rockne, to venerable Cartier Field, to Notre Dame. Few athletic officials of Leahy's age are confronted with the responsibilities which the posts of athletic director and head football coach at Notre Dame carry, but those who knew the quiet Westerner were convinced that he was more than up to the job. A glance at the firm jaw and powerful wrists and into the searching eyes was sufficient to offset the disarming charm of his personal demeanor. Here, truly, was a proper exemplification of that familiar line, "He's a man! He's a man! He's a real Notre Dame man!" Yes, Frank Leahy was ready for the Big Job.

American newspaper readers are accustomed to all of the ceremonies attendant upon the hiring of a football coach—the batteries of photographers he must face, the fusillade of questions by reporters he must answer. As a general rule, the football public has at least an inkling of who the new coach will be before formal announcement of his choice is made.

Such is not the case at Notre Dame, where the selection of a man to guide the school's football destinies is an important job that must be weighed on every count, and the choosing is not completed until the field of candidates has been tested with a fine comb. The problem is a doubly difficult one for the authorities at Notre Dame because of the abundance of coaching talent which has sprung from its own campus.

Following Elmer Layden's resignation as athletic director and head football coach on February 3, 1941, to accept the post of commissioner of the National Football League after a brilliant seven-year career at his alma mater, speculation immediately began on his successor. The first projected list of likely candidates was a veritable Who's Who of football coaching, and every name was that of a Notre Dame man. The second-guessers in South Bend and on the campus compiled a formidable roster that included such men as Jimmy Crowley of Fordham, Harry Stuhldreher of Wisconsin, Buck Shaw of Santa Clara, Maurice "Clipper" Smith of Villanova,

Jimmy Phelan of Washington, Dr. Eddie Anderson of Iowa, Frank Thomas of Alabama, Gus Dorais of Detroit, Charley Bachman of Michigan State, Arthur Bergman of Catholic U., Mal Elward of Purdue, and Harry Mehre of Mississippi. And a few of the cannier handicappers added the name of a young fellow named Frank Leahy.

Seldom does your average sports fan have intimate knowledge of the manner in which a coach is hired. One of the most unusual situations of this type revolves around the route through which Frank Leahy came home to Notre Dame. It's a complex tale that never has been made public before, one which stretches from Notre Dame's administration building to a Florida hotel, and from Leahy's Massachusetts home to a rain-pelted automobile in Salinas, Calif. Now that story can be told.

This complicated transcontinental negotiation, climaxed by Leahy's signing of the contract as athletic director and head football coach, was one of the most astutely guarded secrets in modern athletic history. It had its inception in a campus conversation on a cold afternoon in January 1941, between Layden, who had gained national fame as a member of the Four Horsemen and later as Notre Dame's coach, and Father John J. Cavanaugh, C.S.C., vice president of the university and chairman of the faculty board in control of athletics. A close bond existed between the two men, dating back to Father Cavanaugh's own student days at Notre Dame (he was graduated from the university in 1923, Layden's junior year as a player, prior to joining the Congregation of Holy Cross, the religious order which conducts Notre Dame).

During this campus encounter, the priest noted that "The Thin Man" appeared to be preoccupied and finally asked him, "There's something on your mind, Elmer. Tell me about it."

"Yes, Father, there is, and I'd like to talk to you privately about it. I understand you're going to California within a few days, and I want to have a few minutes alone with you."

"Fine, Elmer. Why don't you drop by my room in Corby Hall tomorrow morning? I'll be leaving for the coast shortly after that, but we ought to be able to settle your problem before I get away."

"Thanks, Father. I'll see you in the morning."

The following morning, Layden told Cavanaugh that he had an

opportunity to become commissioner of the National Football League at a salary of $20,000 a year, with a five-year contract. The result of their conference was that Layden decided to accept the offer.

Before his departure for the West Coast, Cavanaugh visited with Father J. Hugh O'Donnell, C.S.C., president of the university, and told him of Layden's decision. Father O'Donnell, whose multitudinous duties as head of the great institution had not precluded a warm personal enthusiasm for its athletic life, regretted Layden's decision. Nevertheless, he realized that a successor for Layden would have to be named in the near future. O'Donnell then told Cavanaugh that he would arrange a list of eligible candidates during the latter's absence and suggested that they maintain close contact while the vice president was in California.

Following a three-day train trip, Cavanaugh arrived in Los Angeles, where he was a guest of Father Michael Lee in the Beverly Hills section. He didn't have to wait long to learn that Layden had made a speedy decision. He was getting ready for bed one evening, a week after his Corby Hall conversation with Layden, when he received a telephone call from Father John Rockwell, one of Notre Dame's staunchest Pacific coast fans and a particular admirer of Layden.

"Hello. Father Cavanaugh? This is Father Rockwell. Have you heard the terrible news? The barn is burning back home."

"The barn is burning? What do you mean, Father?"

"Yes, it's burning. Layden is lost. Haven't you seen the papers? He has quit Notre Dame."

So it had happened, and so soon. Cavanaugh went out to the corner newsstand and there found the story of Layden's acceptance of the job as commissioner of the National Football league. The stocky, personable priest's work had just begun. It was a monumental chore, this job of selecting a successor for Layden, and almost as difficult was the task of keeping the choice of that successor a secret until he was named.

Early the next morning, Cavanaugh put in a person-to-person call to Father O'Donnell, who had prepared a list of likely candidates for the head-coaching and athletic director positions. The two discussed this roster at some length. Outstanding were the names of

Leahy and of Lawrence "Buck" Shaw, the University of Santa Clara's handsome head coach, who had been a classmate of Cavanaugh's in his undergraduate days at Notre Dame. The vice president promised his superior that he would make every effort to see Shaw during his stay on the coast.

Here Cavanaugh's real problem began, of dodging ambitious newspapermen who had learned through press association reports that he, the chairman of the Notre Dame board of athletics, was in California. It was an assignment that called for no small amount of open-field dodging and running, but he wasted no time in going to work on it. Uppermost in his mind, of course, was the necessity of arranging a meeting with Shaw without disclosing the place or time to the press.

The solution finally struck him with the memory of a visit he had paid to Shaw in San Francisco in 1923. At that time, Cavanaugh was employed as a traveling representative for the Studebaker Corporation, since he had not yet decided to enter the priesthood. Afraid that mention of his own name in a telephone call to Shaw at Santa Clara might betray him, he adopted an alias, relying on Shaw's memory of their 1923 visit to identify him. He telephoned Shaw from the Beverly Hills rectory of Father Lee, his host.

When the connection was at last established, Shaw's ears were greeted by the following cryptic remark:

"Hello, Buck, this is Jimmy Egan. How are you?"

"Jimmy Egan?" answered the puzzled Santa Clara coach. "Sorry, you must have the wrong party. I don't know any Jimmy Egan."

"Now, Buck," continued Cavanaugh, "are you sure you don't remember a Jimmy Egan with whom you visited in The St. Francis Hotel back in 1923? Come on, try again."

The real identity of his caller then dawned on Shaw after he had cudgeled his memory for a few minutes, and he said, "John! What are you doing out here?"

"Buck, I'd like to see you for a while tonight. Can you meet me in Salinas? Jimmy Egan's train will arrive at 7:30 o'clock. O.K.?"

When Cavanaugh stepped off the train in Salinas that night, he was greeted by a driving rainstorm and the sound of the horn in an automobile parked near the station exit. He headed for the car. He and Shaw drove a few blocks to a side street, where Shaw parked the machine. For a solid hour, with the rain beating down on the top of the car, the two men discussed the purpose of the priest's unusual mission.

Shaw, one of the best linemen ever turned out at Notre Dame and later one of its most successful coaching graduates, was pleased that the athletic board had seen fit to consider him as a candidate for the job at his Alma Mater. He told Cavanaugh that he was interested but would be unable to make an immediate decision until he had consulted with the Santa Clara authorities and his family. Cavanaugh pointed out that the final decision would rest with the Notre Dame athletic board, which was scheduled to meet within a few days. After asking Shaw to keep their meeting and conversation confidential, the priest took his leave and caught the next train back to Los Angeles.

The next morning, Cavanaugh headed back to South Bend. On his arrival there, his suspicions that the newspapers would be pressing him were verified. On the train from Chicago to South Bend, one of the first stories to greet his eyes was one speculating on the outcome of a possible meeting between Shaw and himself during his visit to California. This, he realized, was sheer guesswork, for he knew that Shaw would have kept their confidence.

The priest was no sooner off the South Shore Line train than he was greeted by a couple of South Bend reporters, who besieged him with questions. He parried all of these until he could get to his quarters in Corby Hall. He had not removed his overcoat before his telephone began to ring, and another session of verbal weaving and bobbing ensued. But, once again, Cavanaugh came out into the open field, still refusing to make any definite announcement.

He knew the board was to meet on the following Monday night and decided to make a last minute check with Shaw for reference during the meeting. Again, he found himself blocked by the chance that a long distance call from the Notre Dame campus to Santa Clara might give away its purpose. He summoned John Mangan, the elderly Irishman who is one of the university's best beloved characters, and asked him to have one of the school cars ready for a little drive to near-by Marcellus, Mich. Mangan was unaware of the purpose of the ride at the time and was surprised later to discover that this short journey was the final stepping stone on the route that was to bring back a young fellow whom he had been the first to greet back in 1927 — Frank Leahy.

Cavanaugh put through his call to Shaw from Marcellus, and the Santa Clara coach's answer virtually sealed the choice of Leahy as Notre Dame's new head football coach and athletic director. Shaw told him that he had made his decision after talking with both his wife and the president of his university; he had decided to remain at Santa Clara and asked that he be excluded from all consideration when the final selection was made.

The athletic board gathered in the university administration building on the night following Cavanaugh's ride to Marcellus. The field had been narrowed down to Leahy and Shaw and, after the chairman's report on his telephone conversation, the members unanimously voted for Leahy's selection. They felt the choice was a wise one on every count. They were bringing home not only a Notre Dame man, but one whose proven quality of diligence and thorough knowledge of football had established him nationally as an assistant and as an oustanding practical lecturer in coaching schools before he ever became a head coach. And certainly his record at Boston College in the preceding season was one of the nation's best. He had led the Eagles through an undefeated campaign, which was climaxed by the dramatic conquest of a great Tennessee eleven in New Orleans' Sugar Bowl.

Still the road was not clear. There were at least two more perplexing factors before the transaction could be consummated. For one, there was the matter of reaching Leahy in Boston without letting the world know about his appointment. Further, there remained the question of discovering whether he had signed another contract with Boston College and if he would be able to obtain a release from it. The first could be settled and would lead to the solution of the second only by another roundabout phone call.

Eddie Dunigan, the Oak Park, Ill., business executive who had long been a firm friend of Notre Dame athletics, was known to be in Palm Beach at the time. Father O'Donnell chose him as liaison man and instructed Father Frank Cavanaugh, brother of John, to arrange a meeting with Leahy in Albany. Father Frank immediately phoned Dunigan, and Dunigan made his call to Leahy, and reported back. Alexander Graham Bell never played football, but one of the most complex, forward-lateral plays in the history of his invention had clicked.

Now let us shift the scene of this backstage story of a coach's appointment to Boston. There we find our hero himself in the midst of a rather complicated situation, thanks to a strange combination of circumstances.

After the Sugar Bowl triumph, Leahy received two coaching offers from other sources before he ever left New Orleans, and a couple of other opportunities awaited him on his arrival in Boston. But the Boston College authorities had mentioned a new contract to him during the middle of the season, and he had promised to confer with them before making any outside decisions. This contract was duly presented to him, but Leahy did not sign it immediately. Instead, he carried it with him in his inside coat pocket. He withheld his signature, because he felt, with the loyalty to his aids that is characteristic of him, that the terms offered to his assistants — Tex McKeever, Joe McArdle and Johnny Druze — were not adequate to justify his own signature.

Ultimately, the terms he sought for his assistants were adjusted to his satisfaction, but still he didn't sign it, continuing to carry it in his coat. Time and again, John Curley, Boston College's graduate manager of athletics, entreated him to sign it and have done with it. Leahy had brought the Eagles to the gridiron heights in two short years; he had restored New England's prestige in the game; and why shouldn't he stay on to add to his reputation as one of the nation's most brilliant young coaches?

Then came the night of February 3, 1941. Remember that date. It's a significant one in American football. It was the date on which Elmer Layden made his important decision to resign from Notre Dame and take the post of commissioner of professional football. That February night also was the beginning of the chain of events which led to Leahy's return to Notre Dame.

It was six o'clock when Leahy, McKeever and Bill Sullivan (then Boston College's director of publicity and currently the owner of the New England Patriots of the National Football League) dropped into Leahy's office. He was looking for some mail, when Curley, who occupied an adjoining office, stepped out and made another plea relative to the contract.

"Why don't you sign it right now, Frank?" he asked.

"All right, Jack," Leahy suddenly replied. "Got a pen handy?"

Curley produced a pen, but found it didn't have any ink in it. He scurried around the office, refilled it, and handed it to Leahy, who signed the document and handed it to Curley.

"Thanks a lot, Frank," Curley said, and then, in the presence of McKeever and Sullivan, added, "If Notre Dame should ever ask you to go back, we'll be very happy to release you."

Before separating, Leahy and Curley agreed that public announcement of Leahy's signed contract should be postponed until a week later, when the annual "B" football banquet was to be held.

Sullivan and Leahy, that same night, were scheduled to attend a banquet in Haverhill in honor of Gene Goodreault, the Eagles' great end. Before setting out, however, they decided to have dinner at Leahy's home. En route to Haverhill they became temporarily lost in a snowstorm and were slightly tardy in arriving. When they entered the lobby of the auditorium, they were besieged by a score of Boston newspapermen and B.C. alumni.

"What are you going to do, Frank?" they chorused.

Leahy thought they were referring to his unsigned contract. But it took only a minute to realize that they were trying to tell him that Layden had resigned, a fact of which he was completely unaware, and that the job of head football coach and athletic director at his old school was open! Leahy was stunned by the news. He received a further shock when the next day's papers carried a story announcing that he had signed a new contract with Boston College, a story he had thought would not be news until the forthcoming "B" banquet.

Leahy immediately contacted Curley, who told him that he had inadvertently confided to a friend that "Yes — Leahy had signed the new contract." The friend promptly adjourned to a telephone booth in a cigar store near the campus and called the story into a Boston paper. Curley thus was forced to inform the other papers. He further added that Father Maurice Dullea, the new moderator of athletics at Boston College, was out of town at the time and that he would be unable to make any decision on his promise to release him until the priest returned.

The young coach was still in a quandary five days later, when the fateful phone call from Eddie Dunigan reached him in his home. He was one of the principal speakers at a home town banquet in Norwalk, Conn., for halfback Mickey Connolly of the Eagle eleven, and he confided his opportunity to meet with Father Frank Cavanaugh in Judge Paul Connery, a Fordham graduate and a longtime friend.

Judge Connery arranged a special car with a police escort for the ride from Norwalk to Albany. The banquet for Connolly didn't end until nearly midnight, and by the time Leahy reached the hotel in Albany it was four o'clock in the morning. He checked in, got five hours' sleep and then went to Father Frank's room. Their meeting was a reunion between teacher and pupil, for the priest had been his English professor and was rector of Sophomore Hall during his student days at Notre Dame.

Father Frank was amazed at the manner in which Leahy, the South Dakota student, had matured as Frank Leahy, the football coach. He presented Notre Dame's offer, then asked Leahy a number of questions relative to contract terms, only to find himself being quizzed by the young coach. On one point Leahy was emphatic — that the contract permit him to bring his Boston College assistants — McKeever, McArdle and Druze — to Notre Dame with him.

Father Frank then interrupted their chat to put in a long distance call for his brother, Father John, and when the connection was made, Leahy and the Notre Dame vice president went into a telephone huddle. It didn't take long for Father John to realize that Leahy was definitely interested in the position, but was still barred by the fact that he hadn't obtained his release from the Boston College contract.

Later that afternoon, Leahy returned to Boston and within a few days was able to secure a release from Father Francis Murphy, S.J., president of Boston College, and Graduate Manager Curley.

At 3:15 o'clock on the afternoon of February 15, 1941, Leahy arrived on the Notre Dame campus and immediately went to the Main Administration Building where, less than fourteen years before, he had registered as a student, and signed the contract in Father O'Donnell's office to coach the football team that Rockne had once coached and of which he had been a member.

Frank Leahy, a true Fighting Irishman, had come home.

The Notre Dame Years

7

Notre Dame vs. Arizona

SEPTEMBER 27, 1941

NOTRE DAME, Ind. — The Notre Dame Irish this afternoon conducted an interesting experiment which revealed the following facts:

1. A convincing 38-7 conquest of the University of Arizona's Wildcats.

2. One pitcher and several catchers in a multiple battery which practically made this a baseball rather than a football contest.

3. A well conditioned first-string Irish eleven, with a stout supporting cast, which encouraged 20,000 eyewitnesses of the day to suspect that whatever the eight remaining games on Notre Dame's 1941 schedule produce in scoring results, they will deliver a show in which offense is predominant.

The Irish scored six points in each of the first two quarters, added 14 in the third and concluded with 12 more in the final quarter. Their defensive potentialities weren't given a proper test by a light Arizona team which made its only points on a 65-yard pass from Bob Ruman to Bob Johnson in the second quarter. But it can be set down quite definitely that this Notre Dame team, given the ball, will not trifle with any kindergarten shots at the line.

Today, they moved rapidly out of a blend of formations in which the basic Notre Dame shift and the popular T pattern were foremost. Add to this a passing attack which makes this one of the most air-minded teams the Irish have sent out in years, and you can anticipate few dull moments while watching these lads this semester.

The Whit Wyatt of this ensemble is Angelo Bortolo Bertelli. This West Springfield, Mass., sophomore threw 14 passes and completed 11 for 245 yards. In all, the Irish made good on 14 out of 20 passes, one of them being tossed by Don Hogan, late of Chicago's St. Ignatius High School, for the final touchdown. The catchers in this setup included Steve Juzwik, Bob Dove, George Murphy and Tom Miller.

Bertelli can give thanks to grand protection for his pitching assignments to Capt. Paul Lillis and Jim Brutz, the Irish tackles, and Wally Ziemba, the Hammond kid who made his debut as a center this afternoon. And when Bertelli isn't on the mound, there are two other artists ready to go. There's Juzwik at right half and Dippy Evans, who demonstrated with 78-yard touchdown jaunt that he should be one of the fastest fullbacks in the country.

Notre Dame dallied not for long after receiving the kickoff, which Evans toted back to his own 26-yard line. From there in five swift moves, including two passes by Pitcher Bertelli, they romped down to the Arizona 44-yard line before Evans elected to kick. After Arizona, which blew five yards on a first-down reverse, kicked, the Irish really warmed up to their work, proceeding from their own 47-yard mark to the Wildcats' 2-yard stripe, where they yielded the ball on downs.

Major factors in this drive were the consistent driving of Bertelli and Evans, and Juzwik's fondness for sweeping around Arizona's right end. It appeared that Juzwik was en route to a touchdown on the ninth maneuver of the parade, but he was knocked out of bounds on the 2-yard line. On the next play, fourth down, Evans was spilled for a yard loss and Arizona took charge of the ball.

The Wildcats promptly kicked out of bounds on their own 48-yard line. Bertelli actually failed on a pass, but fired his next effort to Dove for a nine-yard profit. Evans then delivered five yards to produce a first down and added two more on the next play. Bertelli then hurled one of his swift passes to Dove for a first down on the Wildcat 19-yard stripe. Evans came through with another three, then Bertelli pitched a shoulder high curve to Dove for sixteen yards and a touchdown.

Juzwik, who only a couple practice evenings ago made forty consecutive conversions, sliced his attempt and the Irish had to be content with a 6-0 advantage.

The second Notre Dame team appeared for duty at the outset of the second quarter, and after permitting Arizona to disturb the house constituency by driving to the Irish 31, where a first down Wildcat pass was intercepted by Bob Hargrave, began the move that indicated they could count as well as the first eleven. This was a fifty-two yard march in which Bill Earley, Jack Warner and Creighton Miller were the main factors. Warner provided the climax with a twenty-one yard toss to Earley for the touchdown, but failed to make the extra point.

Bob Ruman returned the Irish kickoff 23 yards to his own 32-yard line. Bill Lovin was dropped for a two-yard deficit by John Kovath, but on the next play Ruman went in at left halfback and passed to Bob Johnson, who eluded Bob Hargrave and Warner in time to field the ball for a 65-yard gain and a touchdown. The Irish then kicked the extra point. This was consummated with less than three minutes of the half remaining and the Irish varsity soon returned to the ball game.

The top hands opened the second half and required a mere eight plays to make the score 19-7. Only two minutes and 50 seconds had elapsed by the time Juzwik got back in kicking stride and converted the extra point. Bertelli hustled the Arizona kickoff seventeen yards to his 32-yard stripe; then, after adding two yards, turned the carrying job over to Evans, who went thirteen yards in three plays.

Bertelli then fired two strikes in a row, the first to George Murphy who caught it for a ten-yard gain and a first down on the Wildcats' 41. Bertelli struck again by throwing a sinker to Juzwik who scampered thirty-two yards to the Wildcats' 9. Juzwik followed this up by asking Bernie Crimmins to escort him around his favorite beat, the Wildcat right end, for a touchdown.

Toward the end of the third period, Arizona again became annoying, proceeding from its own 27-yard line to the Irish 30; the decisive happening in this march being a pass which Earley knocked into Johnson's arms in an attempt at interception. Ziemba, Dove and Earley soon put an end to this with a set of tackles which cost the Wildcats fifteen yards and caused the latter to kick into the Irish end zone. The first play produced the aforesaid T-formation maneuver, which found Evans hammering at his right guard, shifting to the left once he was in the clear and continuing seventy-eight yards with only Bill Smetana giving anything approximating pursuit. Bertelli returned to add the extra point.

With six minutes of the fourth quarter gone, Bolger rushed in to block Ruman's attempted punt, which eventually went out of bounds on the Wildcat 12-yard line. Hogan then sailed around left end on the next play for a touchdown, but his extra point kick went astray. Hogan and the brothers Miller then needed just three plays from the Arizona 37-yard line to make the score 38-7.

Creighton Miller contributed nine yards in two smashes at the line. Then Hogan, disdaining one would-be tackler, casually lined the ball at Tom Miller, who brushed aside two defenders and caught the pass for a touchdown. Hogan's try for the extra point failed.

8

Notre Dame vs. Navy

NOVEMBER 8, 1941

BALTIMORE, Md. — A Notre Dame bomber, with Angelo Bertelli at the sights, blasted Navy's powerful ship fore and aft this afternoon in Municipal stadium. And when Bertelli ceased firing, the Irish had successfully defended an unbeaten record, 20-13, in the most brilliant battle of the 14-year series with the Midshipmen.

A capacity throng of 64,795, including the regiment of 3,100 naval students from nearby Annapolis, jammed Baltimore's huge Municipal Stadium. They watched Navy's superior line rip wide holes in the Irish forward line to negotiate a 7-7 tie in the second period.

They also saw Navy capitalize suddenly on an alert pass defense to knot the score again at 13-13 in the third period, and finally these hoarse thousands, equally divided in their partisanship, watched the Irish parade to victory with accurate passes, then doggedly defend as Navy's big guns of a brutal running attack blazed away futilely in the gathering darkness of this gray November afternoon.

The veterans of the Notre Dame varsity carried the burden of the play as usual. Jim Brutz and Capt. Paul Lillis at the tackle posts head the list of heroes. Then there was Wally Ziemba, who backed up the right side of the Irish line, Bernie Crimmins who checked Navy's most serious threat by perfectly diagnosing the play and intercepting a pass in his own end zone, and finally the field generals, Harry Wright and Bob Hargrave, who shuttled in and out to direct the team with nearly flawless skill.

But today, the performance of Notre Dame's defensive ends under constant pressure from the zig zag runs to Clark and Busik, literally seemed inspired. John Kovatch, Bob Dove and Jack Barry time and again smashed the Navy interference and brought down the ballcarrier for losses.

The bellwether of the Irish victory marches, of course, was sophomore Bertelli who now has achieved a record for accuracy and distance probably unrivaled in gridiron history for a first-year man. Today Bertelli threw 18 times. He completed 12 passes for a total gain of 232 yards. His season's record, including 3 completions in nine attempt's for ten yards under the impossible conditions of the Army game, now is 52 completions in 89 attempts. Bertelli's passing in seven games has gained 713 yards.

Irish fullback Dippy Evans, who plays defensive left halfback, set the stage for Notre Dame's first touchdown drive on the second play of the second period. Evans stepped in front of Busik's long pass near the east sideline, took the ball from Sammy Boothe, for whom it was intended, then jerked loose from Boothe's clutching hands and fled downfield to Navy's 41-yard line before he was rushed out of bounds.

Evans' stirring run signalled the Irish attack. He followed with a thrust at Navy's left tackle for two yards. The Irish then were penalized five yards for backfield-in-motion, the first of three such assessments, but Bertelli dropped back in front of perfect protection and fired the ball to Bill Earley, his right halfback. Earley took the ball at full speed running to his left and a half step in front of Navy's Alan Cameron on the Middies' 26-yard line. Earley was knocked out of bounds on the Navy 2 by Midshipman John Harrell.

Evans then hit center for a half yard, and on the next play Dippy sliced inside of defensive right tackle and tumbled over and over deep into the end zone for the touchdown. Juzwik rushed back into the game and kicked the extra point.

Bertelli almost pitched the Irish to a second touchdown in the period, but after Notre Dame arrived at Navy's 11-yard line, a pass bounded high in the air from the receiver's hands and Werner of the Navy grabbed the ball and returned it to his own 16-yard line. Soon-after, Navy moved to a tie.

From their own 46-yard line, to which point Clark had returned nine yards with Evans' kick, the Midshipmen's second team swept fifty-four yards in eleven plays. Clark's reverse around the Irish left flank on the third play netted nineteen yards and a first down on the Irish 30-yard line. The Irish line then yielded only two yards in as many rushing plays. A third-down pass was incomplete, but on the last down, Clark passed to Bob Zoeller, his left end, who sprinted in behind Evans to take the ball. Evans' pursuit tumbled Zoeller on the Irish 7.

Clark plunged for a yard and then got three yards at the Irish right end. His next plunge against a Notre Dame five-man line carried within inches of the goal line. On fourth down, against a six-man defensive line, Clark hurled himself over inside of the Notre Dame left tackle. Bob Leonard's kick tied the score.

Evans then took Busik's subsequent kickoff back to the Irish 21, and from here the Irish needed only seven plays to cover seventy-nine yards for a touchdown.

Evans plunged over Navy's right tackle for two yards and added three yards when he ran the same play from a "Notre Dame spread" formation. On third down, Bertelli passed in the left flat to Evans, who with the aid of a terrific block by Matt Bolger on Midshipman center Dick Fedon, made a first down on the Irish 40.

On the next two plays, Bertelli passed to Wright for seven yards and Evans hit right tackle for ten yards and a first down on Navy's 43. Bertelli's third-consecutive successful pass was caught downfield in the middle of the Navy's secondary by Bolger who was stopped on Navy's 17-yard line. Bertelli then passed to Juzwik at the line of scrimmage, a legal screen pass and Juzwik filtered through the secondary, finally evading Dick Opp to cross the goal line. Juzwik missed the kick for the extra point. At the half, the Irish led, 13-7.

Navy then tied the score after four minutes of the third quarter. From his own 19-yard line, Bertelli tried a first-down pass to Dove, failed to lead him sufficiently and Cameron, Navy's defensive right halfback, cut in behind Dove to intercept on the Irish 32-yard line and continued down the west sideline behind hastily formed interference. Dove whirled but could not overtake Cameron who soon crossed the Irish goal line. Leonard missed the point-after kick that would have given Navy the lead.

The Midshipmen made only one first down in the entire third period as Notre Dame dominated the play. The Irish finally got started on its winning drive with one minute of the quarter to go. Earley returned Busik's punt three yards to Navy's 49-yard line. On second down, Bertelli passed to Earley for fourteen yards, then threw 27 yards to Evans for a first down on Navy's 8. Evans failed to gain at right guard and the teams changed goals.

Evans then plunged for two yards at right tackle. On the next play, without a preliminary backfield shift, a maneuver that caught the Navy linemen unprepared, Evans took a direct pass from center and sprinted six yards between Navy's guards to score. Juzwik kicked the extra point for the 20-13 tabulation.

On the next series, Navy took the kickoff and marched from its own 41-yard line to the Irish 3. En route the Midshipmen linked together four-consecutive first downs. Clark led the drive, carrying or passing on 11 of 12 plays. But after a first down on the Irish 6-yard line, and after Clark hit guard for three yards, he lost five on the next play at left end. Clark's next thrust netted a yard, and on fourth down Crimmins intercepted Clark's pass in the end zone. Lillis, Brutz, Kovatch and Ziemba returned to the Irish line when the Navy assault had surged to their 30.

Navy's last desperate effort in the closing two minutes again crossed midfield, but Busik's passes failed before the rushing of Kovatch and Barry, and the Irish took over to stall for 40 seconds with two running plays.

9

Notre Dame vs. Northwestern

NOVEMBER 15, 1941

EVANSTON, Ill. — Notre Dame's undefeated Irish, ever alert opportunists, yesterday let Northwestern's Wildcats amass the incidental statistics while they harvested the fruits of victory. Notre Dame made a touchdown and added the extra point. Northwestern matched the touchdown but didn't add the extra point. Thus, Notre Dame won the 21st game with Northwestern, its 16th victory of the series, 7-6, before a capacity crowd of 48,000 in Dyche Stadium.

The Irish were the first to score. They did it a minute and a half after the start of the second half on a sixteen-yard pass from Angelo Bertelli to Matt Bolger for the touchdown. Steve Juzwik added the payoff extra point. Seven and a half minutes after Notre Dame tallied, Otto Graham climaxed a sixty-yard Wildcat drive with a 4-yard plunge to a touchdown. Dick Erdlitz's effort to add the extra point was blocked by Wally Ziemba, the Irish center.

Notre Dame did a clever job protecting that one-point lead. The Wildcats threatened again in the third quarter and had a first down on the Irish 28-yard line when the period ended. The drive failed when Erdlitz missed a field goal attempt from the 21-yard line early in the fourth quarter. Notre Dame withstood another drive when Juzwik intercepted a pass back of his goal line.

And at the finish, the Irish themselves were pounding away. They were stopped on the 2-yard line after a forty-one yard march, and on the last play of the game Juzwik came back to the Wildcats' 6-yard line after intercepting a pass.

This was Notre Dame's seventh victory, with the only blot on its record being a scoreless tie with the Army. It was Northwestern's third defeat. The Wildcats previously lost close ones to Michigan and Minnesota.

Don Clawson, who scored two of the touchdowns in Northwestern's victory over the Irish last year, had the unhappy experience of giving yesterday's victors an opportunity on which they quickly wreaked revenge. At the start of the third quarter, Juzwik sent the kickoff out of bounds and the ball was put in play on the Wildcats' 35-yard line. On the first play, Clawson fumbled and Bernie Crimmins, the reformed fullback, fell on the ball on the Wildcats' 36.

A Bertelli pass to Harry Wright was good for half the distance to the goal. Juzwik hit center for three yards, then Erdlitz grabbed Dippy Evans for a one-yard loss. Next, Bertelli dropped back to the 25-yard line and shot one of his bullet passes to Bolger who was waiting straight ahead, two yards from the goal line. Bolger stepped over without being hit and the Irish were ahead, 6-0. Then Juzwik booted that aforesaid victory point.

The Wildcats never relinguished the ball from the time they took the kickoff after the Irish touchdown until Graham had slashed through for the Northwestern score.

Capt. Tuffy Chambers received the kickoff and returned thirty-two yards to the Wildcats' 40-yard line. Graham made five yards and another five for an Irish offside penalty gave the Wildcats a first down at midfield. Chambers was held to a yard, but Buckets Hirsch, a sophomore fullback, cracked through for fourteen yards to the Irish 35.

Notre Dame was offside again. Then, after Graham had failed in an attempted swing around right end, he completed a pass to Hirsch which placed the ball on the Irish 14-yard line. Graham made four yards off-tackle, was stopped on the next play and then made it first down four yards from the goal line. Then Graham rocketed over his right tackle for the touchdown.

During the Wildcats' extra point attempt, Ziemba, the offensive center of the Irish, lined up several paces behind teammate John

Kovatch on the outside. Kovatch allowed himself to be blocked out, whereupon Ziemba rushed through the opening and blocked the ball with both hands.

For a time Wright was credited with the vital frustration of the extra point try, but it developed that the guile with which Ziemba and Kovatch collaborated was a carefully rehearsed maneuver.

Late in the third quarter, Bertelli's long pass was intercepted by Bill De Correvont on his own 7-yard line and the flashy senior returned the ball to his 28. Hirsch made six and De Correvont reeled off twenty-seven yards to the Irish 38. Chambers and Hirsch advanced to the Irish 31 and De Correvont failed by inches to make it first down. Hirsch, however, made it first down on the Irish 39 as the third quarter ended.

On the first play of the final quarter, De Correvont was thrown out of bounds on Notre Dame's 21-yard line, and two plays later De Correvont had a first down on the 17-yard line. After two rushing plays were good for only three yards, Graham went in for De Correvont and heaved a pass intended for Bob Motl, which was incomplete. It was at this juncture that Erdlitz tried vainly to kick his team into a 9-7 lead.

Early in this piece we remarked that the Irish were quite happy to yield the general statistics to the Wildcats in exchange for that one victory point. The extent of Notre Dame's generosity in this regard is reflected especially in the matter of first downs, of which the losers made 15 and the winners 7. Northwestern made 144 yards from rushing to 66 by the Irish, and the Wildcats made 78 yards from passing to 58 for the victors.

The game was something less than the aerial circus that had been expected, though passes were vital to the accomplishment of both of the game's touchdowns. Northwestern tried 16 passes and completed 4; the Irish tried 13 and completed 5.

De Correvont, who led the losing Wildcats and has been recently overshadowed by Graham, played one of the sharpest games of his highly publicized and spectacular career. On rushing plays, De Correvont carried the ball 10 times for a total of 64 yards, and his returns of kicks and a pass interception were the flashiest episodes of the game.

In the second quarter, De Correvont got away for a 34-yard run and appeared to be off with the first points of the game behind a front of three blockers. It scarcely was his fault that Juzwik somehow managed to squirm through the interference and throw De Correvont down on the Irish 32.

Bertelli threw all the Notre Dame passes and Graham all but one of those attempted by the Wildcats. Graham carried the ball 10 times for a net gain of 23 yards and Bertelli toted nine times for a net loss of four yards. But remember that Bertelli threw the Irish touchdown and Graham scored the Wildcat touchdown.

10

Notre Dame vs. Illinois

OCTOBER 24, 1942

CHAMPAIGN, Ill. — For three tense, tantalizing quarters that put their skill and courage to a test, Notre Dame today was held in check by the best team that has come out of Illinois since 1934. But the Irish forever kept on the pressure and the Illini finally cracked under the strain. The score was 21-14.

Illinois thus became the second team in a row which Notre Dame removed from the list of the nation's undefeated elevens. Last week, the Irish whipped the previously unbeaten Iowa Seahawks, 28-0.

Notre Dame had to come from behind twice to turn back a foe that gave a magnificent demonstration of poise, precision and, above all, flaming courage. The Illini were not terrified in the least by the magnitude of Notre Dame's victory over the Seahawks. But they were up against a team today that never is willing to settle for a tie.

The most important play of the game was not the touchdown drives or long runs or forward passes. It was Notre Dame's decision early in the fourth quarter to gamble on one play to retain possession of the ball. It was a move that gives coaches the jitters, but a thrill to the fans. And there were 43,476 in the stands to enjoy it.

The score at the time was 14-14 and the Irish had moved the ball from their 23-yard line to the Illini 40. It was fourth down and 5 yards to go. Conservative football called for a punt that might have bottled up the Illini deep in their territory. But it would have meant yielding the ball and you can't make progress on the gridiron when the other team has possession. Notre Dame, whose daring through the years has painted the sky with its name, slipped a short forward pass that was completed for a first down. From there the Irish went on to their third and decisive touchdown.

Illinois didn't fold up, however, after Notre Dame made its third touchdown through a stubborn line, and became the only team to cross the Orange and Blue goal line this season by rushing. It recovered a Notre Dame fumble near midfield with two minutes left to play and advanced to the Irish 27 for a first down. Pete Ashbaugh saved the day for Notre Dame in this predicament by intercepting a pass from Illinois' Art Dufelmeier.

While Notre Dame encountered an Illinois team that obviously was keyed for its maximum effort, it was responsible in part for some of the difficulties it encountered. Its ballhandling was unsteady and occasionally inexcusable. Some of the team's seven fumbles could be attributed to the hard tackling of Illinois, but it didn't account for behind-the-line slips that braked down more than one promising offensive march.

While the game developed some brilliant work by backfield players, it essentially was a battle of two mighty lines tearing each other to pieces and chopping up most of the running plays in the process. It was along the scrimmage strip that play after play perished. Seldom could either team do any consistent marching. Illinois had an edge in the first half, but Notre Dame had a marked superiority in the last two periods.

There were standouts along the line for both sides but none put up a better game than Illinois right guard Alex Agase, whose two touchdowns gave the Illini victory over Minnesota two weeks ago. Save for a couple of minutes in the last quarter, he was in there from beginning to end and the Irish made little headway through his position. He whanged 'em and banged 'em and scattered and slew and when he was taken out of the game for a substitute thousands of Illini came to their feet to give him the salute he had so richly earned. Elmer Engel, Illinois' right end, who today played his third-straight, 60-minute game was another stalwart whose expert diagnosis of Notre Dame maneuvers helped to keep the Irish in check.

But lest you get the impression that Illinois monopolized heroics along the line, we hasten to add that Notre Dame had two ends, Bob Dove and Paul Limont, who proved today they can match any pair of wing men in the country. And a cheer, too, for Lou Rymkus and Bob McBride, who yielded little yardage through the left side of the forward wall.

They gave an early demonstration of Notre Dame's defensive strength by stopping the Illini in their tracks for three downs on the 3-yard line right at the beginning of hostilities. Bob Neff then shared their glory by recovering an Illinois fumble, staving off momentarily the first Illinois touchdown.

Angelo Bertelli, Notre Dame's famous forward passer, had trouble finding open targets in the first half against Illinois' tight defense, but he hit his stride in the closing periods and wound up the day with a record of nine completions in 18 attempts.

The Irish made 14 first downs as compared with nine for the Illini and they rolled up 232 yards from scrimmage against Illinois' 191. None of the ballcarriers for either team acquired more than a fair average. Don Griffin and Jim Smith shouldered most of the offensive work for the Illini and neither was able to strike a 4-yard average. Anthony Butkovich turned in 6 yards per try, but he lugged the oval only six times. Ashbaugh clicked over 4 yards per carry for Notre Dame but Corwin Clatt was the player who did most of the work for the Irish. His average was less than 4 yards, but he made 20 trips with the ball which was almost twice as many as any other man on the field.

Clatt, incidentally, got his team in trouble shortly after the opening kickoff when he fumbled on the second play after the Irish received the kickoff. Myron Pfeifer recovered for Illinois on the Irish 20. Griffin, with an amazing burst of speed, whirled around his right end to the 3-yard line where he was tossed out of bounds by Creighton Miller.

Griffin tried three times to go over for the touchdown through McBride's guard position, but on fourth down the ball still was a yard from the goal line. On fourth down, he fumbled and Neff fell on the bounding ball on the 3.

Bertelli, who averaged 43 yards on his punts, then kicked to the Irish 30 from where Griffin and Butkovich gained 6 yards in two plays.

Griffin, while faking a pass, held the ball at the level of his head and slightly behind while Butkovich came around and picked the ball off his hand. The old Statue of Liberty maneuver caught the Irish napping and Butkovich went all the way for a touchdown. Jim McCarthy kicked the extra point to give Illinois a 7-0 lead.

Before the first quarter ended, Notre Dame got a break when Griffin fumbled on his 16, which was recovered by the Irish's Dove. Clatt and Ashbaugh then ripped through the Illinois middle for 6 yards, and Clatt cracked the same hole for a first down on the 5 where he was grounded by Walter Correll. Clatt went over for the touchdown on second down, the first man to score on Illinois from scrimmage this season. Bertelli kicked the extra point and the score was tied, 7-7.

Livingstone's fumble of a punt put the Irish in trouble again in the second quarter when Engel recovered for Illinois on the Irish 35. The Irish regained the ball when Wright recovered Good's fumble on the Irish 35. Afterwards, Livingstone was thrown for a 16-yard loss when he fumbled again and Bertelli punted to Good who raced back to the Irish 35. Smith gained 11 yards on another Statue of Liberty play. Good then faded deep and threw a pass that sailed over Bertelli's head and into the arms of Ray Grierson for Illinois' second touchdown. McCarthy added the extra point and the Illini again were in front, 14-7.

Illinois threatened again in the second quarter when Illini defensive back Steve Sucic intercepted Bertelli's pass and ran 13 yards to the Irish 20 where he lateraled to Butkovich, who carried on to the 11. The Illini could make no headway against the aggressive Irish line, however, and Notre Dame took the ball over on downs.

Bertelli's good punt, which rolled dead on the Illini 6-yard line, put the Orange and Blue in a hole in the middle of the third period. Correll kicked to Ashbaugh and the Notre Dame flyer soared 40 yards down the sideline to the 1-yard line where he was tackled by Smith. Bertelli plunged over for the touchdown and added the extra point to tie the score, 14-14.

Late in the third period, Illinois moved down to the Irish 23 but was stopped dead at that point, and in less time than it takes to write it Ashbaugh gained a first down on the Irish 42. Notre Dame advanced steadily to the Illini 40 where it was fourth down and 5 yards to go.

That was the situation described in the lead of this story where Notre Dame gambled on making a first down by a forward pass that succeeded.

Livingstone and Clatt alternated in moving the ball to the Illini 21. On the next play, Bertelli fumbled but Clatt fell on the ball at the 12. Clatt then smashed through his right guard for 6 and an offside penalty against Illinois put the ball only a yard away from the goal line. Cowhig then scored standing up, the third time this season he has made touchdowns without hitting the ground. He crossed the Iowa Seahawks' goal in that fashion twice last Saturday. Bertelli again added the extra point to conclude the scoring for the day.

11

Notre Dame vs. Michigan

NOVEMBER 14, 1942

NOTRE DAME, Ind. — Michigan's mighty men, with power and speed to match their firm resolve, this afternoon wiped out the memory of bitter defeat 33 years ago that had topped the Wolverines from their throne as the football champions of the West. For today, before an all-time record crowd of 57,000 gathered in Notre Dame's buff brick stadium, Michigan drove to a smashing 32-20 triumph.

The ghost of Michigan's defeat in 1909 by Notre Dame, a beating that has rankled ever since, finally has been laid to rest. But before that triumph was irretrievably written in the third period as the Wolverines rushed for three touchdowns, the Notre Dame players proved again that although they may be whipped they live up to their familiar name of Fighting Irish.

Notre Dame scored first. Michigan matched this and went on to lead, 13-7, early in the second quarter. Then the Irish roared back to leave the scarred battlefield with a 14-13 advantage at the intermission.

Then came the deluge. Michigan power and Michigan speed could not be halted. In 15 thrill-packed minutes, the Wolverines ripped through the Irish line and raced around the flanks to score three times.

Michigan marched 59 yards after the second-half kickoff for the touchdown which put it into a lead that was never relinquished. The Wolverines then seized first on a fumble and next on an intercepted pass to touch off the subsequent drives. During this Wolverine assault, brilliant in conception and executed without flaw, the Irish had the ball only for six plays.

Michigan could not be stopped. Probably on this afternoon no collegiate team could have halted the Wolverine powerhouse plunges and sharp thrusts which began with smooth deception and were consummated in slashes that always carried into the group of Irish secondary defenders. The Wolverines played with inspiration and determination.

Michigan scored five touchdowns — according to the record book it has been 26 years since a team scored like that on the Irish. Back in 1916, Army whipped Notre Dame, 30-10. And as for 32 points, this mark had withstood the challenges of football elevens from coast to coast since 1905 when Purdue blanked Notre Dame, 32-0.

In this comparison, however, one can not forget Notre Dame's three touchdowns. The Irish rallied to score in the fourth period to mark up their third, and with 10 minutes to play were in scoring position again after an interception.

But Michigan calmly took this counterattack in stride, immediately regained the ball by intercepting an Irish forward pass, and moved ahead steadily to control the battle.

This game, above all others this year, was offensive in character. Only five punts were made in 60 minutes, so thoroughly did each team dominate the contest upon obtaining possession. Between them, the rivals piled up 34 first downs and nearly 500 yards in gains from rushing. In this last statistic — yards gained by rushing — Michigan had an advantage of 319-170, figures that accurately reflect respective merits.

Michigan's four backs moved precisely. They handled the ball without error and with a speed which baffled their opponents, who early found that a five-man line could not possibly cope with the attack. It is impossible to single out one man for the headlines of victory. Indeed, since Michigan made only two major substitutions this afternoon — Don Robinson at halfback and Walter Frelhofer at right guard — the triumph justly belongs to Michigan's starting

Notre Dame was penalized for being offside and immediately eleven.

Capt. George Ceithami, Michigan's senior quarterback, ran the Wolverine team confidently and with keen perception of Irish defensive weakness. His main weapon was big, speedy Bob Wiese who plunged for 114 yards in 26 attempts. Wiese's fake spins also were a foundation for Paul White's slashing drives at the Irish right tackle. Then there was Tom Kuzma. His straight plunges seldom could be stripped.

Up in front were Merv Pregulman, Al Wistert, Julie Franks, Phil Sharpe and Elmer Madar — all 60-minute men. Mader confounded the Irish passing attack by his position in the secondary covering the man-in-motion on either side, and Wistert and Franks were in every scrimmage.

Notre Dame's men had their inning but despite Angelo Bertelli's passes to Bob Dove, John Yonaker and Capt. George Murphy, and despite Corwin Clatt's plunges, Notre Dame today met a team superior by all measurements.

There was no forecast of Michigan strength, however, in the early minutes. The second time the Irish had the ball after the kickoff they drove 44 yards for a touchdown on eight plays. Bob Livingstone, the Irish sophomore left half, went inside left tackle on a quick opening for 14 yards. Creighton Miller plunged for 3 yards and Clatt's successive drives of 5 and 7 yards accomplished another first down. Creighton Miller then took Bertelli's lateral and skirted left end for 10 yards.

Clatt lost a yard and Livingstone netted two on a Bertelli lateral. On third down, with Michigan in a seven-man line and four secondary defenders in a row, Bertelli passed to Dove in the end zone for the score as White fell to his knees trying to cover. Bertelli's placement gave the Irish the lead, 7-0.

Seven and a half minutes had been played. Michigan received and with the stimulus of Kuzma's 24-yard return, marched to the Irish goal line. Wiese hit left tackle for 3 yards and Kuzma circled Murphy's end for 8 more. Kuzma then broke loose over Neff's tackle for a first down on the Irish 25. On the next play, Wiese failed to gain on a sweep to the outside but White drove over guard for 6 yards and Kuzma followed at the same spot for 4 more and a first down.

substituted Herb Coleman, Ziggie Czarobski and Paul Limont in the line. White ripped over Czarobski for 4 yards and Kuzma, on a spin play, was stopped one foot from the goal line. On the next attempt, Ceithami sneaked over behind Pregulman. Jim Brieske came from the Michigan bench to kick the extra point.

Livingstone's fumble of a lateral from Bertelli, with the ball being recovered by Madar on the Irish 36, signalled Michigan's following attack on the next to last play in the first period. Wiese plunged for 6 yards as the quarter ended.

Despite an offside penalty and Kuzma's incomplete pass, Michigan marched on because of Madar's run around Notre Dame's right end to the Irish 25-yard line. Wiese spun through center for 19 yards. Kuzma got a yard and added 2 more on a fake plunge by Wiese and a lateral from Ceithami. White was stopped at right end. It was now fourth down and from the sideline came Brieske and Robinson.

The men went through the preparations for a place-kick but even as Notre Dame's Limont charged in to block, as Brieske went through the motion of kicking, Robinson ran the ball around the right flank to score. Then Brieske missed the try for the extra point. Michigan led, 13-7.

Notre Dame received, moved from its own 20-yard line to Michigan's 43, and Bertelli punted on fourth down. Kuzma took the ball and fumbled. Capt. Murphy recovered for the Irish on the Wolverine 12. Clatt then plunged for 2 yards and again for 8 and Creighton Miller drove over guard for the score. Bertelli's placement gave the Irish the lead, 14-13.

In the remaining seven minutes of the half, Michigan marched 60 yards to Notre Dame's 4-yard line but the Irish stopped Kuzma and Wiese in three plays and took over when Kuzma's fourth-down pass was incomplete. The half ended a minute later.

Michigan's victory quarter, the third, followed. John Creevey kicked off for Notre Dame and purposely booted out of bounds. It was short, however, and the Wolverines started from their own 41-yard line.

White swept around right end for 8 yards and repeated for 16, cutting inside the same Notre Dame defensive position. Wiese hit center for 5 yards, White went over right tackle on a reverse for 2, and Wiese spun through center for a first down on the Irish 23. After Wiese plunged for a yard, Kuzma passed to Madar on the Irish 9-yard line.

Kuzma plunged for a yard, White got 5 at the vulnerable right tackle and then drove again at the same position to score standing up. Four minutes and five seconds had been played as Brieske kicked the extra point, which put Michigan ahead, 20-14.

Michigan's Pregulman then kicked off to Creighton Miller, who returned 17 yards but fumbled when tackled and Madar recovered on the Irish 25-yard line. Michigan scored in seven plays with Kuzma, White and Wiese overpowering the defense. Kuzma's power drive at left tackle carried over from the 2-yard line for the score. Brieske missed the extra point attempt.

Notre Dame received the kickoff and on fourth down, from his 30-yard line, Bertelli punted and the Michigan parade was renewed at the Irish 36 by virtue of Kuzma's sparkling 29-yard return down the east sideline.

Kuzma bolted through the line for 15 yards. A wide lateral from Ceithami to Robinson turned the Irish right end for 9 yards. Robinson went through right tackle for a first down on the Notre Dame 4-yard line, but the Irish would not yield and took over on downs on the 3.

On his second play, Bertelli tried to pass from his own end zone. He was hurried and threw high and short. White, who had returned to the Michigan backfield, intercepted on the Irish 24. From here Michigan drove to the goal line. White got 9 yards. Kuzma went 9 more. Robinson went over for the score, but Michigan was set back to the Irish 16 for illegal use of the hands. Kuzma retrieved the situation with a 15-yard pass to Sharpe and then plunged for the score. Brieske missed the extra point kick and Michigan led, 32-14.

Notre Dame replied with a 65-yard assault for its last touchdown. In this, Bertelli successively completed passes of 5, 11 and 19 yards, with John Yonaker catching the last two. Clatt then plunged for 4 yards and, on a fake pass play by Bertelli, Creighton Miller took the ball on the Statue of Liberty play and went around Michigan's right end to score. Bertelli failed to add the extra point.

Notre Dame then had the ball only once until the last three minutes when another air foray finally was checked by Wiese's interception at Michigan's goal line.

12

Notre Dame vs. U.S.C.

NOVEMBER 28, 1942

LOS ANGELES — Football's biggest college crowd of 1942 — upward of 95,000 — cheered and booed today as Notre Dame defeated Southern California, 13-0, in the most bitter battle of their 17-year-old series. The Irish struck late in the first and second quarters to sweep to victory.

There were 17 penalties inflicted, 6 on the Trojans and 11 on Notre Dame, not counting the penalties refused by both sides. They totaled 145 yards. Three Notre Dame players and one Southern California man were banished.

A handful of Southern California players rushed onto the field after a particularly vicious Notre Dame tackle at one stage of the game, and the contest ended in a free-for-all with a few players and spectators participating. Cooler heads on both sides intervened, however, and the disturbance was settled within 5 minutes without the aid of police.

Bill Sexas, the Southern California right guard, and Bob McBride, the Notre Dame left guard, were banished early in the third period and Jim White, the Irish right tackle, was chased a few moments later for protesting to referee Louis G. Conlan on a holding penalty. Late in the game, Notre Dame right guard George Tobin was removed for protesting too vigorously that he had been roughed.

Apparently the Trojans were not prepared for the sharp blocking and tackling of Notre Dame today and they became embittered as they saw a potential Rose Bowl bid slipping from their grasp. Coach Frank Leahy of Notre Dame visited the Trojan dressing room, however, to apologize to Coach Jeff Cravath and the U.S.C. players for Notre Dame's part in the unpleasantness.

The much advertised arm of Irish quarterback Angelo Bertelli was directly responsible for the victory. He pitched a beautiful pass to right halfback Creighton Miller for a 48-yard gain and the first touchdown with only two minutes of the first period remaining. Miller took the ball cutting to his left through the secondary in full stride. The ball led him just enough, and he continued on a diagonal into the end zone without an enemy getting within five yards of him.

The second toss was shorter, and into the flat zone to sophomore left half Bob Livingstone. He caught the 3-yard toss on the 10-yard line, faked Trojan fullback Bob Musick so successfully that the latter fell down, and then zipped 10 yards into the end zone. Bertelli missed the first extra point kick and sophomore quarterback John Creevey kicked the second with 3½ minutes remaining in the second period.

The first touchdown was preceeded by Livingstone's 1-yard gain after the Irish had taken a punt on their 49, the first time they hit Trojan territory. The second climaxed an uninterrupted drive of 80 yards.

Southern California came back to make its most serious threat of the day after the first touchdown, with Mickey McCardle's 53-yard pass to Ralph Heywood, the longest gain of the 82-yard drive that moved the ball from the Trojan 17 to the Notre Dame 1-yard line. There the Irish stopped McCardle after a 4-yard gain with inches needed for the first down.

Bertelli completed 6 out of 11 passes with none intercepted. Southern California tried 30 passes, completed 13, with many of them in the flat zone for short gains or no gains.

On the final play of the first half, Trojan sub left halfback Jim Hardy was trapped while trying to pass and was chased back 17 yards to midfield before he unleashed the ball. Tom Miller, the Notre Dame sub left half, picked the ball out of the arms of Trojan tight end Joe Davis on the 10-yard line and ran back to his 40 with most of the play occurring after the gun had sounded.

This was overshadowed, however, by the day's final play, which touched off the fuse under the powder keg of emotion built up throughout the third and fourth quarters. Earle Parsons, the fourth Trojan left halfback to see action, returned a Bertelli punt 13 yards to his 28, then tried a desperation pass. Bertelli snatched it on his 48-yard line, raced across the turf, reversed his field and streaked back to his right, got pinned and finally lateraled to Irish right guard Harry Wright. Wright in turn lateraled to Creighton Miller and blocked a path to the Trojan 35 where Miller was finally downed. While he was still prostrate, the stands began emptying their aroused customers and the melee was on.

Notre Dame's running attack was led by sophomore fullback Corwin Clatt, who made 55 yards on 13 attempts to come off on top in his duel with Musick. The latter carried 14 times for 44 yards. Tom Miller with 48 yards, and his brother, Creighton Miller, with 44, also contributed heavily to the Notre Dame total and to the enjoyment of the game by their father, Harry Miller, the 1908 Irish captain, and their Uncle Don, a 1924 halfback and one of the fabled Four Horsemen.

After an exchange of kicks at the outset, the Irish appeared to be moving on Livingstone's 14 yards in two attempts and Bertelli's apparent first-down pass to Bob Dove, but the arbiters said that Bertelli was not back 5 yards and, for this first infraction of this rule in two years of play, the Irish were forced to punt. Heywood's return punt was brought back 17 yards by Livingstone to the Trojan 49. Livingstone picked up a yard, then Bertelli threw his scoring pass to Creighton Miller.

The McCardle to Heywood pass gave the Trojans a first down on the Irish 26, and the men in the striped shirts ruled that Heywood had been tackled too forcibly, thus moving the ball to the 11 as the quarter ended. Musick made 4 yards at center. McCardle's running pass missed and Musick hit center for 2 yards. On fourth down, McCardle hit the Irish left tackle under a full head of steam, but three members of the Irish secondary met him forcibly at the 1-yard stripe and a measurement showed he was lacking inches of a first down.

Bertelli punted out to the Irish 30 and Notre Dame was penalized 5 yards for being offside. Speedy Trojan right halfback Howard

Callahan lost 6 yards on a reverse and Musick lost 2 more, with Notre Dame refusing an offside penalty. The Trojans then drew a 15-yard penalty for using an illegal formation and Heywood kicked into the end zone.

It took them most of the period, but the Irish hammered and passed their way 80 yards for the second touchdown. Livingstone got 7 yards in two trips and Clatt added 9 for a first down on his 36. Bertelli passed to Bob Dove for 14 yards a moment later, then Creighton Miller, Livingstone and Clatt made it first down on the Trojan 37. Bertelli hit Murphy with a 17-yard pass. Livingstone rounded right end for 3. Bertelli's aerial missed, then he found Clatt for 6 yards in the flat zone. On fourth down, Clatt wriggled and stretched for 2 yards and a first down on the 9.

Clatt got 3 yards at tackle, and sub right half Bill Earley lost 2 on a sweep. Here the Irish were penalized 5 yards for stalling, of all things, thus putting the ball on the 13. Bertelli promptly rifled a pass to Livingstone for the touchdown.

Trojan fullback Dirk Manning returned the third period kickoff to his 33-yard line to launch a drive which was materially aided by an interference penalty. Manning got 15 yards, McCardle added 5 and the Irish drew 5 yards for defensive holding, making it first down on the Trojan 42. When two plays and a 5-yard penalty for being offside left the Trojans 2 yards in arrears, McCardle winged a long pass downfield intended for Trojan end Joe Davis. Earley nudged the latter, however, and the pass was ruled complete on the Irish 14.

Here the Notre Dame line braced. Musick made 2 yards. Two passes by Musick to Heywood and Manning lost 2 yards and a fourth down pass was incomplete. Then on a short gain by Clatt, McBride and Sexas were removed from the game for fighting. Clatt then ran 21 yards, but White was accused of holding on the play and was banished while Notre Dame took a 15-yard penalty.

Leahy said after the game that he believed that the fast whistle employed on the West Coast led to the charge that Notre Dame was piling on and around Trojan feelings. Coach Cravath, who later visited the Notre Dame dressing room with U.S.C. President Rufus B. Von Klein Smid, agreed in making his apologies to the Irish squad. He said that the Trojans thought the whistle unusually slow when they played Ohio State at Columbus earlier in the year. Thus, when Notre Dame players hit an already-tackled player before he was down or completely stopped, the local contingent felt that they were being roughed.

It was the third-straight victory for the Irish over the Trojans and their tenth in the series which started in 1926.

13

Notre Dame vs. Michigan

OCTOBER 9, 1943

ANN ARBOR, Mich.— Notre Dame's football team, presenting an attack pointed with deception and grounded on speed of maneuver, whipped the University of Michigan, 35-12, this afternoon. In doing so, Frank Leahy's squad avenged the worst defeat the Irish ever had received in the 11-game series and satisfactorily assuaged memories of that afternoon 11 months ago when Michigan won at Notre Dame.

The heralded battle of the undefeated midwestern contenders for national collegiate honors measured to the advance script but the marginal notes narrowly missed being farcical and would have been if the decision had not been dramatically written before the denouncement.

Michigan's all-time record crowd, an enthusiastic and extremely partisan throng which actually exceeded the announced attendance of 85,688, watched the march of events that became ludicrous in the second half by the collapse of the electrical timing system.

These thousands, hundreds of them service men who were seated on chairs along the sidelines and end lines, cheered Notre Dame's initial lightning thrust when Creighton Miller ran 66 yards for a touchdown and Angelo Bertelli, the director of the T attack, place-kicked the extra point.

Michigan followers were heartened by the Wolverines' counter-drive which scored but failed to even up the score early in the second period. Merv Pregulman was unable to add the extra point because a momentary fumble by Elroy Hirsch, who held the ball, destroyed the rhythm of the placement.

But Notre Dame, swinging into high speed, struck through the air immediately after the kickoff and Fred Earley, the relief man for Miller, sprinted 69 yards with a pass from Bertelli. Before the end of the half, Jim Mello climaxed another air assault by plunging over from Michigan's 2-yard line. Bertelli's extra point kick gave the Irish a 21-6 lead at the intermission and only the more rabid of the Wolverine partisans refused to admit Notre Dame superiority.

Then came the third period which will be remembered as the "long third quarter" of collegiate sport even as sports fans recall the Dempsey Tunney long count fight and the vagaries of Cornell's fifth-down scoring pass against Dartmouth.

Thirty-five plays generally are par for a period of football. When these had been consummated and the huge electric clock still showed more than eight minutes to go in the third period, the press representatives knew the timing device had failed.

Actually 47 plays were run off in the third period during which Notre Dame added two touchdowns, the first on a quarterback sneak by Bertelli and the last a second touchdown by Miller on a pass from Bertelli.

The teams changed goals and began the last period. Then, after nine plays from scrimmage, the public address system bellowed to the thousands that 2½ minutes remained to be played. Actually the final quarter was limited to 18 plays and seven minutes. The rival coaches, Frank Leahy of Notre Dame and Fritz Crisler of Michigan, agreed that since 23 minutes had been played — an assumption, of course — in the third period then the last period should be seven minutes. Fifteen minutes of playing time constitute one quarter.

In this brief period, Michigan was stopped one foot from Notre Dame's goal by the second-team Irish line. Then on the last play of the game, Capt. Paul White of Michigan took Hirsch's pass to go 13 yards for the consolation score. Hundreds rushed onto the field as the timer's gun sounded, but retreated far enough for Pregulman to try for the extra point. He failed and the final margin of Notre

Dame's victory, 23 points, tied the mathematical differences Michigan established in 1898 and again in 1902. Notre Dame failed to score in each of these games.

Notre Dame's only other victory in the series, which again is terminated temporarily with today's game, was registered on old Ferry Field in 1909 by an 11-3 score. The hero of that conquest was Harry Miller, the first of the famous family of Miller brothers in Irish gridiron history and among whom is Don Miller, the left halfback of the 1924 Four Horsemen eleven.

This afternoon Harry Miller sat in Michigan's huge sunken bowl and watched his son, Creighton, spark the Irish rushing attack. Literally his 66-yard run for the first score set the tempo for a great Notre Dame team. Only Bertelli, who today proved his mastery of the intricacies of the T-formation and his superb control of forward passes, could rival Creighton Miller.

Bertelli attempted eight forward passes and completed five of them for 138 yards. Two were incomplete, one in the second quarter and another in the third, and a second-period pass also was intercepted. Two throws by Bertelli were carried all the way and, as previously recounted, another touchdown was set up by passing.

But Notre Dame's attack, while founded on Bertelli's passes, was equally brilliant in quick-opening thrusts into a Michigan line. Mello, a slashing fullback, and Miller ripped through for 253 yards between them. Julie Rykovich, at right half, was the foil from which many of these drives were sprung.

Michigan's line played valiantly and none was greater in defeat than Pregulman and Bob Hanzik, the Wisconsin end converted to a tackle.

Michigan had its stars. Big Bill Daley, the thundering fullback who led the drive a week ago against Northwestern was never greater. Daley carried the burden for the Wolverines, and gained 135 yards on 24 rushes. When he left the game near the end of the interminable third period, he received an accolade of unreserved applause from the thousands regardless of collegiate allegiance.

Daley also played a spell at left half, as predicted, when Michigan called on Jack Wink, the former Wisconsin quarterback, who was the surprise performer of the day. When Wink entered the game, Bob Wiese moved to fullback.

The game began on a note of frustration when Rykovich's fumble of the opening kickoff, recovered by Michigan's Capt. White on the Irish 39-yard line, was nullified by Michigan's offside penalty. Michigan repeated the kickoff and each team had one turn at attack before Notre Dame took possession on its own 34-yard line where Wiese had punted out of bounds.

On the first play from scrimmage, Miller hit over defensive right guard on a quick opening, shot by the linebacker, cut to his right and sprinted downfield with an escort of green-shirted blockers who took out all defenders. Bertelli's extra point kick gave Notre Dame a 7-0 lead after 5 minutes and 45 seconds had been played.

Michigan received and its men, still fresh, put together a drive of three first downs and 10 plays before failing on downs on the Irish 9-yard line. Michigan did not get into production again until the start of the second period and it was Daley who signalled the drive when he intercepted Bertelli's pass and returned 18 yards to Michigan's 48-yard line.

Wiese plunged for 2 yards and Daley roared off left tackle for 23 yards. White failed on a reverse and Daley passed (he was now playing left half as he did last year at Minnesota) to Art Renner for a first down on Notre Dame's 4. Bertelli made the tackle. Daley then plunged between defensive left guard and tackle for the touchdown after which came Hirsch's fumble and Pregulman's failure on the try for the extra point.

John Lujack returned Michigan's kickoff 10 yards to his 24-yard line and the Irish scored in five plays. Earley made 12 yards at defensive right end and then Notre Dame was offside, Mello failed to gain and Bertelli's first pass was incomplete. Bertelli threw again and this time Earley took the ball running to the west sideline behind all defenders and continued to the goal line. The play gained 69 yards.

Michigan received and yielded on a fourth-down touchback punt by Wiese. Five plays later, Miller ran 58 yards to score but the Irish were convicted of holding and were set back to their own 42-yard line. The drive was renewed but failed at Michigan's 1-yard line.

Notre Dame began again on the Wolverine 36 where Hanzlik grounded Wiese's punt. John Zilly took Bertelli's first-down pass down the east sideline and was run out on the Wolverine 2. Mello plunged off-tackle for the score and the halftime 21-6 lead.

Rykovich set up Notre Dame's fourth touchdown with a 42-yard return of Wiese's kick in the third period. He was stopped on the Wolverine 31. Mello hit for 4 yards and Miller ran to the Wolverine 10-yard line. Mello got 8 more yards and Bertelli sneaked over for the touchdown.

Notre Dame's last touchdown march went a total of 65 yards in 8 plays with Rykovich, Mello and Miller carrying. Miller's quick-opening thrust of 28 yards was the principal ingredient and he completed the drive by taking Bertelli's pass downfield over Fred Negus' head to erase the last 26 yards.

At this point, the length of the quarter became apparent and subsequently was followed by the shortening of the last period. Michigan's sturdy determination was rewarded on the last play of the game.

14

Notre Dame vs. Navy

OCTOBER 30, 1943

CLEVELAND — Notre Dame turned in its lowest score of the season today and its largest in history against the Navy, to vanquish the previously undefeated Middies by a score of 33-6. The Irish showed a record Cleveland crowd of 82,000 superb play in all departments. The great Notre Dame defense stopped the Navy's vaunted running attack, all but nullified Navy's frenzy of forward passes, and the alert, talented and powerful Irish backs, under the direction of departing Angelo Bertelli, scored in every period through passes, on long dashes and on plunges. Notre Dame, indeed, still is America's No. 1 football team but Navy may have lost its No. 3 rating on the sun-washed turf here today.

The Irish did not start piling up tallies at once against the belligerent young sportsmen from Annapolis. The first score of the game came after 11½ minutes. Julie Rykovich, the ex-Illini freshman, negotiated a 49-yard gain to the goal. Rykovich took a 24-yard pass from Bertelli, whirled, and ran unmolested the remaining 25 yards. Left tackle Don Whitmire blocked Bertelli's try for the extra point.

In the third minute of the second period, another pass by Bertelli blossomed into a touchdown. Putting the ball in play on the Notre Dame 48-yard line, Bertelli passed 17 yards to Creighton Miller, who did a tight rope dance down his left sideline for the remaining 35 yards to the goal line, an overall gain of 52 yards. Bertelli kicked the extra point for the Irish.

Navy ducked the shutout before Notre Dame scored again. After the midway mark in the second period, Navy got possession of the ball on the Navy 48 when Hillis Hume intercepted Bertelli's pass. Hal Hamberg then clicked on a series of passes to Hume and Bill Barron. The one which scored was to Barron, a gain of 29 yards. Vic Filos was assigned to kick the extra point but never got a chance as Roe Johnston fumbled the pass from center.

Notre Dame was all keyed up after returning from the lecture room at the start of the second half. Rykovich returned the kickoff to the Irish 31 and Jim Mello, who was both tricky and powerful all day, whizzed 38 yards. Miller then sped 23 yards to the Navy 8. Mello and Miller rammed three times to make it fourth down on the 2. Then Notre Dame forgot the T-formation for one play. Lining up in a single-wing formation, Bertelli passed to John Yonakor at the back of the end zone for the third Irish touchdown. Bertelli added the extra point.

The Irish scored their fourth touchdown with 2½ minutes to go in the third period. Mello intercepted Hamberg's pass and zigzagged 40 yards before he was downed on the Navy 7. Rykovich went to the 3. Miller then plunged over his right guard for the touchdown and Bertelli converted.

It appeared up until the closing minutes that Notre Dame might miss counting in the fourth period. But the most thrilling and longest run of the day, a 71-yard gallop by Vic Kublitski, saved the record. Hamberg had clicked again on a series of passes which had carried to the Notre Dame 14. Then the Irish took over on downs.

Johnny Lujack, who is to succeed Bertelli next Saturday as the Notre Dame quarterback, made 7 yards. Then Kublitski, the former Gopher who played his best game for Notre Dame today, ran 71 yards. A great block by George Sullivan on the 35-yard line had enabled him to keep going, apparently to a touchdown. Jim Pettit popped out of nowhere and knocked Kublitski out of bounds at the 9. Rykovich and Lujack went to the 1-yard line and Bertelli went over for the final score of the game. He failed to kick the extra point.

The 33 points the Irish made today were seven more than they ever made in any of their previous 16 games with the Middies. The prior tops was 26-2, which was accomplished by the national champions of 1930 in the game which dedicated Notre Dame Stadium.

The extent to which the Irish stopped the Navy ground attack was reflected bluntly in the statistics. Navy made seven first downs to 14 by Notre Dame, but none was from rushing. Navy had a net loss of seven yards from rushing and a gross loss of 31 yards. While Navy was running backwards from scrimmage, Notre Dame piled up a total of 332 yards from rushing.

Navy made 188 yards from passing as compared to 122 by Notre Dame, but the total was not imposing from the average per attempt. Hamberg connected on 8 of 38 passes.

In his farewell game, Bertelli was his usual brilliant self when the chips were down. But statistically he was somewhat below his own 1943 par. Bertelli threw nine passes, completed four and had 3 intercepted.

Two Irish fullbacks, Mello and Kublitski, were the long-range travelers of the day. Mello made 125 yards in 17 tries and Kublitski ripped off 112 in six tries. The ever agile Miller accounted for 68 yards in 16 efforts.

The Irish, who returned to South Bend immedately after the contest to start preparation for the clash with Army in New York next week, were a bit disappointed that the Cadets fell out of the untied class today. But the Irish had consolation in contemplating their national rating. They now have won all six of their games and have scored 261 points to their opponents' 31.

Leahy quickly took charge of the ailing B.C. program in 1939 and turned them into big-time winners.

Four Horsemen Jimmy Crowley's all-Notre Dame staff at Fordham consisted of *(left to right)* Frank Leahy, Ed Hunsinger, Crowley, Earl Walsh and Glen Carberry.

Charlie O'Rourke *(left)* escapes a Tennessee tackler in the 1941 Sugar Bowl.

Leahy and B.C. captain Ernie Schowtzer *(right)* at opening of 1939 preseason drills.

With one second remaining in the 1941 Sugar Bowl, the scoreboard tells the final story.

Leahy and assistant coach John Druze teach the fundamentals of the center-to-halfback snap to onlooking members of the 1939 B.C. squad.

The Fighting Irish defense stopped powerhouse Northwestern for a 7-6 victory in 1941.

Elmer Layden *(right)* hands over the Notre Dame head-coaching reins to Leahy at opening of 1941 Spring drills.

All-America halfback Creighton Miller was one of the leaders in Notre Dame's 1943 National Championship campaign.

Angelo Bertelli (48) scampers for big yardage against Arizona in 1941.

The Fighting Irish battle toward the goal line against Navy in 1943.

As assistant coach Ed "Moose" Krause observes, Leahy charts the defenses which the Fighting Irish planned to use in the 1943 season.

Angelo Bertelli and other members of the Notre Dame squad are sworn in for military service at mid-season of 1943.

Assistant coach Hugh Devore led the Fighting Irish in 1945 while Leahy was in the Navy.

Leahy, a student manager and assistant coach John Druze *(right)* prepare to watch the game films of an upcoming Fighting Irish opponent.

All-Americans John Mastrangelo, Ziggie Czarobski and Johnny Lujack join Leahy to check the plays they hope will click against Navy in 1946.

Leahy *(far lower left)* shakes down the thunder during a student pep rally in the Notre Dame Fieldhouse.

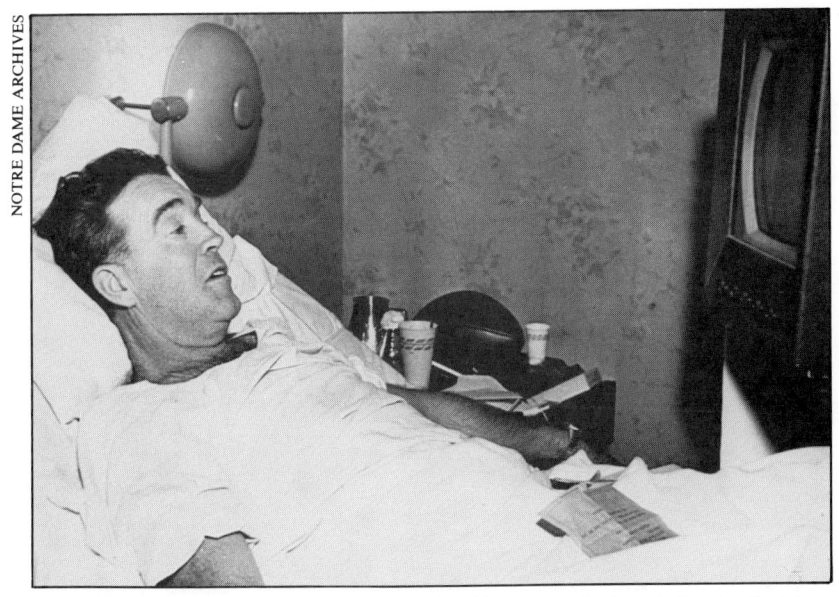

After being stricken ill in 1946, Leahy watches his troops via closed-circuit television against U.S.C.

Chicago Bear quarterback Sid Luckman, while serving as a volunteer assistant coach to Leahy, instructs a trio of Fighting Irish quarterbacks on T-formation ball-handling fundamentals during 1947 Spring drills.

Leahy assistant coach Ed "Moose" Krause and the Fighting Irish team on the sideline prior to kickoff of 1947 Army game.

Bing Crosby *(front middle)* visits with the Notre Dame football squad following the 1947 U.S.C. game.

A pair of Leahy's all-Americans, Johnny Lujack *(right)* and George Connor *(middle)*, inked lucrative pro football contracts with Chicago Bears owner George Halas *(left)* following the 1947 season.

All-America fullback Emil Sitko during a preseason workout in 1948.

Lancaster Smith (20) returns a punt 85 yards for a touchdown against Pittsburgh in 1948.

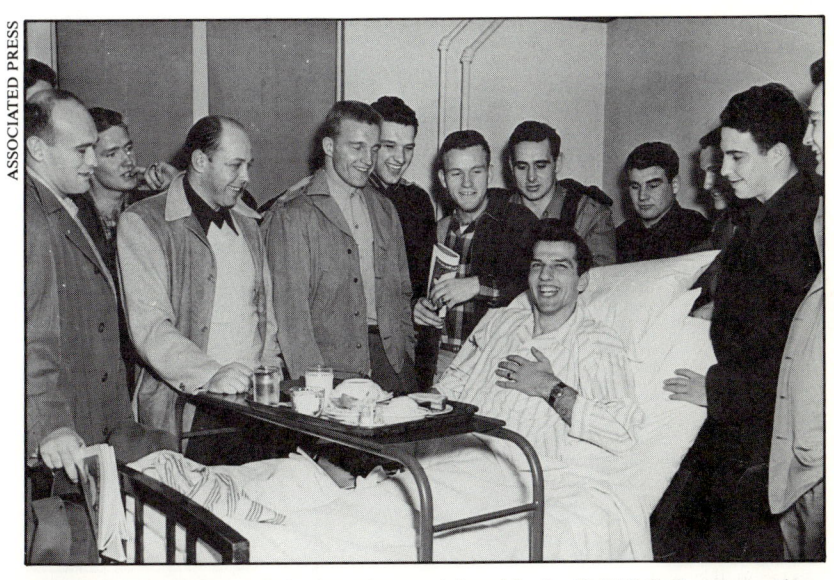

Irish quarterback Frank Tripuka, who was injured in the 1948 U.S.C. game, enjoys a post-game visit from his teammates.

Long-time friend and former college teammate, Fred Miller *(right)*, served Leahy as a volunteer assistant coach from 1946-53.

Leahy celebrates Notre Dame's third national championship in four seasons with 1949 all-Americans Jim Martin *(left)*, Jerry Groom *(middle)* and Leon Hart *(right)*.

Halfback Joe Heap (42) romps for a long gain against Georgia Tech in 1953.

Irish Fullback Neil Worden (48), with an escort by Don Penza (83), gallops downfield for 55 yards against U.S.C. in 1953.

In January 1954, Leahy announced to the press and the Notre Dame student body that he was resigning as head football coach.

15

Notre Dame vs. Army

DECEMBER 6, 1943

NEW YORK — One of the greatest teams that ever has come out of Notre Dame today removed Army from the list of the nation's undefeated, 26-0. It was the most decisive triumph scored by either side in football's oldest continuous intersectional series since West Point's 27-0 victory in 1925.

The glittering figure in Notre Dame's star-studded cast was an 18-year-old boy named Johnny Lujack who today was given the assignment of replacing Angelo Bertelli, who last week moved into a marine base after enshrining himself forever as one of the all-time greats at a university whose records are crowded with gridiron satellites.

Lujack convinced 76,000 spectators who filled Yankee Stadium to overflowing that he is well equipped to carry on where Bertelli left off. He directed his forces flawlessly. He threw two touchdown passes in the process of completing eight out of 17 for a total gain of 182 yards. He scored another himself.

On three or four occasions it was Lujack who brought down Army ballcarriers with nothing between them and the goal line except bright sunshine and green turf. His choice of plays was Phi Beta Kappa caliber. He didn't leave the game until two minutes before the final gun. What more could anyone ask, unless it was to ride the two Army mules that kicked and bucked up and down the sideline while Cadet cheerleaders sought in vain to win the game with lung power.

While Lujack was the great man in Notre Dame's greatest 1943 victory, he was by no means a nonpareil. Creighton Miller, whose father was making gridiron history for the Irish before this series began, was the best ballcarrier on the field. He not only gained more yardage than any other player for either team but he was the hardest to bring down. It was the safety man who frequently caught him before he could break into the open.

While Miller was giving Army's rooting section alternate attacks of chills and fever with his slippery running, two other Notre Dame backs, Jim Mello and Vic Kulbitski, were wearing down the West Point line with their plunges between tackles. Bob Kelly, another 18-year-old back, who only last season was leading Leo High School to Chicago's high school championship, rounded out a backfield that rates with the Four Horsemen or any other Notre Dame combination you can recall.

It wasn't so much the size of the score that makes Notre Dame's victory impressive. It was the caliber of the opposition. This was no ordinary Army eleven. It had rolled through its schedule against eastern teams without losing a game. It had a starting front made up mainly of men who were holdovers from 1942. It included only one plebe, a fullback from Southern California named Glenn Davis, who, incidentally, was the Cadets' best ground gainer.

Army's line was as big as Notre Dame's and equally experienced. But it lacked some of Notre Dame's aggressiveness. It was an Irish tackle, Jim White, who clinched victory for his team by stealing the ball — a legal act on a gridiron — from Army's Davis in the third quarter. That bit of enterprise gave Notre Dame the ball on West Point's 8-yard line, from where Lujack chucked a pass to John Yonakor for the touchdown that gave Notre Dame a 13-0 lead.

Army's ends, John Hennessey and Robert Mackinnon, were outstanding. Hennessey was a star in Chicago's Catholic High School league three years ago.

Notre Dame lost no time giving evidence of its offensive punch. Army center Casimir Myslinski kicked off out of bounds and the ball automatically went to the Irish on their 35. From that point they put together four first downs, three by rushing and one by passing, that moved the ball to West Point's 2-yard line, where the Cadets held for downs.

George Maxon, the Army right halfback, punted to Kelly at midfield and the former Chicago high school phenom sped back to the Cadets' 31. He then picked up 2 yards off his left tackle, after which Lujack passed to Yonakor, who caught the ball in the end zone for Notre Dame's first touchdown. Lujack's kick for the extra point was wide.

A short time later a long pass, Lujack to Yonakor, put the Irish on West Point's 19, but a 15-yard penalty for holding and a stiffening Army defense forced Lujack to punt, with the ball sailing over the goal line.

Notre Dame was on its way to a touchdown in the second quarter when a forward pass interception by Army's left halfback Carl Anderson on the 10-yard line ended the threat. Anderson raced back to midfield before Lujack broke through a cordon of Cadet blockers to make the tackle.

Army put on its most sustained drive shortly after Anderson's run. Davis was the big ground gainer in the Army assault, but misfortune struck him in the shape of a fumble on Notre Dame's 14-yard line, with Herb Coleman recovering for the Irish on their 13.

Miller's alertness enabled Notre Dame to capitalize on a break early in the third quarter. Davis fumbled when he was tackled hard by Mello, the ball bouncing into the arms of Miller who sidestepped four Cadet tacklers and went to Army's 13 before he was brought down by Maxon.

Again, Army showed it had a defense much stronger than any the Irish had encountered elsewhere this season. Mackinnon stopped Mello after a 2-yard advance and Cadet tackle Joe Stanowicz held Kelly to 3 yards. Miller's 2-yard smash through the middle left the Irish 3 yards short of a first down. On the next play, Lujack fired a pass intended for Yonakor, but it was batted down in the end zone by Cadet defensive back Tom Lombardo.

It was after this magnificent stand that disaster struck the Army. Jim White, one of the finest tackles in 1943 football, stopped a plunge by Davis and in the process stole the ball out of the Cadets' arms and moved to the 8-yard line before he was tackled.

Lujack sneaked through center for 3, but Mackinnon nailed

Mello for a loss of 10 yards. Lujack passed to Miller for 9, and on fourth down rifled another to Yonakor in the end zone for Notre Dame's second touchdown. Fred Earley kicked the extra point.

Army flared back with a march featuring some fancy running by Ed Kenna. Kelly halted the parade by intercepting a pass from Kenna on the Irish 15.

Notre Dame later went 72 yards for its third touchdown after getting the ball on its 28. There were no long runs involved in this drive. The farthest trip was 12 yards by Kulbitski on the first play. Kelly got 5 more at center and then caught a pass from Lujack for a first down on Army's 44. Miller picked his way over right guard for 8, then went through the opposite side for 6. Kulbitski cracked through center for 3 and 6 yards, and Miller earned a first down on the Cadets' 18. Miller and Mello, who relieved Kulbitski, alternated in carrying the ball to the 8-yard line. Mello went off his right tackle for 5 yards and then smashed into center for 2. Lujack scored on a quarterback sneak. Earley's extra point kick was good, thus making the score 20-0.

Kulbitski then set up Notre Dame's final touchdown by intercepting an Army pass on the Cadets' 30. Kilbitski rammed over center for 7 yards and Rykovich, weakened by an attack of dysentery that had kept him in a hospital for several days, gained a first down on the 13. Kilbitski's 6-yard advance was almost nullified by a 5-yard penalty. Earley sped around right end for 10 yards. Kulbitski was held for no gain, but on the next play Earley crashed over for a touchdown. His extra point attempt was blocked.

16

Notre Dame vs. Iowa Pre-Flight

NOVEMBER 20, 1943

NOTRE DAME, Ind. — The greatest team this correspondent ever has seen at Notre Dame today defeated the Iowa Seahawks, 14-13, to retain its rating as the No. 1 unit of intercollegiate football.

Only the greatest team in Notre Dame history could have beaten an opponent the calibre of the one it faced today. Iowa Pre-Flight, sparked by Dick Todd, who for six years was an outstanding performer in the National Football League, thrilled 45,000 spectators from the opening kickoff to the final gun.

Never have we seen a game with better blocking, surer tackling, finer line play, more spirited ball-carrying, or more intelligent direction of team tactics. It was a battle of two mighty lines tearing each other to pieces and chopping up running plays in the process. Brilliant backs had only occasional chances to glitter. The real actors were up front along the line of scrimmage. It was there that plays perished. Seldom could either backfield do any consistent marching. It was chiefly a battle of strangled offense.

It remained for Fred Earley, who only recently reached his 18th birthday, to clinch victory for the Irish. His team, for the second time in this thrilling game, had come from behind to tie the score late in the last quarter. Twice in last week's game Earley had failed to add the point after touchdown. It didn't matter then, because Notre Dame had a commanding lead. Today his accuracy determined the outcome of a game that was even in every other way.

Earley didn't fail when the pressure was on. His kick sailed squarely between the uprights and that was the last seen of him for at least half a minute. Teammates swarmed all over him with congratulatory slaps on his head and back. Earley gave evidence today they haven't taken the foot out of football.

Those who had expected Notre Dame to overpower the Seahawks as it had all of its college opponents were stunned at first half developments. It was Iowa Pre-Flight's backs — Todd, Art Guepe and Jimmy Smith — who were prancing through the line. It was Todd's toe which twice kicked the ball out of bounds inside the Irish 5-yard line, thereby keeping the pressure on Notre Dame until they yielded a touchdown at the end of the first quarter.

Todd, incidentally, was the most dangerous ballcarrier on the field. He averaged six yards in his 13 trips, sending chills up and down the spines of Notre Dame adherents every time he got the ball. He was carried off the field with a broken jaw a few minutes before the end of the game and everyone in the stadium came to his feet to cheer a player who almost had removed the nation's No. 1 eleven from the narrowing list of undefeated and untied teams.

While Todd had the highest rushing average, Creighton Miller, Notre Dame's all-America halfback, gained the most yardage. He carried 20 times for 48 yards, including a 6-yard dash for the touchdown that tied the score at 13-all.

Statistics bear out the equality of the teams if the score is not sufficient evidence. The Seahawks made 14 first downs, one of which was on a penalty, and Notre Dame earned 12. Pre-Flight gained 197 yards by rushing to Notre Dame's 187, but the Irish had an edge in forward passing, 97 yards to 58. John Lujack, whose generalship, defensive play and kicking were high spots in Notre Dame's victory, completed seven of his 15 passes. The Seahawks clicked with six out of 18. Jimmy Smith, who formerly played for Illinois, threw two of the Seahawks' successful passes, Todd two, Guepe one, and Bob Higgins one.

Pat Filley, the Notre Dame captain, lost the toss before the opening kickoff. It was the first time he had called the wrong turn this season. Then things happened to the Irish.

Pre-Flight couldn't gain after taking their kickoff, but neither could Notre Dame when its turn came. On fourth down, Lujack's punt was deflected by Nick Kerasiotis, the former Bear lineman, and went out of bounds on the Seahawks' 44. The Iowans made one first down before the Irish line began to operate, at which point Todd punted out of bounds on the Irish 4-yard line.

Miller got only a yard at right tackle, Lujack went through center for 5, and Mello's plunge was just short of a first down. Lujack punted high and long to Todd, who was brought down on the Seahawks' 47. The Irish held for three downs and Todd again put them in a hole by kicking out of bounds on the 2. Three running plays left Notre Dame a yard short of the required distance and Lujack punted from his end zone out to the 37.

Pre-Flight turned on a terrific burst of running power and the Irish momentarily cracked under the pressure. Smith dashed around Notre Dame's left end for a long gain. Todd and Smith then made only 2 yards apiece, but on the next play Smith again whirled around end for a first down on the 9. Mertes got a yard at left guard, and Guepe went through the opposite side of the line for a standup touchdown. It was the first time this season that the Irish had trailed an opponent. Bernard McGarry kicked the extra point as the first quarter ended.

Notre Dame's line still wasn't operating effectively on offense and the Irish backs couldn't gain after taking the kickoff. Lujack punted to Todd on the Seahawks' 20 and he was smothered on the 24. From that point the Pre-Flight boys passed and rushed their way to the Irish 13. Runs of 17 and 10 yards by Todd and Todd's 27-yard pass to Bob Timmons were the big factors in the Seahawks' parade.

Here Notre Dame made its stand, and with it came a turn in the ball game. George Sullivan, the 17-year-old substitute for Jim White at left tackle, threw Smith for a 2-yard loss. Smith banged through his right tackle for 5. Lujack then nailed Guepe, who had caught a lateral from Smith for a yard loss. On fourth down, Notre Dame end John Zilly barged into the Pre-Flight backfield so fast that Smith, in an attempt to get away a touchdown pass, threw wildly and the Irish took possession of the ball.

The Irish threatened for the first and only time in the first half shortly before time ran out. Lujack hurled a pass to John Yonakor for 30 yards and Yonakor carried for 20 more before he stepped out of bounds on the Iowa 9. Bob Kelly picked up 3 yards at left guard but the gain was canceled on his attempted left end run. On the next play, Lujack's pass to Yonakor fell incomplete. He then clicked with a 4-yard pass to Kelly as the gun ended the second quarter.

Known as the greatest third-quarter team in 1943 football, the Irish lived up to their reputation today. McGarry kicked out of bounds intentionally to open the second half and it was Notre Dame's ball automatically on its 35. Down the field came Miller, Lujack, Mello and Kelly. Once again they were the unstoppable backfield that had crushed some of the greatest teams in the land. Their famous line — Limont, White, Filley, Coleman, Perko, Czarobski and Yonakor — suddenly had come to life.

Mello cracked the Seahawk middle for 3 yards. Miller danced through right guard for 5. Lujack made it a first down on his 48. Mello rammed through right tackle, was halted for a flash, but broke away for 17 yards. Miller hit center for 5, then dashed around right end for 23 yards and a first down on Pre-Flight's 12. Notre Dame was penalized 5 yards for being offside, the first one of the game, and Timmons of the Seahawks threw Lujack for a 1-yard loss. However, it took more than those discouragements to halt the Irish now. Lujack flipped a pass to Kelly for 15 yards and Mello went over center for a first down on the 7. Mello made 2 yards at center and Lujack's lateral pass to Miller gained 3. Kelly pushed through center for a touchdown. Fred Earley was sent in to kick the extra point which tied the score at 7-all.

A few minutes later it looked as if the Irish were on their way to another touchdown, but the Seahawks held on their 18. The young men from Iowa City then put on one of their finest drives of the game, a march that carried to the Irish 6.

Miller broke away for 8 yards, but then disaster struck the Irish. Lujack fumbled the ball trying to hand it to Miller and the Seahawks' George Tobin, who last year won a monogram at Notre Dame, recovered on the Irish 13. On the first play, Todd passed to Dick Burk on the 3-yard line and Burk stepped over for a touchdown. McGarry's try for the extra point hit the west upright and bounced back into the field, a break that saved the day for Notre Dame.

It was now the fourth quarter and those who were watching Notre

Dame for the first time figured the scoring was over. They soon learned why the wearers of the Blue and Gold were called the "Fighting Irish."

Mello returned Pre-Flight's kickoff to the Notre Dame 45. Miller then ripped through center for 8 yards and Kelly earned a first down on the Seahawks' 43. Mello got 4 yards at right guard and Miller 5 at center. Lujack's bullet pass to Yonakor was completed for a 12-yard advance, Miller pranced off right tackle for 7, and Mello banged behind center for 2. Miller gained a first down on the 6 and then broke through right tackle for a touchdown that tied the score. Then came Earley's extra point kick which sent up a victory cry that threatened to shake down the thunder from the sky.

Pre-Flight had one more chance to pull the game out of the fire when Perry Schwartz, the former star of the Brooklyn Dodgers, recovered a fumble by Miller on the Irish 33. The Seahawks tried desperately to click with forward passes but four-straight attempts found the ball still on the 33-yard line. Notre Dame took possession and froze the ball with two running plays until the gun ended a thrilling game.

17

Notre Dame vs. Iowa

OCTOBER 26, 1946

IOWA CITY, Ia. — Notre Dame this afternoon ruthlessly smashed the 25-year-old tradition of the tall, corn country that the Irish cannot win a football game in Iowa City.

In less than three minutes, almost before the last of the capacity crowd of 52,311 had squeezed into their seats, Notre Dame scored its first touchdown against the University of Iowa and then rambled on smoothly to triumph, 41-6.

The Hawkeyes, who 25 years ago this fall whipped the Irish to end Notre Dame's domination of the west and whose iron men of 1939 upset another fine Notre Dame eleven on this gridiron, today contributed to their own disaster. But in the second half, Notre Dame, led by Johnny Lujack, added three more touchdowns and proved convincingly its right to challenge undefeated Army next month for the national championship the Cadets have held for two years.

Notre Dame now has beaten Illinois, Pittsburgh, Purdue and Iowa, and only Navy remains before the climactic battle in New York with Army. This was Iowa's second licking of the campaign and, while defeat perhaps had been expected, few had believed that Notre Dame, or any team, could completely contain Iowa's attack or score so readily against the burly Hawkeye line.

Lujack's share in Notre Dame's victory was not readily noticeable, for Iowa fumbles made his task quite simple. It suffices, however, to note that his 33-yard touchdown pass to Terry Brennan in the third minute of the game, complemented by Fred Earley's extra point kick was sufficient to win.

Statistically, Iowa had the ball for 59 rushes and passes, while Notre Dame had the ball for 62 plays, which is unusual, considering the touchdown ratio of 6 to 1. Moreover, Iowa's line thoroughly demonstrated in the opening period that it was a match for the Irish varsity but progress afoot was painfully slow. Notre Dame, always alert, seized on each Hawkeye misplay to compound Iowa's woe.

Here was a football game in which Notre Dame's partisans might have compassion for opponents, who gradually collapsed under the weight of their misfortunes until the Irish had absolute command at the end.

Lujack completed seven of his 11 passes. His judgment was without fault. Yet, at all times, it seemed that Notre Dame was playing with thoughts of later games. Certainly the Irish, individually, did not have the impetuous drive which characterized their recent victory over Illinois.

Iowa's initial error, a fumble by Dick Hoerner on the third play of the game on Iowa's 29-yard line, established the motif. Lujack recovered the ball. Once more, Notre Dame's extremely tight defense was in evidence for Lujack, who was playing safety, came up fast to get the ball almost at the line of scrimmage. Notre Dame was employing a five-man line, three linebackers, two defensive halfbacks and Lujack.

Lujack was thrown for a 4-yard loss by Earl Banks, a 205-pound Iowa guard from Chicago, on the first play. Lujack intended to pass, but no Irish lineman blocked Banks who roared in for the tackle. On second down, Lujack missed on a pass. On third down, Terry Brennan sprinted around right end, outran the Hawkeye defenders to the end zone, turned and there was Lujack's pass, an easy catch. Notre Dame had scored.

The touchdown spurred the Hawkeyes. After a punt exchange, following the kickoff, the Hawkeyes opened on their own 42-yard line, had 12 consecutive plays and reached the Irish 11-yard line. The 13th play was the jinx. Hoerner shot into the line and again he fumbled under the fierce impact. This time, Pete Ashbaugh, a substitute for Lujack, recovered on Notre Dame's 8-yard line.

Lujack returned to punt as the first period ended.

Notre Dame next gained possession on its 38-yard line. Five plays later, the Irish clinched the decision. Principal ground gainer in this drive was Lujack's long throw which Leon Hart, who was substituting for Frank Koskowski at right end, grabbed on the Hawkeye 11.

The pass sailed over the head of field judge John Fahey, who did not see that Hart had lightly pushed the defending back to make the reception. This was the first foul on several pass plays and, while four penalties were called later, it set up the touchdown from which Iowa never recovered.

Earley's extra point kick was partly blocked and Herb Schoener recovered for Iowa to nullify the try. Notre Dame led, 13-0.

Notre Dame's third touchdown encompassed 80 yards in seven plays for a 20-0 advantage. Lujack dominated the assault. On third down, he threw for 17 yards to Hart. Two plays later, Mike Swistowicz gained 11 yards on a Lujack throw. The Irish lost 15 yards on a holding penalty. Bob Skoglund then caught a Lujack pass for 15 yards.

On the next play, Jim Mello dropped the ball as Lujack handed off from the T-formation for a power thrust at Iowa's right tackle. Lujack got the ball on the bounce, hit at the point of attack, and went down the east sideline behind perfect blocking for a 42-yard touchdown run. This time, Earley had the required blocking and his kick sent the Irish into a 20-0 lead.

Iowa got its consolation touchdown immediately. Forty-six yards were covered on a ruling that Ashbaugh had interfered with Jack Dittmer on the Irish 10-yard line on a pass by Emlen Tunnell. On the same play, Notre Dame was called for roughing Tunnell and, of course, Iowa took the larger gain as the roughing penalty was for only 15 yards.

Tunnell then struck over defensive right guard for 5 yards. On the next play, his pass to Dittmer was incomplete, but he later hit Lou King a foot short of the Irish goal line. On fourth down, Hoerner ran wide around the left end to bounce into the end zone. Bob Sullivan's extra point kick was wide and Notre Dame led, 20-6, at the intermission.

Bob Smith fumbled to end Iowa's first thrust in the second half. Thereafter, the bottom dropped out of the contest for the Hawkeyes. Notre Dame went 50 yards in 10 plays for a 27-6 score and this ended the work for many of the Irish varsity, which had started the third period. Emil Sitko got the touchdown standing up from the Hawkeye 3 and Earley kicked the extra point.

Iowa had the ball for only seven plays in the fourth period while Notre Dame was scoring twice. The Irish covered 62 yards for the first of these. In this attack, field judge Fahey called interference on a third-down pass by Lujack. On Notre Dame's 15th consecutive play, Sitko powered over from the 3-yard line for the score.

The final Notre Dame drive added up to 69 yards, which were gained in 11 plays by such hard hitting third-string backs as Bill Gompers, Floyd Simmons, Cornie Clatt and Larry Coutre from the Hawkeye 26-yard line. Gompers swept around right end after a fake plunge, and had an open field to the goal line. Earley then established the final figures with a place-kick.

18

Notre Dame vs. Army

NOVEMBER 9, 1946

NEW YORK — West Point's famous touchdown twins, Glenn Davis and Doc Blanchard, today ran into a defense they couldn't penetrate and Army was held to a scoreless tie by Notre Dame before a capacity crowd of 75,000 in Yankee Stadium.

The final count was a true index to the comparative strength of the nation's top two football teams. Both had scoring opportunities, but the fury of the opponent's defense always staved off a touchdown.

It was a battle of two mighty lines tearing each other to pieces, and chopping up all running plays in the process. All-America backs were merely members of the supporting cast. The real actors were up front along the scrimmage strip. It was there that plays perished. Neither backfield could break loose. Neither could do any consistent marching. It was primarily a contest of strangled offenses, each usually choked on its own side of the 50-yard line.

This was the fourth tie between the gridiron's oldest intersectional rivals. The series stands at 23 victories for Notre Dame and seven for Army. Notre Dame's performance today ended West Point's string of 25 consecutive triumphs. It was the first time the Cadets had been held to fewer than 19 points in three years.

There's an old military saying that it's not the individual or the Army as a whole but the everlasting team work of every bloomin' soul. That sums up, succinctly, the workmanlike job turned in by both teams today. There seemed to be no stars, but perhaps they were all stars. Individuality was welded into the mass. There was no one great climax run to turn the stands upside down. Rather there was smooth, machine-like precision that kept chewing away at the opponents' defenses. Parts were constantly replaced, yet so smooth was the gearing that the tempo never slackened and the pressure never softened. It probably was one of the most thrilling scoreless ties ever played.

Davis and Blanchard played the full 60 minutes. So did Notre Dame's Johnny Lujack, whose twisted ankle was a matter of national concern 48 hours ago. Blanchard carried the ball 20 times for an average gain of approximately three yards. Davis made 17 trips for an average of one and a half yards. These figures do not include a Davis-to-Blanchard pass that was good for 25 yards.

No matter the statistical notations, one broad fact marked Notre Dame today with a stamping no observer could misread. Its 5-3-2-1 defense operated expertly to halt Davis' sweeps, Blanchard's power drivers and Arnold Tucker's forward passing. The team had spirit and drive and eagerness. Its desire to hurry with the ball resulted in five fumbles, three of which were recovered by Army. It had the fire and fight of Rockne's great teams.

West Point excelled in return of punts, where Davis' great speed gave the Cadets a margin of 40 yards. Notre Dame had an edge in first downs and in yards gained by rushing. Each team made 52 yards by forward passing and they had identical 40-yards punting averages.

While there were no glamour boys on the Yankee Stadium turf today, how about a cheer for Terry Brennan, Notre Dame's plucky left halfback, who kept dividing the Army line like Moses sundered the Red Sea? Brennan averaged five yards in 14 ball-carrying efforts. And how about the expert field direction and brilliant defensive play of Lujack, without whom Notre Dame would have had little chance of stopping Army today? And what would have happened if there had been no George Strohmeyer and Jack Zilly to sift into the Cadets' backfield to break up plays behind the scrimmage line?

The alertness of John Mastrangelo and the aggressiveness of George Connor and Bill Fischer figured prominently in Notre Dame's stand. Mastrangelo twice recovered loose balls at times when Army seemed ready to make its victory move.

While West Point accepted the tie as a moral defeat, there were heroes aplenty on the Cadet side of the line. Army's ends, George Poole and Hank Foldberg, turned in one of their greatest performances. Art Gerometta, who learned his gridiron fundamentals in Gary, Ind., etched his name in West Point records with his magnificent play at guard. So did tackle Gobel Bryant. Center Jim Enos brought fans in Army's section to their feet when he recovered a Notre Dame fumble near the game's end to guarantee his team at least a tie.

Army got a break soon after the opening kickoff when it recovered Emil Sitko's fumble on the Irish 25-yard line. Davis and Blanchard alternated in thrusts at the Irish line, but after four tries the ball was half a yard short of a first down and Notre Dame took possession on its 16.

Brennan and Sitko collaborated for two first downs, but when Lujack lifted his attack to the air, the drive bogged down and the Irish quarterback punted to Davis, who returned 14 yards to his 35. Army put together two first downs before Notre Dame settled down and forced Davis to punt.

Neither team could gain consistently the rest of the first quarter, but early in the second period Lujack clicked with a forward pass to Bob Skoglund on the Cadet 41 to start an 84-yard march. Lujack almost was trapped before he could get the ball away but he operated with a calm that belied the pressure.

Bill Gompers, who had relieved Sitko at right half, broke through center for nine yards and Gerry Cowhig, whose average for the day was in excess of five yards, raced to the Cadet 13. He was aided by blocking that sprang up magically.

Lujack then passed to Cowhig for two yards and Gompers darted through the middle of the Cadet line for 6. Lujack tried to sneak through center for a first down but he was held without gain. Gompers ran wide to the left and was crowded out of bounds on the 4-yard line, where Army took over. That was the closest either team came to winning this terrific ball game.

Shortly before the end of the first half, Army again got a break but couldn't capitalize on it. Brennan fumbled when he was smacked by an Army tackler and Harold Tavzel recovered for Army on the Irish 35. Blanchard made only two yards at right guard and three Army passes, two thrown by Tucker and one by Davis, were broken up by Notre Dame's alert secondary.

Irish eyes were smiling when Army's Elwyn Rowan, a substitute for injured Ug Fuson, let the ball squirt out of his hands and Mastrangelo of Notre Dame fell on it at the Cadet 34. Sitko nibbled at the line for a yard and Brennan gained only two. Army's Tucker ended the scoring threat by intercepting Lujack's pass on the 12-yard line and returning to the Cadet 42.

Blanchard then came through with his longest run of the day. He found a hole in the right side of the Notre Dame line and went tearing goalward with only one man in his path. Unfortunately for Blanchard, that defensive player was Lujack, who never misses his man. Mr. Inside, as Blanchard is known on the gridiron, was dumped on the Irish 47. On the next play, Tucker whipped a pass over center to Foldberg that carried to the Irish 20, but Brennan, who, next to Lujack, was the busiest man in the Irish backfield, broke Army's heart by grabbing one of Tucker's passes on the Irish 8.

Brennan wasn't satisfied with a forward pass interception. On the next play, he sped around his right end for 22 yards and a few seconds later caught a pass from Lujack on the Irish 44 just as the third quarter ended.

There now was a spark to the Notre Dame offense that lifted fans out of their seats. Army's Enos put out the fire, however, by recovering Cowhig's fumble on the Irish 43. Army later failed to convert a fourth-and-one play and Notre Dame took over on its 34. The battle was seesawed the rest of the way with neither team getting close to the other's goal. The game ended with the ball at midfield in Army's possession.

19

Notre Dame vs. Army

NOVEMBER 8, 1947

SOUTH BEND, Ind., — Army's first courtesy call on Notre Dame resulted in disaster today as the curtain was lowered on the most famous of all football rivalries.

Thirty-four years ago, in the game that launched this intersectional relationship on the Plains of West Point, unheralded Notre Dame startled the football world with a history-making aerial display that threw the heavily-favored Cadets into confusion. Today, a record stadium crowd here of 59,191 saw the Fighting Irish discard their favored instrument of attack and tear Army's defenses apart with a running offense that left the experts in confusion.

With Terry Brennan as the chief scourge in a whirling attack on the flanks and Mike Swistowicz and Emil Sitko playing heavy roles, Frank Leahy's green-shirted operatives ripped and raced against one of the most respected lines of the year as they had in no other game of the season.

After the blazing Brennan had taken the opening kickoff and sped 97 yards down the sideline to score without a hand being laid on him, the Fighting Irish compiled the almost staggering total of 361 yards along the ground in registering three more touchdowns and fell 10 yards short of consumating another assault of 76 yards.

The final score was 27-7 and the margin of the victory in this valedictory to a rivalry that has been the most publicized and one of the most profitable the gridiron has known was almost the same as in the inaugural game. The series opened in 1913 with Notre Dame the winner by 35-13.

Not since 1943 has Notre Dame, now more than ever the nation's ranking college eleven and unbeaten in a 15-game sequence, scored so brilliant and crushing a triumph over West Point as it rolled up today. The Irish won from an opponent that had gone undefeated for four seasons until it was the victim of a shocking reversal at the hands of Columbia on Oct. 25 by a margin of 21-20. Indeed, Notre Dame had failed to come out the winner in any of the previous three games, and, more than that, had been held scoreless in all three.

It can well be imagined with what riotous rejoicing each successive touchdown was greeted by the vast majority of the great throng that sat heavily bundled against the nippy weather. The breaking off of the relationship between the teams, commonly accepted as forced by Army, has not been accepted in too kindly a spirit out here, though Notre Dame people have kept their feelings to themselves.

Also, the memory of those humiliating 59-0 and 43-0 drubbings that Earl Blaik's Black Knights administered to the Irish in 1944 and 1945, respectively, when Doc Blanchard and Glenn Davis were the twin terrors of the girdiron, still rankled after the frustration of last year's scoreless tie.

Today was the day of reckoning and atonement for the worst pair of defeats in Notre Dame football history, for expressing with touchdowns the resentment and hurt that the Fighting Irish feel in being dropped after so many years of friendly relationship in one of the most bitterly and yet cleanly fought rivalries the sport has known.

The crowd came with high expectations of seeing its heroes prevail as the favorites by 13 points and they won precisely as they were expected, but the manner of their winning was entirely at variance with preconceived notions.

Johnny Lujack, the celebrated all-America quarterback and passer par excellence, and Frank Tripucka, his accomplished understudy, were the two men above all others who were counted on to bring the victory. It was their great accuracy and poise in firing aerials that were supposed to bring the touchdowns against an Army team whose line was fancied to be a match for the huge, powerful Notre Dame forwards in stopping a running attack.

But Notre Dame had other heroes today. The two men who had engineered the Irish's five previous triumphs this season with their passing, while the running attack was bogging down, were in eclipse. It was the ground operations that sent Army's fighting but baffled operatives down in their worst defeat in years. It was Brennan, scorer of the first two touchdowns; both in the opening quarter; Swistowicz, Sitko, Bob Livingstone and Jim Martin, breaking loose on end-around plays, who held the spotlight.

Lujack, as the master pilot calling the plays against Army's 6-3-2 and 6-2-2-1 defenses, to exploit the weaknesses on the flanks, and handling the ball faultlessly and with beautiful deception, was certainly as valuable a worker as any on the field. His fine defensive work, both against running plays and passes, and his kicking, were factors in the victory, too.

But in his specialty, the pass, the famous quarterback failed to measure up to expectations and on two or three occasions he was glaringly wide or short of the mark, even though four of his eight tosses were completed for 27 yards. Tripucka threw only two passes and both failed.

Army's pass defense was better than any one had anticipated, but Leahy, knowing how intensely West Point was working all week to stop the Irish's aerial operations, crossed up the Cadets by relegating the air arm to a minor role. He had been well advised that Army lacked its usual strength and experience on the wings, that it was particularly potent from tackle to tackle.

So Leahy sent his team out with an offense that concentrated on the flanks. The result was that his fast carriers swept the flanks all afternoon and the Army ends, storming in too sharply, had one of their most horrible days in many years of brilliant West Point end play.

Scoring their three touchdowns after Brennan's electrifying gallop of ninety-seven yards with the opening kickoff, the Fighting Irish went eighty yards twice and then forty-seven yards.

In their first eighty-yard advance they used only one pass, for twenty-three yards. Twelve running plays ate up the remainder of the yardage. They went forty-seven yards in ten plays, and there was just one short toss before Livingstone went across, and on their eighty-yard advance in the final quarter they went the full distance without a single aerial in eleven rushes. Larry Coutre made the last eleven yards.

On the seventy-six-yard assault that was stopped on Army's 10-yard line in the second quarter, seven running plays accounted for the entire gain. After the failure of Notre Dame's ground attack to break loose in its previous games, its disruptive speed, deception and power today against a line rated as highly as Army's were little short of dumbfounding.

Army's running attack, too, was far more impressive than its air operations. It completed only five of fourteen passes for 40 yards, whereas along the ground the cadets picked up 168 yards. They made thirteen first downs, eleven by rushing, but they could not put enough of them together. Invariably they would fail of a first down by a yard or two and have to kick.

Just once Army sustained its attack. That was near the end of the third period and early in the fourth. Starting on their 43, the Cadets went 57 yards to score in the final quarter and all but 11 yards were made along the ground.

Fullback Rip Rowan, their chief gainer with his hard running; Amos Gillette, who displaced Winfield Scott at right half and was a fast, determined runner; Arnold Galiffa and Bobby Jack Stuart were the ballcarriers and Rowan went across for the score. Incidentally, it was the first time that Army has scored against a Notre Dame team coached by Leahy, who was in the Navy in 1944 and 1945.

Army's blocking was not up to standard today and suffered sharply by comparison with the fine protection afforded the Notre Dame ballcarriers when they broke loose. Time and again the Irish forwards, particularly Ziggy Czarobski, Bill Fischer, Capt. George Connor and Leon Hart, swarmed in to smother the Cadet runner.

Army did not handle the ball cleanly, either, and its fumbling of kicks and kickoffs was conspicuous. The West Pointers may have been trying a little too hard. They had all of the fight characteristic of Army teams, but perhaps they were a little nervous in their first appearance here and made mistakes that were costly.

The biggest paid attendance in the seventeen-year history of the stadium welcomed the West Pointers on their first appearance in the

Notre Dame Stadium and exulted in their defeat, bringing the rivalry to an end for an indefinite period. Among the few who did not enjoy the afternoon's proceedings were 300 members of the first, or senior, class of the United States Military Academy.

The Cadets and their superintendent, Maj. Gen. Maxwell D. Taylor, were late in getting to the game. Their train was held up en route by a derailment on the line. They did not reach the stadium until a quarter of an hour before the kickoff.

The West Pointers paraded behind the Notre Dame band and lined up on field in a column of platoons. It was a novel sight in the stadium — the faultless files of young future officers in their gray ulsters, and an impressive one, even though they constituted no more than a detail compared with the 2,200 who composed the entire corps.

The crowd was more tardy in taking its seats in the compact red brick stadium than it has been in arriving at the Yankee Stadium, scene of the game since 1925 with the exception of 1930. The West Pointers were scheduled to march in at 12:30 and at that time fewer than half the seats were occupied.

The difficulty of obtaining food and transportation in the city, with its jammed hotels and restaurants and clogged streets, was responsible in good measure for the slowness with which the stadium filled up. Never before has South Bend been so inundated with visitors, whose numbers were equal to almost half the population of the city. Thousands of local residents, unable to get tickets, saw the game on television sets that were installed in numerous buildings on the Notre Dame campus.

Southern California's line — rated one of the best in the country was no match for Notre Dame's speed boys, Emil Sitko and Bob Livingstone, and their hard running fullback, John Panelli, who were forever breaking through the Trojan wall for big gains.

Livingstone, due largely to his 92-yard touchdown gallop in the fourth period, had the best total of the Notre Dame ballcarriers. He averaged 16.7 yards in eight trips. Sitko carried 11 times for an 11.8 average, but Panelli, whose 3.9 percentage was weak by comparison, nevertheless was the player the Trojans couldn't stop.

Notre Dame started the scoring the first time it had the ball. Conner recovered a fumble by U.S.C.'s Varl Lillywhite immediately after the opening kickoff. The Irish moved from the Trojans' 37 to the 13 where it was fourth down and four. Fred Earley rushed in from the bench to kick a field goal.

That was the only score in the first period, but before the quarter ended the Irish were back on their opponents' 3. Notre Dame controlled the ball so effectively in the opening session that U.S.C. ran only nine plays, exclusive of two punts.

Sitko went over for the first touchdown on a plunge from the 1-yard line to climax a march of 82 yards, during which the Irish linked five first downs. Earley's kick added the extra point.

Southern California showed it's only offensive spurt late in the second quarter when it moved 44 yards for a touchdown in nine plays, after Powers had intercepted a pass from Lujack and was downed on the Irish 44. Powers ran to the 32 on the following play and his pass to Jack Kirby earned a first down on the 14. The first-string Irish line then returned to the game, but it couldn't stave off a U.S.C. touchdown.

Gray picked up 5 yards over right guard. Powers' pass to Gray netted only a yard, but on the next play Kirby dashed outside Notre Dame's left tackle for a touchdown. Tom Walker added the extra point and the teams left the field at the half with Notre Dame ahead, 10-7.

20

Notre Dame vs. U.S.C.

DECEMBER 6, 1947

LOS ANGELES — Notre Dame today convinced 104,953 spectators, the largest crowd ever to see a sports event on the Pacific coast, that it belongs among college football's all-time great units by burying previously undefeated Southern California, 38-7.

Three minutes before the end of the one-sided contest, the vast Coliseum throng rose to its feet to cheer Johnny Lujack, the brilliant field leader of the Fighting Irish, who was motioned to the sideline to receive an enthusiastic handshake from Coach Leahy.

Lujack's performance was brilliant and, above all, workmanlike. He made no mistakes. His passing was accurate, as it was expected to be, but his team today didn't rely on Lujack's marksmanship. It ground the Trojans into the soggy turf by one of the most devastating running attacks this historic field has seen.

Today's score was the biggest ever rolled up in the 19-year rivalry between the famed intersectional foes. The victory gave Notre Dame a record of nine-straight victories for the season, the first time since Knute Rockne's 1930 campaign that the Irish whipped every opponent on their schedule. It also marked the 18th consecutive game that Notre Dame has gone undefeated.

This was a battle of a good team against a great one. The Trojans were only 3 points behind at halftime, but any question about the outcome was dissipated on the first play of the third quarter, when

Emil Sitko broke outside his left tackle and raced 76 yards for a touchdown. He dodged past two defending backs, picked up his interference and crossed the goal line standing up. Capt. George Conner, who played one of his greatest games today, blocked out Southern California's Gordon Gray on the 25-yard line, the only Trojan who had a chance to overtake the fleet runner.

From that moment the excitement of close and uncertain combat was missing. The Irish substituted one unit for another in an effort to hold down the score, but the reserves moved with the precision of the regulars. The record gathering had to get its thrill out of seeing Southern California, the Pacific coast's representative in the Rose Bowl on New Year's day, doing its best in a hopeless cause and Notre Dame playing football which, for variety, proficiency and the knack of doing the right thing well, had reached gridiron perfection.

The Irish piled up 397 yards to U.S.C.'s 118 on running plays and had a margin of 64 yards to 55 in passing. Lujack completed five of his seven tosses and Frank Tripucka clicked once in two efforts. Four different Trojan passers — Jim Powers, George Murphy, Dean Dill and Wilbur Robertson — threw 29 aerials but connected only eight times.

The weather, too, may have accounted for the fact that the spectators were in no hurry to gain their seats. Flurries of snow fell at intervals for most of the morning, and the temperature was not far above freezing. The weather cleared before the kickoff, and the field, protected by tarpaulins, was dry and fast.

Notre Dame won the toss and elected to receive. Jack Mackmull kicked off and the ball went out of bounds. That was unfortunate for the Cadets, for on the next kickoff Brennan picked up the ball on his 3-yard mark in front of the goal posts, cut to his left for the sideline and went all the way.

One man had a shot at him right after he got under way, but by the time he had passed his 20-yard line he was clear and beyond catching. Galiffa tried to overhaul him, but the Notre Dame halfback outsprinted him and the crowd roared deliriously with joy.

Army took the next kickoff and made a first down and then had to kick. Notre Dame, starting on its 20, again went all the way. Army was helpless to stop its sweeps and dashes off the tackles. Lujack pitched to the towering Hart for twenty yards and Martin carried for fifteen on an end-around play. Brennan went across from the 3-yard mark, finding a big hole at left tackle. Fred Earley, who had kicked the first extra point, missed on his second try and Notre Dame led by 13-0 with more than six minutes of play remaining in the quarter.

Army now came back strong and made two first downs, with Gillette the big gainer. But it was stopped at the Irish 35, the nearest it got to a score in the first half.

Early in the second period, Notre Dame started on its 14 and again had the crowd roaring as it swept Army off its feet. Sitko, Swistowicz, Lujack and Brennan gained big chunks and a 23-yard dash around left end by Swistowicz put the ball on Army's 10. Here the Cadets rose up so fiercely that Notre Dame had to give up the ball sixteen yards back on the 26.

Notre Dame got a break when Ed Gradoville, in kicking formation, fumbled the pass from center on fourth down and had to run for it. Notre Dame took possession on Army's 45. But the Cadets fought back so savagely that the Irish was unable to gain and had to punt.

A fumble by Brennan, recovered by Galiffa, gave Army a break and the ball on its 47. Then came a beautiful 30-yard pass by Galiffa. Scott was down under the ball and got it in his hands, but a big groan went up from the 300 Cadets as he dropped it, inside Notre Dame's 25-yard line. Another pass was intercepted by Lujack before the half ended.

Largely as the result of Army's fumble of the second-half kickoff, Notre Dame started on the Cadets' 45 and got to the 38 but was stopped. Late in the period the Fighting Irish launched their 47-yard march to their third touchdown.

A penalty against Army for pass interference came at the start of the drive. Livingstone, who found himself in the Navy game; Swistowicz and Bill Gompers carried the ball the remaining distance and Livingstone went across from six yards out. Army now made its only sustained drive of the game. It began late in the third period and ended early in the fourth with Rowan going over from the 1-yard mark.

If that Army score frightened any in the crowd, their fears were speedily dissolved. Notre Dame took the next kickoff on the 20 after a touchback and went all the way, eighty yards. Martin, Livingstone, Swistowicz and Coutre were the ballcarriers. Coutre broke through left tackle, shook off a clump of tacklers and went eleven yards for the score.

Trojan hearts beat wildly when Livingstone was downed on the Irish 24 after returning the third-quarter opening kickoff. Then came the 76-yard touchdown sprint by Sitko that broke U.S.C.'s morale. This was the Notre Dame they feared, the team that is dangerous anywhere on the field. Earley's extra point kick boosted the score to 17-7.

Lillywhite kicked off to Livingstone who fumbled the ball, with Paul Cleary recovering for the Trojans on the Irish 35. Lujack pulled his teammates out of this embarrassment by intercepting Powers' pass and running 15 yards to his 47.

Notre Dame marched straight up field to score its third touchdown in eight plays. Panelli carried the ball over the goal line and Earley added the extra point. The score now was 27-7.

Southern California got another chance in the fourth period when it's George Davis recovered a Coy McGee fumble on the Trojan 47. John Rossetto picked up 19 yards and Dill passed to Stan Cramer for 4. Plunges by Dill and Mickey McCardle moved the ball to the Irish 11 for a first down. Here the Irish braced and took over on their eight.

On the next play, Livingstone darted through an opening outside his left tackle, side-stepped a defending back and outran everyone to the goal line. Earley again added the extra point.

The final Irish touchdown was made by tackle Ul Smijewski who intercepted a lateral pass from U.S.C.'s Robertson. The big lineman ran 30 yards for the score. Earley wound up a perfect day by kicking the extra point that made the count 38-7.

21

Notre Dame vs. Purdue

SEPTEMBER 25, 1948

NOTRE DAME, Ind. — Notre Dame and Purdue each scored four touchdowns this chill, sunlit afternoon in Notre Dame Stadium before a record crowd of 59,343 gathered for the opening game of the campaign. From this basic equality, the rival kicking specialists, Steve Oracko of Notre Dame and Rudy Trbovich of Purdue, who took no other part in the game, fought for victory.

Oracko, who had missed his first three kicks for extra points, got them back with a fourth-period field goal and then was successful on his point-after try following Notre Dame's fourth touchdown. Trbovich missed the second of his four attempts. Thus, Notre Dame, victor by a 28-27 score, now has been undefeated in 19 consecutive contests.

Few games have been more replete with thrills — long passes, clever runs, unusual plays, and errors. No game could be closer. In the final analysis, the Irish were victors because they followed the ball more carefully and, in particular, took advantage of Purdue's mediocre punting.

Norbert Adams' fumble, which was recovered by Bill Walsh, permitted continuance of Notre Dame's first-period scoring drive. George Punzelt, Purdue's erratic kicker, punted only 6 yards and out of bounds in the second period and Notre Dame seized the opportunity, again, this time going 36 yards in five plays, with Emil

Sitko getting his second touchdown. In the last period, Jim Martin partly blocked Punzelt's punt. Irish fullback John Panelli alertly grabbed the loose football, burst through two tacklers and ran 70 yards to score.

Notre Dame then made its final touchdown when Leon Hart rushed Bob DeMoss as the Boilermaker quarterback attempted a lateral near his goal line. Hart deflected the ball and Irish substitute right tackle Al Zmijewski intercepted it and ran 8 yards for the touchdown.

Purdue's line consistently was outplayed in the first 20 minutes as Notre Dame led, 12-0. After only one first down in this time, the Boilermakers rallied with sophomore halfback Neil Schmidt sparking the attack. Schmidt was the fastest back on the field, and completely covered Terry Brennan of the Irish on his sprints for long passes. Schmidt also caught a 51-yard pass when Brennan was covering him.

Purdue's first attack was halted by a pass interception by Irish reserve halfback Frank Spaniel in Notre Dame's end zone. Spaniel mistakenly tried to run and was dropped on his own 2-yard line. Irish quarterback Frank Tripucka then saw his third-down pass intercepted by Adams and Purdue scored in three plays from the Irish 35. Adams caught DeMoss' scoring pass for the final 18 yards and Trbovich's extra point kick left Notre Dame in front, 12-7, at the intermission.

Purdue received the second-half kickoff and drove 74 yards in 15 plays, while running at the Irish ends consistently. Bob Agnew plunged 2 yards for the touchdown, giving Purdue its 13-12 lead. Here Trbovich missed the kick for the extra point, a failure which eventually cost a tie.

Notre Dame regained its lead 18-13, on Panelli's 70-yard run with the partly blocked punt.

Early in the last quarter, DeMoss passed from behind his goal line, which was intercepted by Irish defensive back Mike Swistowicz and returned to Purdue's 20. On fourth down, with the ball on Purdue's 16, Oracko then kicked a field goal from an angle.

Notre Dame led, 28-20, with three minutes to play after the Hart-Zmijewski interception. The Boilermakers immediately rallied with Bob Hartman pitching. Ken Gorgal relieved DeMoss at quarterback and passed 24 yards to Bob Grant in Notre Dame's end zone but Swistowicz interfered. The penalty put the ball on the Irish 1-yard line. After a 5-yard penalty for being offside, DeMoss passed to Harley Jeffery on the last play of the game for the touchdown. Trbovich's extra point kick established the final score, 28-27.

22

Notre Dame vs. Northwestern

NOVEMBER 13, 1948

NOTRE DAME, Ind. — Notre Dame, after the unusual experience of trailing, 7-6, rallied in the sixth minute of the final period with a 63-yard march to beat a brilliant pack of Northwestern Wildcats, 12-7, before a capacity crowd of 59,305 this afternoon. The success of this final game of the always tense and exciting Notre Dame-Northwestern series was the 23d conquest of the Wildcats by the Irish.

The victors had their hands full at all times as they proceeded in the business of extending their victory string to 20-straight and their sequence without defeat to 26 games. The Wildcats lived up to expectations at the very outset by surging to the Notre Dame 9-yard line. In this advance, the Purple had a foot to go for a first down but the Irish were able to stop Frank Aschenbrenner in a stack-up on fourth down. Taking over at that point, Notre Dame penetrated 91 yards in a drive that terminated with fullback John Panelli going over from the 1. The Irish, who had not operated in Northwestern territory in the first 11 minutes of the game, had that first touchdown in 13:25 of the opening period.

After Panelli had scored the game's first points, Steve Oracko went in and kicked the ball between the uprights but the points were taken off the scoreboard because a Notre Dame back was illegally-in-motion. Oracko failed in his second try after the 5-yard penalty.

We'll give you the detail of the 91-yard advance a bit later.

The score remained 6-0 for the Irish until 10:25 of the third period. Shortly before this juncture, Bill Gay had intercepted a pass and returned it to Northwestern's 24. Things looked bad for the Wildcats when they were assessed 15 yards for roughing, which move the ball down to the Northwestern 9.

Frank Spaniel was tossed for a 4-yard loss by Joe Zuravleff. Irish quarterback Frank Tripucka then tossed the ball crossfield and Art Murakowski leaped high, catching the heave on the 10-yard line near his right sideline.

Holding close to the sideline, the Wildcats fullback galloped without much of a challenge until a near tackler had been blocked in midfield. At the Northwestern 30, Murakowski had only Tripucka to beat for a touchdown. When Tripucka made his try, Murakowski had just enough room between his path and the sideline to swerve out of the Irish quarterback's reach. Murakowski then pranced without escort to the touchdown.

Jim Farrar took his tape measure onto the lawn, measured his stepping distance, and booted the extra point that gave the Wildcats a 7-6 lead.

Near the close of the third quarter, Northwestern got possession of the ball when Murakowski recovered a fumble by Larry Coutre on the Northwestern 41 but the Wildcats couldn't get an advance moving and Aschenbrenner kicked to Gay, who returned to the Irish 37. It was from this point the Notre Dame victory march proceeded as the game went into the fourth period.

John Landry made 11 yards on two tries and after Gay had added a yard, Landry ripped off 12. Notre Dame was penalized for backfield-in-motion after which Bill Wightkin made 7 yards on another of the several end around plays the Irish employed successfully during the afternoon. Landry then went to the Northwestern 30, Gay made three yards and Landry hit off-tackle for 12 to the Northwestern 15. Gay smacked up the middle to the 10. Landry and Gay each hit off-tackle before Gay finally dived over for a touchdown. Oracko again failed to add the extra point and the scoring was over for the day at 5:20 of the fourth quarter.

A fumble which Bill Fischer recovered on the Northwestern 8, a 36-yard Irish pass ruled incomplete because of pass interference, and two futile tries for field goals by Oracko were among the elements that kept excitement at high pitch till game's end.

And now to go back to the detail of that 91-yard march that gave Notre Dame the first points of the afternoon. Terry Brennan started things with a 9-yard gain, then added 8 more. Brennan went 5 yards, then 22 for a first down on the midfield line. Panelli and Mike Swistowicz stepped in and carried for a first down at the Northwestern 38. After an incomplete pass, Brennan carried 6 yards and Swistowicz 1. It was fourth down and 3 to go for the Irish, whereupon Panelli ran for a first down at the Wildcat 11. Two plays later, Leon Hart was forced out of bounds a few feet short of a touchdown on another end around maneuver and from there Panelli went over the score.

Brennan was the high mileage gent insofar as the victors' rushing was concerned, making 78 yards on 12 tries, while Gay traveled 70 on 11 tries. Murakowski was the heavy duty fellow for the losers, making 74 yards on 19 totes and, of course, his 90-yard sprint on that pass interception.

23

Notre Dame vs. U.S.C.

DECEMBER 4, 1948

LOS ANGELES — Notre Dame was unbelievably behind, 14-7, only two and one-half minutes were left, and 100,571 fans in the Coliseum today were sure the football upset of the year was unfolding before them.

Southern California had just scored for the second time in this last quarter and now Charley Peterson, a 215-pound tackle, was kicking off. A yard in advance of his goal line, Bill Gay of the Irish, who once played football at Chicago's Tilden High School, fielded the ball.

He cut sharply to his right and his blockers moved in that direction, too — one huge blob of green — cutting a swath along the sideline for the 170-pound halfback. The rapid trip ended just 13 yards from the Trojans' goal line. The Irish, in a desperate race with the clock, then put over the tying touchdown with 35 seconds left.

Now Gay had done his part, but Notre Dame still needed one big point off Steve Oracko's goal-kicking shoe. It went straight and true over the cross bar, and another of those astounding Irish gridiron miracles had happened.

The final score was 14-14 against a thrice-beaten Pacific coast team which had been figured at least three touchdowns inferior.

And, children, today's Irish will recite in later years, that's how Notre Dame kept alive its undefeated string, running it to 28 games and marred only by two ties. The other smudge was a scoreless deadlock with the Army in 1946. But today's tie ended Notre Dame's 21-game winning streak.

The Irish played in that rocky last half without Frank Tripucka who was felled on the final play of the first half, when he carried the ball deep in his own territory. It was feared the senior quarterback suffered fractured ribs and a bruised kidney.

The Irish not only were forced to overcome the loss of Tripucka, but the indignity of losing the ball seven times — six by fumbles and once on an interception. Despite four of those bobbles showing up in the first half, Notre Dame was ahead, 7-0, at the end of the first half.

At the end of the scoreless first quarter, the Irish were on their own 48-yard line. On the fourth play of the second period, Tripucka, from the Southern California 45-yard line, hit gigantic Leon Hart with a pass over the middle. Hart, an all-America end today, both on offense and defense, took the ball on the 40. He was smacked hard and almost downed after his first strides, but recovered and, with virtually every Trojan on the field chasing him, ran for a touchdown after swerving to the right.

As the game wore on, with the Irish still plagued by their own mistakes, but keeping the Trojans from capitalizing, Hart's dynamic touchdown loomed larger and larger.

Late in the third quarter, Jack Kirby of Southern California intercepted a pass thrown by Tripucka's substitute, 18-year-old Bob Williams of Baltimore, who took over the job and ran the team like a veteran.

That interception was taken back 3 yards to the Irish 42. On the first play, Dean Dill, third and best of the Trojan T quarterbacks, was knocked down for five-yard loss before he could pass. On the next play, he chose to run and reached the 40. Then Kirby made a leaping catch of Dill's pass and was knocked out of bounds on the 18. On the last play of the period, Kirby smashed to the 15.

On the first play of the final quarter, the Irish swarmed in toward Dill to keep him from passing, but left the middle unprotected. Seeing the hole, Dill ran to the 5-yard line. Bill Martin bulled to the 2, Art Battle drove to the 1, and then Martin went through a hole at Notre Dame's right guard. Dill then kicked the tying point and the

Coliseum caught on fire, vocally.

After the kickoff, Williams fumbled while back to pass and Southern California's Ed Henke recovered at midfield. Then Dill punted out on the Irish 5. Notre Dame had to kick and Kirby returned to the Midwesterners' 42. After a 5-yard penalty for too many time-outs, Kirby ran 17 yards.

Now five minutes remained in the game. Battle was stopped on the 30, but Ernie Tolman made a leaping catch of Dill's pitch on the 13. On second down, Dill, while back to pass, again saw that inviting gap down the middle and slammed to the six. Battle struggled to the 3 and, on the next play, Martin again found a hole on the defensive right side and went over. Dill's kick put the Trojans in front, 14-7.

That was when the press box began to buzz. Where had Notre Dame last been defeated? It was the last game in 1945 when Great Lakes whipped the Irish, who were coached by Hugh Devore, 39-7. Leahy? His last defeat at Notre Dame had been by Great Lakes, 19-14, way back in 1943.

Then came the kickoff and Notre Dame's Gay stopped this defeat speculation with his 86-yard return. A minute and a half remained when Williams, on a quarterback sneak, reached the 8. Williams then passed to Gay in the end zone but it fell incomplete. Williams again pitched and again Gay dashed into the end zone where Gene Beck, the Trojan linebacker, was called for interference.

That put the ball on the Trojan 3. John Panelli smashed up the middle to the 1. Then Emil Sitko, striking low and hard, found enough daylight to tumble over for the touchdown. Oracko completed the comeback story with that large one-pointer to even the score at 14-all.

The Irish then recovered their own onside kickoff and, on the last play of the game, Williams ran 14 yards to the Trojans' 34.

Southern California, in the last analysis, made its victory bid with a passing attack — 31 aerials of which 17 were good for 130 yards. The stout Irish line yielded only a net of 74 yards. Notre Dame's total offense ledger showed 304 yards — exactly 100 more than Southern California made.

Tripucka completed 2 of seven passes for 46 yards, Williams 3 of nine for 28.

Gay, who had been in a running mood before his game-turning dash, was the top ballcarrier on the field.

24

Notre Dame vs. Tulane

OCTOBER 15, 1949

NOTRE DAME, Ind.—Notre Dame took highly-touted Tulane seriously for the first 10 minutes of today's football entertainment before 58,196 in Notre Dame Stadium this afternoon. In that brief span, Chicagoan Larry Coutre made three touchdowns and his fellow townsman, Steve Oracko kicked two points for a 20-0 Irish lead. Thereafter, the game was conducted on a northern hospitality basis to a 46-7 final score.

Thus, did Notre Dame bust an abortive national title bubble by ringing up its fourth-straight victory and prolong its favorite statistic to 32-straight games without a defeat. The Irish's winning string began with the 1946 season and is composed of 30 victories and two ties, one with Army in 1946 and the other with Southern California in the last match of last season.

Notre Dame employed 53 men in pursuing the northern hospitality theme but even so, the lads who supplemented Coutre and his first-string buddies wore no hobbles. Frank Spaniel made the score 27-0 in the last two minutes of the opening period and thereafter the Irish added six points in the second period, seven in the third and six more in the final quarter. Oracko kicked four extra point conversions and three were blocked.

Here are the salient features of the scoring:

Touchdown No. 1 — Made by Coutre from the 14-yard line after the contest was 2 minutes and 45 seconds old. Shortly before this first score, Notre Dame had been forced to kick after a 15-yard penalty. The kick was brought back and Tulane was penalized 15 yards for roughing the kicker. It was Notre Dame's ball on the Tulane 36. A Bob Williams-to-Emil Sitko pass was good to the 19. Five yards were added on the ground. Then Coutre went over tackle, standing up. Oracko kicked the extra point.

Touchdown No. 2 — Six minutes after his first touchdown, Coutre ran 81 yards to score again. Seconds before, Notre Dame had been set back to its 16 by a 15-yard penalty for clipping. Spaniel went to the 19, then Coutre ran 81 yards for a pay-off. Oracko converted.

Touchdown No. 3 — Coutre went over from the Tulane 2 as the clock hit the 10-minute mark in the first period. The ball had reached the 2 on a 53-yard pass maneuver, Williams to Bill Wightkin. Oracko's extra point kick was blocked.

Touchdown No. 4 — This one was made on a 34-yard Williams-to-Spaniel pass play. Leon Hart set up the touchdown by recovering a Tulane fumble on the Irish 49. Sitko, Hart and Jim Barrett carried to the Tulane 34, despite being slowed by a 15-yard illegal use of the hand penalty. Then came the Williams-to-Spaniel toss and the touchdown. Oracko converted.

Touchdown No. 5 — Notre Dame started on its 20 after Tulane had kicked through the end zone. Big factor in the advance was another long Williams-to-Wightkin pass, good for 44 yards to the Tulane 15. There was a loss to the 18. Then a Williams-to-Hart pass which was good for the touchdown. Oracko failed to add the extra point. This scoring was in the ninth minute of the second period. The half ended with Notre Dame leading, 33-0.

Tulane touchdown No. 1 and only — After three minutes and 25 seconds of play in the third period, Tulane got the ball on a punt. Two plays later, Bill Bonar passed to George Kinek who ran unpursued 76 yards along his left sideline for the touchdown. Euel Davis converted.

Notre Dame touchdown No. 6 — Spaniel went over for his second touchdown from the Tulane 12 with six minutes remaining in the third period. Oracko converted.

Notre Dame touchdown No. 7 — Jim Barrett ran 59 yards, which was aided by spectacular blocking by John Petitbon and others. Oracko failed to add the extra point.

The final accounting in the matter of first downs showed Notre Dame with a dozen, Tulane with seven. Tulane had a slight edge in pass yardage, 186 to 179, but the Green Wave, lulled perhaps, by success a week earlier in its 40-0 conquest of Southeastern Louisiana State College and early-season defeats of Alabama and Georgia Tech, was swamped in the rushing department. Notre Dame romped for 230 net yards to Tulane's 23.

25

Notre Dame vs. Michigan State

NOVEMBER 5, 1949

EAST LANSING, Mich. — Notre Dame advanced along the victory trail this afternoon with power and incredible skill in forward passing to smash Michigan State's courageous Spartans, 34-21. An overflow throng of 51,277 watched the Irish take command, 14-7, at the intermission and tally three more touchdowns before Michigan State's counter-attack established the final score.

Notre Dame now has won six consecutive games this season and has advanced to 34 games in four years without defeat, although this summary has been punctured by ties with Army and Southern California.

There was no question of the outcome of today's battle, waged under clear skies that tempered a chill northwest wind, after the Spartans expended pent-up energies and emotions in a blazing first period. Michigan State accomplished five first downs in two futile assaults before Notre Dame converted a first down. This was half of the Spartans' total of first downs.

The Irish, when once under way, recorded 18 first downs while producing five touchdowns.

Williams' accurate passing — he completed 13 of 16 passes for 178 yards — was sensational. The air attack was dictated by the Spartans concentration on seven- and eight-man defensive lines which left the secondary vulnerable to short, riflelike throws to the ends or lobbing tosses over the undermanned defending backfield.

Even so, Notre Dame's ground assaults, led by Emil Sitko and Frank Spaniel, rolled up 291 yards on 63 rushing plays as compared to State's 81 yards on 40 attempts. Sitko averaged 5 yards for 18 carries and Spaniel 7 yards for 10. Williams himself carried six times, including once when the Irish quarterback raced 40 yards on a dash off left tackle for Notre Dame's third touchdown.

Williams played without relief when the Irish had possession. His work today was as brilliant and intelligent as that of any of his great predecessors.

As the battle developed, it soon became apparent that Michigan State could not entertain hope of ending Notre Dame's victory march. Despite jammed line defense and smashing tackling, the Spartans could not cope consistently with the Irish's power. But Michigan State justified its own record of five victories this year and thoroughly satisfied its constituents by its sturdy play.

This was the most rugged football we've seen this year, an opinion officially recorded after the game by Trainer Hugh Burns of the Irish. In the third period, Michigan State's substitute fullback Leroy Crane suffered a knee injury and will miss the Spartans' remaining games.

Michigan State's air attack in the last period, when the Spartans trailed, 24-7, fought on as furiously at the conclusion as at the beginning. Gene Glick's passing — he completed six of eight throws and all five of his attempts in the second half — was a high point of the closing rallies. In the main, however, State was forced to yield ground before Irish perfection and Williams' consummate strategy.

Michigan State received the kickoff by winning the choice and the first surge failed after two first downs. Al Dorow punted out on Irish 21-yard line. The Irish returned the kick on fourth down and Williams' spiral was brought back 10 yards by Horace Smith on Michigan State's 41.

Spartan halfbacks Ev Grandelius and Lynn Chandnois ripped into the Notre Dame line, despite the Irish shift to seven men and with aid of a pass from Dorow to Dorne Dibble advanced to Notre Dame's 7-yard line. Grandelius smashed for 5 yards and fullback Jim Blankhorn got a yard at left guard. On the next play, Blankhorn fumbled and Notre Dame linebacker Jerry Groom made the recovery on his own 5-yard line.

Notre Dame now got its initial first down, but after one more, Chandnois relieved the pressure by intercepting of Williams' high pass over the head of intended receiver Larry Coutre. This was the only interception of the day and afterward Williams completed 10-consecutive passes before a failure.

This sent the game scoreless into the second period. Then Notre Dame struck and a 25-yard return by Bill Gay of Dorow's punt set up the first touchdown on Michigan State's 24.

Coutre advanced 4 yards, but was stopped on his next rush. On third down and faced by an 8-man line with three Michigan State secondary men spaced in a row, Williams tossed the ball to Notre Dame's left half, Ernie Zalejski, who took the pass at the goal line and ran over for the touchdown. Steve Oracko kicked the extra point and the Irish led, 7-0.

Five minutes later, Gay fumbled Dorow's punt and recovered, but he was downed on the Irish 11-yard line. On the first scrimmage, Williams handled the ball badly in a handoff to Coutre and the ball bounced around freely with Coleman finally gaining possession for the Spartans on the Irish 5. This compensated for Michigan State's first-period fumble at the goal.

Grandelius took the ball from Leroy Crane's spin turn and advanced to within a foot of the goal. Grandelius then smashed for the touchdown and George Smith kicked the extra point to tie the game, 7-7.

The clock showed 7:45 until intermission when Notre Dame presented its longest assault for the touchdown which established the 14-7 halftime score. Coutre returned the kickoff 8 yards to his 11-yard line. Subsequently, a penalty for illegal use of the hands put the Irish back to their 5-yard line, but in 16 legal plays Notre Dame went all the way.

Williams carried for 10 yards and then completed the penalty deficit by passing to Leon Hart for a first down on the Irish 34. Sitko and Coutre went 8 yards, and on third down Williams lateraled to Sitko who finally was chased out of bounds on the Irish 47.

Sitko lunged for 3 yards but the Spartans' jammed line tossed Coutre for a yard loss. Williams then passed to Coutre for 6 yards, but it still was short of the required distance. On fourth down,

Williams tossed downfield to Bill Wightkin for a jumping catch in front of the Spartans' secondary and a new start on Michigan State's 22. Wightkin almost escaped his enveloping tacklers.

State dropped into a seven-man line with one linebacker and Zalejski swept left end for 9 yards. Sitko then crashed through with uncanny timed blocking and it was first down on State's 9.

Williams carried off-tackle and the threat of a lateral gave him 5 yards. Coutre took the quick-opening handoff to drive 2 yards. Sitko was stopped inches short, but State was offside and the ball was moved two feet back to the 1-yard line with the advantage of replaying the down.

Coutre again failed — the Spartans fought furiously — but Williams sent a flanking back wide to the left with the left end split out and, with this deployment loosening the defense, Coutre split the line for the touchdown. Oracko's extra point kick made it 14-7.

Notre Dame chose to receive to start the second half and here again was evidence of Irish power and skill for they did not release the ball until they had moved 79 yards in eight plays to take complete control of the game.

Coutre returned the kickoff 10 yards to the Irish 21. Gay turned left end for 12 yards. Coutre and Spaniel, who replaced Gay, picked up 6 yards. Then Sitko, on a delayed plunge with Williams taking a pass, went to the Irish 48. Spaniel and Sitko, the later carrying twice, moved to Michigan State's 40.

Williams carried again. You might think Notre Dame was using a new offense akin to the effectiveness of Oklahoma's split-T, as perhaps the Irish were, for Williams burst through the line outside tackle, raced past the defending halfback and finished at the end zone.

A high pass from center handicapped the extra point attempt which was hurried, lacked timing, and was wide. Notre Dame led, 20-7.

Notre Dame's fourth touchdown was instituted late in the third period and consummated in the fourth. It numbered 10 plays and covered 59 yards. Williams jump pass to Wightkin was a feature. It predicated a fake jump and lateral to Coutre which lost 4 yards but, on the next play, Williams tossed to Wightkin for 12 yards. Coutre made 4 yards and a first down on State's 20. Williams then fumbled and recovered as the third period ended.

Sitko slashed for 4 yards and repeated against the tight line, sidestepped Chandnois and ran 16 yards to score. Oracko's extra point kick produced Notre Dame's 27-7 lead.

The next time the Irish had the ball, they moved 35 yards in eight plays after State had gambled on fourth down and failed. The scoring play was on third down from the Spartan 33 with Hart taking a lob pass in the end zone.

Hart was completely free and Williams, at the last second, cut down his speed to make the touchdown toss a picture play of Michigan State's ineffectual secondary defense. Notre Dame now led, 34-7.

In the closing minutes, Glick was sent in to pass. With the ball on the Spartans' 11, he hit Chandnois who was in the clear only to be staggered by a diving try by John Petitbon after which Sitko caught the carrier. The pass gained 84 yards and gave the Spartans a first down on the Irish 5-yard line.

Glick then passed over Petibon to hit Bob Carey in the end zone for the touchdown. George Smith kicked the extra point.

Michigan State duplicated its air attack for its last touchdown. This time Notre Dame had failed on fourth down on the Irish 44-yard line. Glick threw to Bob Carey for 37 yards, who made a spectacular catch despite two defenders. Then Glick passed over Gay's head to Dibble in the end zone for the score. Smith's extra point kick ended the scoring at 34-21, with 1:12 left to play.

26

Notre Dame vs. S.M.U.

DECEMBER 3, 1949

DALLAS — Notre Dame today added the final star-spangled chapter to its golden 1949 football season by defeating Southern Methodist, 27-20, before an overflow crowd of 75,428 in the Cotton Bowl.

The Mustangs, playing without their ace passer, Doak Walker, lived up magnificently to their reputation for wide open, daring football. They were the only team that stood up to the nation's No. 1 collegiate unit for 60 minutes. There never was a moment when the Fighting Irish looked like certain winners.

This was Notre Dame's 10th-straight victory and the 38th game it has played without defeat. It also marked the fourth-consecutive season the team has played without a setback.

Today's triumph belongs to the Notre Dame line. Twice the Irish stopped Southern Methodist inside their 5-yard line, once on the 4, and again with the Mustangs only a foot from a touchdown. The defensive work of Jerry Groom, Bob Toneff, Leon Hart, Jim Martin, John Helwig, Jim Mutscheller and Bob Lally should be engraved in stone at Notre Dame Stadium for future generations of linemen to admire.

There were defensive greats in the Notre Dame backfield, notably John Petitbon, Billy Gay and Mike Swistowicz, but it was the speed and fury of Notre Dame's line that enabled the Irish to survive this thrilling contest undefeated.

The offensive star of a battle that surged from one end of the field to the other was Southern Methodist's Kyle Rote, the best all-around back Notre Dame has faced this season. He passed, he ran, and he caught. His trickery found the Irish, widely rated as Phi Beta Kappa in gridiron technique, completely off guard on two or three occasions.

Notre Dame knew Rote was almost as efficient a pitcher as his disabled teammate, Walker, but they hadn't counted on his brilliant running. He carried from the tailback spot in Matty Bell's single-wing offense 24 times for a net gain of 115 yards, more than any other player on either team. He completed 10 of his 24 passes for 146 yards and caught a pass that was good for a 15-yard gain. Every time he handled the ball he gave Notre Dame partisans, of whom there were many thousands, a bad case of jitters.

While Rote piled up more yardage than any other back, his average was exceeded by Notre Dame's Emil Sitko, who covered 6 yards per try in 14 carries, and by Billy Barrett, with a 5-yard average, and Larry Coutre with 4.5.

Bob Williams, the 19-year-old Irish quarterback, excelled as a passer, completing 11 of his 18 pitches for 165 yards, including two that went for touchdowns.

Frank Leahy shut the door of the Notre Dame dressing room for five minutes after the game, barring visitors while he paid tribute to his all-victorious squad. This is what he told them:

"You are the greatest football team I ever coached. My thanks for your cooperation in every way through the season. As soon as we are dressed, all of us are going to get into a bus and visit the cathedral to offer up a prayer of thanksgiving for the success we have enjoyed. Before you do any celebrating send a telegram to your father and mother thanking them for the privilege of letting you play for Notre Dame."

The first outsiders to get into the dressing room were S.M.U. head coach Matty Bell and Doak Walker, who was kept out of his final game as a collegian because of an injury suffered last week.

Both Bell and Walker praised the Irish for their terrific will to win. Walker said that while he regretted his inability to play, he got satisfaction enough just watching Notre Dame operate. The whole

Irish squad gave both Bell and Walker a rousing cheer they long will remember.

The dressing room hospitality was in sharp contrast to the fury of one of the greatest ball games in which either team had ever engaged.

This was the third meeting of Notre Dame and Southern Methodist and the third time they played thrilling ball. The Irish won, 20-14, in 1930 and 20-19 in 1939.

The Mustangs gave evidence of the character the contest would take immediately after they received the opening kickoff, which Raleigh Blakely returned 10 yards to his 24.

Rote fired a pass to Zohn Milam for a first down on his 35. He then tossed to Dick McKissack for five yards and to Rusty Russell, the son of S.M.U.'s backfield coach, for a first down at midfield. Rote's fourth-straight pass, this one also to Russell, was knocked down and S.M.U. was penalized 15 yards for holding.

Fred Benners, who completed six of his 10 passes, threw his first toss into the arms of Notre Dame's Groom, who always seemed to be in the right place when the Irish were in trouble. Groom returned the interception to the Mustangs' 31.

Frank Spaniel whirled around his right end for 7, but a 15-yard penalty for clipping braked down Notre Dame's first drive. Coutre was held to 2 yards at right guard and Williams' pass to Spaniel went astray. Williams was trapped for a 4-yard loss before he could pass, and on fourth down he punted over the S.M.U. goal.

Rote, faking a pass from the Mustang 20, swept around left end to his 38 before Gay brought him down. Rote then passed to Milam which earned a first down on the Irish 47. Here Notre Dame braced and Rote punted out of bounds on the the Irish 16.

It looked as if Leahy's squad were in difficulty when Williams' pass sailed out of bounds on the Irish 32. But Petitbon saved the day by intercepting Benners' pass, intended for Milam, and returning 10 yards to the Irish 27.

Notre Dame now went to work and looked like the team that has leveled nine opponents in a row. Williams passed to Spaniel for 9 yards and Coutre broke through center for a first down on the Irish 42. Spaniel then bolted over right tackle for 5 yards and Hart, on an end around, powered his way to the S.M.U. 45.

Coutre, who was running like he did in early season, dashed off right tackle for 10 yards and Sitko added 3 inside the same spot. Coutre was trapped for a 10-yard loss on a wide pitchout from Wiliams. There was an obvious sigh of relief from the S.M.U. stands as the Texas fans thought the Irish finally were stopped, but they soon learned that Notre Dame is most dangerous when opponents seem to have its offense checked.

Williams, a study on poise and precision, faded back while Bill Wightkin sped downfield. Wightkin got behind Rote, the defending back, to catch Williams' long pass on a dead run. He gathered in the ball on the S.M.U. 12-yard line and there was nobody between him and the goal. Steve Oracko's extra point put the Irish ahead, 7-0.

Southern Methodist came within a foot of scoring the tying touchdown early in the second quarter. It got the ball on its 16-yard line where Notre Dame's Williams has punted out of bounds.

Rote, taking the ball on a direct pass from center, handed off to John Champion, who whipped a forward pass to Milam, who was standing all alone on the Irish 40. It was the first pass Champion had thrown this season and the maneuver caught Notre Dame flat-footed. Milam set out for the goal, but was overtaken by Petitbon and forced out of bounds on the 6-yard line.

Here it was that Notre Dame proved its defensive might. Rote battered at center, where he was held to 2 yards by Groom. The S.M.U. ace then picked up 3 yards at left tackle before he was dumped by Petitbon. It was third down and only a yard to a touchdown. Rote again hit center, but Groom was there and when the pile was unscrambled Rote had made only 2 feet. It was fourth down now and pay dirt was only 12 inches away. Rote again piled into the middle of the Irish line and the ball wound up exactly where the effort had started. Climbing up from the bottom of the scramble was Mike Swistowicz, whose number was blotted out by the mud on his shirt. Notre Dame had held and took possession of the ball.

Most quarterbacks would have punted out of that gloomy area at once, but not Williams. He tried to sneak behind center but got nowhere. He then tried a pass from behind his goal, but it was knocked down. Sitko then banged over left guard for 7 yards, and Williams then got away a beautiful kick that rolled dead on the Mustang 35.

Jim Martin hurled Champion for a 5-yard loss, but that was only a minor disaster for the the Mustangs. On the next play, Gay intercepted a pass from Rote and raced back 18 yards to the Mustang 34. Barrett went inside his right tackle for 2 yards and Sitko ran to the 20. Williams' pass to Wightkin was good for 10 yards, but the play was called back and Notre Dame penalized 15 yards for holding. Williams then hurled a long pass to Ernie Zalejski, who caught the ball in the end zone where he had to outmaneuver three defending backs. Oracko missed the extra point kick and the score was 13-0.

An offside penalty nullified another Notre Dame touchdown shortly before the end of the half. Williams then passed to Hart, who crossed the Mustangs' goal line standing up, but the play was called back and the Irish were set back 5 yards. Time ran out a moment later.

The Irish were on their way to another score in the third period when it lost the ball on the Mustang 13, where Zalejski's fumble was recovered by Jack Halliday of S.M.U.

Notre Dame got back to the Mustang 38 a few minutes later, where again Zalejski fumbled and Bill Richards recovered for the Methodists. That break inspired the Mustangs and they scored soon afterwards.

Rote scooted around his right end to Notre Dame's 44, where Petitbon caught him. One play later, Rote faked a pass and went around his right end to the 21. On a handoff from Rote, Champion legged it to the 3-yard line, where Petitbon cut across field to stop him. On the next play, Rote rammed over right tackle for the score. Bill Sullivan's kick made the score, 13-7.

Notre Dame's third touchdown was set up when Mutscheller intercepted a pass from Rote on the Mustang 22. Williams passed to Hart, who lateraled to Spaniel for a first down on the 12. Barrett, Landry and Hart, the latter operating from fullback, moved to the 3-yard line in three carries. Barrett then went over right tackle for a touchdown. Oracko's kick increased Notre Dame's lead to 20-7.

Notre Dame's third touchdown instead of discouraging S.M.U. served only to put more fire into the Mustang's attack. Blakely was downed in his tracks on the Mustang 28 after taking Oracko's ensuing kickoff, but then Champion showed why he bears the name. He caught a pass from Rote on his 45, cut back toward center and ran to the Irish 1, where Notre Dame's Lally crowded him out of bounds. Rote hit behind right guard for the score. Sullivan added the extra point and the score was 20-14.

A 15-yard penalty after the next kickoff set back the Irish to their 1-yard line. Williams later punted to Richards, who sped back 25 yards to the Irish 14. Rote then got around his left end to the 3. Groom held his next charge to a yard, but on third down Rote crashed over left tackle for the tying touchdown. Sullivan came off the bench to try for the point that would put S.M.U. ahead, a feat no other team has accomplished against Notre Dame this season. Again it was Groom who arose to the occasion for the Irish by breaking through the S.M.U. line and blocking the kick. The score then stood, 20-20, with nearly 10 minutes left on the clock.

Notre Dame then proved why it is rated the No. 1 team of 1949. Spaniel returned the kickoff from the Irish 10 to their 43. Sitko, running with terrific drive, moved to the Mustang 20 before he was forced out of bounds. A disheartening penalty canceled the gain and moved back the ball to the Mustang 49-yard line.

Barrett dashed around left end for 8 yards and Sitko went inside left tackle for a first down on the 35. Spaniel, Sitko and Hart collaborated in moving the ball to the 20. Gay drove inside his right tackle for 8 yards and Barrett moved to the 6-yard line, where Richards nailed him. Barrett, on the next play, sneaked around left end for a touchdown. Oracko's extra point kick was good and Notre Dame again was ahead, 27-20, never to relinquish the lead.

It took another desperate goal line stand to hold off the stubborn Mustangs, however. Fancy stepping by Rote gave S.M.U. a first down on the Irish 28 and Benners' pass to Russell was completed on the 5.

Hart knocked down a pass from Benners, and Mutscheller held Rote to a 2-yard gain. Groom and Lally each had a hold on the ball when they intercepted a pass from Rote on the 2.

Barrett, Sitko and Hart alternated in rushing the ball out of the danger zone and there was no serious scoring threat by either team the rest of the way.

27

Notre Dame vs. Purdue

OCTOBER 7, 1950

NOTRE DAME, Ind. — The Fighting Irish of Notre Dame, unbeaten in 38 gridiron struggles, two of which were ties, came to the inevitable end of their successive victory trail today on their own field before 56,746 spectators.

The Irish, so thoroughly outclassed that their hope only was a forlorn one by the time the battle had reached the halfway mark, fell before an elusive, tireless, skilled Purdue Boilermaker team by a resounding 28-14.

And the Irish, unwilling to give up in the face of almost hopeless odds, avoided an utter rout only by storming their way to touchdowns in the third and fourth quarters.

The Boilermakers, a pack of condensed football fury from the very outset, stunned everybody, except their own rooters, by shoving the Irish around relentlessly throughout the first quarter, although not scoring until the last couple of minutes. Their fury mounted in the second quarter when they drove about the soggy premises for two more touchdowns, going into the halftime recess with a 21-0 bulge, which was enough to indicate that the victory string was about to snap for sure.

Shoved around as they had been, the Irish bounced up menacingly in the third period to slightly change the outlook. They eventually scored again following a Purdue fumble. They still were marching when the period ended, and on the first play of the final quarter they were back within reach of a foe that could run, pass and smash. They then were only seven points from a tie. But the Boilermakers took care of that a few minutes later, scoring their final touchdown on a pass pitched by the spectacular Dale Samuels, who is Chicago Lindblum High School's contribution to Purdue.

The team statistics tell the story of how the Irish were cut up. The vanquished did pile up a margin of their own in rushing, but most of this yardage was reeled off in struggling to get out of their own territory. And they didn't accomplish that until late in the second period when they reached the Boilermaker 47 with the help of a 15-yard penalty. But what the Irish did on the ground was taken back in the air with a total of 158 yards, all but seven of this total being piled up by Samuels' amazing pitching.

Samuels was the spectacular boy in his passing duel with Notre Dame's Bob Williams who was pretty slick on his own account, but there was other busy lads in the Purdue backfield. The Irish couldn't figure out one Neil Schmidt. His No. 40 was here, there and everywhere. In 14 carrying jobs he shaved 80 yards from the Notre Dame defense and also snared three passes for 71 yards. And there was more trouble originating in the shoes of John Keretes. He ripped and ran for 81 yards in 23 assaults and scored two touchdowns.

When the clock on the wall ticked off the final second in a drizzly, darkening atmosphere, the Irish had to go way back to Dec. 1, 1945 to recall their last defeat. The Great Lakes Navy team did it that day, 39-7, at Great Lakes in the final game of the season. The two ties encountered by the Irish since then were 0-0 with Army in 1946 and 14-14 with Southern California in 1948.

The Boilermakers also forced another Notre Dame record into the discard. The Irish had won 28 in a row on their home gridiron. Their last previous setback at Notre Dame was with the compliments of Michigan, 32-20, in the eighth game of the 1942 season. And the Irish hadn't lost to Purdue since 1933 in a series that now stands at 14 Notre Dame victories, five for Purdue and two ties.

The Boilermakers' fury burst with the inital kickoff which Mike Maccioli received on his 10-yard line, where he stumbled. On the first play, Samuels sailed one of his long passes, but Maccioli missed it by a hair's breadth. Maccioli then ran for four yards and, on the next play, Schmidt went tearing down the field on an 86-yard jaunt to cross the Irish goal line. The scoring venture was called off because Schmidt had stepped out of bounds on his own 24.

The break didn't phase the Boilermakers in the least. They bounced back with Samuels' pass to Maccioli for 18 yards and Notre Dame then drew a 15-yard assessment for holding. Kerestes shot through for a first down on the Irish 22. The Boilermakers tore on until they reached the five-yard line. Two plays later, Kerestes was tackled on the Irish 1. Here Notre Dame went on the offensive for the first time.

The Irish moved out toward midfield, but soon had to punt and the ball rolled dead on the Boilermaker 26. In two smashes, Kerestes made it a first down. Samuels then pitched twice to move the Boilermakers to their 49. Schmidt ripped through center to the 32. After Maccioli had gained a yard, Samuels threw to Schmidt and the pass was allowed because of interference by Dave Flood on the one-yard mark. On the next play, Kerestes smashed through the left side of the Notre Dame wall for the first touchdown and the versatile Samuels kicked the extra point.

The Boilermakers opened the second period with a pass interception by Dick Schnaible who scooted away for 45 yards to the Irish 15. The Boilermakers drove to the 4 for a first down, but this advance bogged down when Schmidt momentarily fumbled a lateral from Samuels for an 8-yard loss. Maccioli, on a reverse, stepped out of bounds on the 7 and Notre Dame took the ball when a pass was knocked down by linebacker Jerry Groom in the end zone.

The Irish, even with Williams trying two passes, couldn't advance. They punted and the ball rolled out on their 41. Samuels promptly let fly with a long heave into the arms of Schmidt, who was only 6 yards from the goal line when he brought it down. Kerestes smashed through for 2 yards and went through again, this time to score. Samuels' kick made it 14-0.

The Boilermakers didn't waste much time assembling their third touchdown, which came late in the second period. They had gone into Purdue territory and a fourth-down pass by Williams was grabbed by an ineligible receiver. The Boilermakers then took possession of the ball on their 44. Kerestes advanced 7 yards and, after a pass had failed, Schmidt reeled off 10 yards. After a five-yard penalty against Purdue, Schmidt lugged the ball up to the Irish 30. Samuels missed on a pass to Maccioli, but followed with one to Schmidt in the end zone for the score. Samuels kicked the extra point and it was 21-0.

Notre Dame kicked off to open the third quarter and between a Purdue offside penalty and a fumble by Phil Kiezek, the Irish found themselves on offense with the enemy goal only 10 yards away. The loose ball was captured by Dick Cotter. Bill Gay sauntered around right end for 7 and, after John Landry had failed to gain, Williams shot a pass to Jim Mutscheller for the touchdown. Joe Caprara added the extra point kick.

By the time the third period closed the Irish were in a choice spot, 21-7, although not many minutes earlier they were on their one-foot line where Samuels was stopped in attempting a quarterback sneak from one-yard out. After an exchange of punts the Irish were on their own 43. Billy Barrett sprinted around right end for 30 yards. Smacks by John Petitbon, Landry and Barrett sent the Boilermakers back to their 10-yard line as the period ended.

On the first play of the last quarter, Petitbon weaved through to the right side of the line for the touchdown and Caprara kicked what proved Notre Dame's final point. The Boilermakers now led, 21-14.

In the wake of its last touchdown, Notre Dame quickly ran into its final batch of grief. The Boilermakers took the kickoff on their 41. Kerestes picked up 4 yards and Maccioli toured over right end to the Irish 43. Samuels then threw to Maccioli, who dropped the ball. The same play was tried again with similar results. Determined to make it click, Samuels threw another to Maccioli and this time the latter went over the goal line with the ball tucked safely in his arms. Samuels completed the day's scoring with his fourth point-after-touchdown.

28

Notre Dame vs. Michigan State

NOVEMBER 10, 1951

EAST LANSING, Mich. — Before it happened, football fans throughout the world said the meeting here today between Michigan State's undefeated Spartans and Notre Dame's hopeful Irish was to be the game of the year.

Spartan partisans in the overflow crowd of 51,296, who saw their speedy, powerful and resourceful heroes score in every quarter in a 35-0 conquest, were ready to vote it the game of the century.

Startled Notre Dame enthusiasts, who were off to a bad day when Dick Panin, the Spartan junior halfback, ran 88 yards to the winning touchdown in the Spartans' first play from scrimmage, were wondering what manner of catastrophe had befallen their heroes.

The score was shocking enough. The realization that the Notre Dame offense did not penetrate Spartan soil until the second play of the final period was unbelievable to those who, through the years, so rarely have seen the Irish thwarted at every turn.

On that second play in the fourth quarter, Ralph Guglielmi's pass to John Lattner carried to the Spartan 36, which was Notre Dame's closest threat of the amazing afternoon.

A few seconds after the big "invasion," Notre Dame was forced to kick and, with five minutes to go in that final period, the Irish hope of averting their first shutout since the Army 0-0 game in 1946 vanished and faded into the Spartans' fifth touchdown.

The final touchdown grew from Johnny Wilson's interception of a forward pass and return to the Irish 32. The rest of this crowning touchdown effort included two passes by Al Dorow. The first went to Capt. Bob Carey which carried to the 12. Ellis Duckett then took a pass from Dorow in the end zone to wind up the Spartan touchdown spree, after which Carey booted his fifth extra point kick for the final score.

The total brought out two historical notes. It was the biggest defeat ever suffered by a Notre Dame team coached by Frank Leahy, and the worst defeat suffered by the Irish since the 48-0 wartime setback at the hands of the Army in 1945.

The only points the Spartans needed for victory, that touchdown of Panin's on an 88-yard run when the game was only two and a half minutes old, of course, was the big thrill play of the day. Panin suffered a broken nose and a possible broken rib during the game, but kept on playing.

Notre Dame had received the opening kickoff and had come back for its farthest advance in the first three quarters, to the Irish 41. Then Billy Barrett punted to the Spartan 12.

On the first Michigan State play from scrimmage, Panin broke through right guard and set sail from his own goal line in a fast-pumping gallop. He soon ran away from all pursuers except the rapid John Petitbon who got near enough to nip one of Panin's heels as he sped over the goal line with the payoff touchdown.

The Spartans scored again in the first period. This one, like the first, began to grow after a punt. Factors in this production were Don McAuliffe, the passing combo of Dorow and Paul Dekker, Panin who went to the 1-yard line, and Vince Pisano who went over for the touchdown from there. In this gang-up, the Spartans went 68 yards in six plays.

The second period began with the Spartans on the Notre Dame 43. Panin ran to the Notre Dame 30 then fumbled, but Carey recovered for a first down at that point. On the next play, Carey made a diving catch of a Dorow pass on the 5. An offside penalty put the ball on the Irish 1. McAuliffe went over for the score on the next play.

The first half statistics did not relieve the shock which Notre Dame partisans derived from the halftime score of 21-0. In the first half, the Spartans made 14 first downs to 4 for the Irish. Michigan State gained 317 net yards in the first half to Notre Dame's 80. The victors' total included 254 yards from rushing to 61 for the Irish.

The Spartans' fourth touchdown was made in 6:23 of the third period and came about when Carey leaped high to spear a fourth-down Dorow pass in the end zone. This was the climax of a 74-yard advance.

The victory was the 13th straight for Michigan State since it was upset by Maryland for the only setback in nine games last year. The present string includes last year's conquest of Notre Dame by a 36-33 score.

This year, the Spartans have shut out Notre Dame, Oregon State, 6-0; and Michigan, 25-0. They also have beaten Ohio State, 24-20; Marquette, 20-14; Penn State, 32-20, and Pitt, 53-26.

They have Indiana and Colorado coming up, yet while they are undefeated and have been rated all season among the nation's top five, they will have no bowl to play in, come New Year's Day because of their embryonic Big Ten Conference tieup.

But bowl or no, Coach Biggie Munn of the Spartans was a proud and happy man after the game. "Our team was just real ready," he said. "When your players go right, they just go right. We went right today."

Commenting on Panin's big run, Munn said, "We had three opening plays lined up. We didn't need the other two."

Leahy, who suffered through the worst defeat of his Notre Dame coaching career, said, "Now I know how some of those other coaches felt." Leahy felt very blue. But he had a bright word for the Spartans.

"They were a really great ball team. They were ready, and they were the best team we've played this season. We were never in the ball game. I'm sorry we didn't do better," he apologized.

For more than a week weather has been more of a cause for alarm than any of the player personnel phases. Last Tuesday, this capital city in the heart of Michigan snow belt, literally was buried in that white stuff which poets call beautiful. Since the storm abated late Wednesday, the area has been dedicated to digging out, with special emphasis on Macklin Field.

When they arrived inside the stadium, the spectators found the only snowless area in the countryside. But it took a lot of slushy doing to arrive at the scene of action. Inside the stadium, not a flake of snow, slick of ice or puddle was to be seen, either on the field or in the stands, thanks to husky bulldozer operations, manned by experts with an inspired mission.

29

Notre Dame vs. North Carolina

NOVEMBER 17, 1951

CHAPEL HILL, N.C. — Notre Dame's football team, knocked down for a count of nine by Michigan State week ago, today climbed to its feet and defeated North Carolina, 12-7, for its third-straight victory over the Tar Heels.

The starting backfield for the Fighting Irish was made up of kids in their baptismal year of varsity competition. Two of them, Tom Carey of Chicago and Ralph Guglielmi of Columbus, Ohio, engineered the payoff drives. Carey a year ago was leading Mount Carmel to the high school championship of Chicago.

North Carolina, which is experiencing the most dismal season in several years, brought a flaming spirit into today's fray that thrilled the capacity crowd of 44,500.

The Tar Heels had trouble getting off the defensive until late in the third quarter, but once they got into attacking position they sent shivers up and down the spine of the Notre Dame coaching bench. They had a dangerous passer in Connie Gravitte, a fine runner in Jack Cooke and a power-driver named Allen Mueller, who suited up today for the first time this season.

Notre Dame's alertness against Gravitte's passes, more than any other factor, staved off North Carolina's victory bid in the closing moment. The decisive play of the dramatic fourth quarter was John Lattner's interception of Gravitte's pitch from the Irish 29, with less than two minutes to play.

A few minutes earlier, it was Gene Carrabine, another yearling, who knocked down a pass from Gravitte which was intended for Cooke at the goal line. If Carrabine had failed, North Carolina would have had a touchdown and a 13-12 lead. Those were situations that featured this hard, cleanly played and fast moving game.

Notre Dame threw a more varied offense against the Tar Heels than it had employed in any previous contest. It ran more plays from the I-formation, but instead of shifting into the T, the Irish frequently came out of the tandem lineup into the old Notre Dame box. They further confused the North Carolina defense by getting off plays with no shift at all.

Coach Frank Leahy said after the game North Carolina compared favorably with any other foe Notre Dame has encountered except Michigan State.

Statistically the contest was highlighted by Capt. Jim Mutscheller's 54th forward pass reception, an all-time record for a Notre Dame player. He broke Leon Hart's old mark of 49 last week against Michigan State. His four catches today accounted for 60 yards. Guglielmi completed six of his 11 passes for 74 yards and Carey clicked with three of 5 for 33. John Mazur hit his target only once in six attempts and had a pass intercepted.

Notre Dame never would have whipped North Carolina today without those rugged linebackers, Dick Szymanski, Dan Shannon and Jack Alessandrini. A salute also to defensive line tackle Sam Palumbo who gave the Tar Heels' running game more trouble than any other player on the Irish side of the line.

It was apparent both teams were a trifle jittery in the first period. There was loose ball-handling by both sides, but the breaks were about even. The Irish lost the ball three times on fumbles and the Tar Heels twice.

The first bobble that could have been important was committed by Lattner. It was recovered by North Carolina's Dick Lackey on the Irish 35. Bill Gaudreau pulled the boys from the north out of this jam by intercepting a pass from Frank Wissman on the Irish 9.

Notre Dame applied heavy pressure against the Tar Heel line, but it wasn't until the second quarter that it got its offense clicking. The Irish took the ball on their 45 where Bud Wallace had punted out of bounds. They soon hit high gear.

Carey flipped a pass to Mutscheller for a first down on the Tar Heels 39. Paul Reynolds, who was Notre Dame's leading ground gainer with 80 yards in 22 carriers, was trapped for a loss of six yards by North Carolina's Joe Dudeck, one of the strongest defensive players of the game. On the next play, Carey handed off to Lattner, who sped to the 4, but the play was nullified by a 15-yard holding penalty.

Lattner, who was Notre Dame's punter in the absence of injured Billy Barrett, kicked to the Tar Heel 11 where the receiver, Bud Carson, was dropped in his tracks by Tom Seaman. The Tar Heel offense was stopped dead by the Notre Dame line and Wallace again punted out on the Irish 45.

This time Notre Dame went the distance in a parade skillfully directed by Carey. Reynolds bolted over right guard for 12. Francis Paterra, who got his first real shot at varsity football today, nibbled at center for two yards. Carey's pass to Reynolds moved Notre Dame to the Tar Heel 33.

Reynolds powered his way for eight yards in two carries and Paterra broke through the Tar Heels' right guard for a first down on the 12. Worden banged inside his left tackle for 3 yards and added six at center. Reynolds gained a first down on the Tar Heel 1. Then he leaped over a pile-up at left guard for the touchdown.

The Irish had another scoring opportunity later in the second quarter after Reynolds had caught a pass from Carey on the Tar Heel 15. Mazur then relieved Carey at quarterback and tossed a long pass which Mutscheller caught, but the head linesman ruled he had stepped out of the end zone. Two more Mazur passes faltered, and on fourth down Menil Mavraides attempted a field goal from his 22. But, like his first extra point try, it went to the left of the uprights.

Notre Dame traveled 74 yards in an unbroken march for its third-quarter touchdown. It opened on the 16 where Lattner was downed after taking Wallace's punt. It was engineered by Guglielmi with the same fine assortment of plays that marked Carey's earlier drive.

Worden darted through the left side of the Tar Heel line for 12 yards. Lattner got through his left guard for a first down on the Irish 40. Reynolds hit the other side for a first down on the Tar Heel 45. This looked like the Notre Dame of old.

Worden powered through the middle for four yards and Guglielmi passed to him for a first down on the Tar Heel 28. Lattner's 5-yard gain was offset by a 5-yard penalty, but Guglielmi fired a pass that Worden caught on the 18. Worden banged through the sagging Tar Heel line for another first down on the 6.

The Irish were penalized five yards for taking too much time on the next play, but Lattner got it back through his left guard. Worden, grand marshal of the big parade, whirled around right end for the touchdown. Mavraides again missed the extra point attempt.

It took that second Notre Dame touchdown to rouse the Tar Heels. They soon got the ball on the Irish 37 where Lackey signaled for a fair catch on Lattner's punt. On the next play, Gravitte hurled a long high pass to the right that Cooke caught over the head of Notre Dame's Carrabine. He went the rest of the way unmolested. Abie Williams kicked the extra point and North Carolina was back in the ball game.

Notre Dame reached the Southerners' 18 a few minutes later. Mazur then came in to replace Guglielmi and his first play was a forward pass tl at North Carolina's Bill Kirkman intercepted on the 20. He lateraled to Carson, who raced to the Irish 46. A 15-yard penalty momentarily slowed the Tar Heels, but Mueller ran over Notre Dame tacklers for a 24-yard advance.

Gravitte's pass to Adler was completed on the Irish 33. Mueller found a hole at his left tackle and ran to the Irish 20. Plunges by Cooke and Gaylord, coupled with an offside penalty against the Irish, moved the ball to the 7.

Here Notre Dame braced for the magnificent stand that broke the heart of Carolina. On fourth down, Carrabine knocked down Gravitte's pass.

The Tar Heels never quit trying. They soon were back on the Irish 29 for a first down. But Notre Dame invariably had an operative in the right place at the right time. Lattner intercepted Gravitte's pass and sped back 18 yards to his 33. That, in effect, was the ball game. Notre Dame advanced to the Tar Heels' 22 just before the gun, but a 15-yard penalty put an end to the scoring threat.

30

Notre Dame vs. U.S.C.

DECEMBER 1, 1951

LOS ANGELES — An unfigurable, but flaming individualist named Ralph Guglielmi today led Notre Dame to victory over Southern California in the 23d game of a series that began in 1926, before any of today's contestants were born.

The score was 19-12 and marked Notre Dame's 14th triumph against seven defeats and two ties in football's oldest continuous intersectional competition.

Guglielmi, the 18-year-old freshman, who a year ago was leading the Grand View High School team of Columbus, Ohio, was the big man of this furiously contested game. He completed eight of 13 passes for 161 yards. He carried the ball when a yard was necessary for a first down. His choice of plays belied his inexperience in college ball.

Guglielmi proved today he is the leader Notre Dame has needed all season. Coach Frank Leahy used senior quarterback John Mazur for the scoreless first period, but switched to his No. 2 field general at the start of the second quarter and he stuck it out to the finish.

The young man from Columbus was a study in poise. Time after time he darted and procrastinated while the play developed, literally playing tag with foes who tried to rush him. He sometimes hesitates a split second too long before firing the ball, but he'll get back lost yardage on his next pitch. He's that kind of player. Kinda like a

Mississippi riverboat gambler, it's all or nothing with him.

The game was played before 55,783 spectators who sat through smog and mist to the finish. Lights were turned on at halftime, but players barely could be identified from the Alpine heights of the Coliseum press box.

This wasn't the case of a weak team looking good and a good team looking weak. Southern California, which closed out its season with a record of six victories and 3 defeats, didn't look bad. Until Guglielmi engineered Notre Dame's third touchdown drive, the Trojans were in the game every minute.

The final Irish score, however, took the heart out of the U.S.C. team. The players were battered, dispirited and done at the end. There was no mistake about what had happened to them.

Today's triumph was Notre Dame's seventh of the season against two defeats and a tie. Considering that its traveling squad of 40 players averaged only 19½ years in age, Notre Dame followers can look to 1952 through rose-colored glasses.

Lest anyone think today's victory was a one man attainment, we hasten to add that Guglielmi was supported by a backfield that gives promise of developing into one of Notre Dame's greatest offensive units.

John Lattner gave a brilliant, all-around performance. He played both ways, on offense and defense, and was superb in his twin duties. Neil Worden had his best day as a Fighting Irishman. He carried 22 times for 91 yards, including a touchdown sprint of 39 yards — a play cleverly conceived and brilliantly executed. John Petitbon ended his career in a blaze of glory.

There are young backs coming along like Paul Reynolds and Joe Heap who will be somewhere near Petitbon's caliber in another year.

Bob Toneff, the 230-pound left tackle, and Capt. Jim Mutscheller made their last game for Notre Dame one they will long remember. Toneff made more tackles and showed more aggressiveness than in any other game this fall.

Southern California's Frank Gifford was a Trojan star that remained undimmed in the gloomy afternoon. He ran 17 times for 67 yards and connected with five of his 8 passes. It usually took two Notre Dame tacklers to bring him down.

The Trojans used the single-wing offense almost exclusively, but they once caught the Irish defense flat-footed on a T play that sprang Jim Sears for 25 yards and a first down on the Irish 5 just before U.S.C.'s second touchdown.

Notre Dame employed the T with variations that included single- and double-wing maneuvers. It switched its forward pass defense from the zone to man-to-man without appreciable results. The Trojan pitchers, Dean Schneider, Gifford and Sears, completed 10 of their 21 passes.

Notre Dame was in trouble early in the first quarter when Lattner fumbled on his 25 and George Bozanic recovered for the Trojans on the Irish 27. Gifford's pass to Al Carmichael was knocked down and Gifford was held to 3 yards at center. Dan Shannon, who was carried off the field late in the contest after a lip injury, hurled Gifford for a yard loss. On the next play, Gifford's pass to Charles Greenwood was broken up and Notre Dame took over on its 25.

Worden sped to his 38 on a trap play through center, but the offense bogged down and Lattner punted to the Trojan 32.

Southern California began to move effectively about two minutes before the end of the first quarter after getting the ball on its 35. Gifford shot a pass to Schneider for a first down on Notre Dame's 43. Harold Han then broke through the middle to the 27. Gifford added 4 yards as the period was concluded. Han stepped through over right guard for 4 and Gifford powered his way to the Irish 14. Han darted behind center for 6 yards, then Gifford swung wide to his left, evaded Notre Dame's Bill Gaudreau and scored at the extreme corner of the field. Gifford missed the extra point attempt.

If U.S.C. fans thought that score would break the spirit of the Notre Dame kids, they learned their mistake almost immediately. The Irish took the ensuing kickoff on their 23 and they didn't yield possession of the ball until it was planted behind the Trojan goal line on the 13th play.

This was Guglielmi's opportunity to demonstrate his leadership and he knew what to do when the big chance came. His jump pass to Chet Ostrowski was good for 16 yards after Lattner had been stopped without gain. A 15-yard penalty was assessed against the Irish, but no minor setbacks could stop this gang.

Worden plunged over center for 2 yards and a 5-yard penalty was accessed against U.S.C. Guglielmi then passed to Reynolds on the

Irish 35. The Columbus sharpshooter next hurled to Petitbon who carried to the Irish 48. Petitbon's jab at center netted only a yard and a Guglielmi-to-Petitbon pass was knocked down. With all the poise of a Johnny Lujack or Otto Graham, Guglielmi whipped a pass to Ostrowski that advanced the ball to the Trojan 16.

The confused Trojan defense had trouble flagging down Lattner on the 3. Worden banged at center for a yard. Lattner then nibbled at right guard for another yard. On third down, he went through the same spot with yards to spare for the touchdown that evened the count. Bob Joseph's extra point kick was blocked by Dan Zimmerman.

The Los Angeles unit, due mainly to Gifford's running and passing, soon had a first down on the Irish 23. Gifford moved to the 15 before Dave Flood, who played a strong defensive game, brought him down. Gifford tried to get through the right side of the Notre Dame line but he was hit so hard by Shannon that he dropped the ball. Lattner recovered for the Irish on their 14.

Heap's running and Guglielmi's passing soon put Notre Dame on the Trojan 46. The attack sagged when Guglielmi was trapped for a big loss and Lattner punted to Sears who was dropped in his tracks by the Notre Dame ends. Sears fumbled as he went down and it appeared from the stands that a green-shirted Irishman had fallen on the ball, but in the pileup a Trojan apparently gathered it into his arms. At any rate, the referee ruled it was the Trojans' ball. The half ended a few plays later with the score tied, 6-6.

Southern California capitalized on a break soon after play was resumed. Dick Nunis, the Trojan back, intercepted Guglielmi's pass intended for Ostrowski on the Irish 33. Toneff threw Carmichael for a 3-yard loss and Shannon broke up Schneider's pass to Carmichael. Schneider, who shifted the Trojan offense from single wing to the T, hit Sears for a first down on the 5. Sears then swept around his right end behind a wall of defenders for the touchdown. Gifford again missed the extra point attempt.

Gene Carrabine crushed Trojan hopes of a third touchdown by intercepting Sears' pass to Carmichael on the Irish 27. It took the Irish only eight plays to travel to the U.S.C. goal line.

Lattner, Heap and Worden alternated in making a first down on the 37. Worden made 9 in two plays and Lattner dashed to the Trojan 47. Lattner, whose ball-carrying average was 4.3 this afternoon, went over center for 8 yards. Guglielmi then moved two flankers to the right and sent Worden spinning to the left. U.S.C.'s secondary was pulled over to meet the threat supposedly directed to the right and Worden dashed across the goal without a Trojan hand touching him. Joseph missed the extra point try and the teams again were tied, 12-12.

The Trojans roared back before the third quarter ended and were hammering at the Irish goal with a first down on the 8-yard line. Notre Dame's Flood stopped Sears at center and Shannon saved the occasion for the Irish by intercepting Sears' pass in the end zone.

The decisive touchdown came in the final period after Notre Dame got the ball on its 39. It was Guglielmi's pass to Lattner that set up the score. Lattner did some fancy stepping after catching the ball and he was at the foe's 30 before the harassed Trojan secondary grounded him.

From that point the Irish ground out a touchdown the hard way. Lattner for 2 yards, Worden for 4, Worden for 2 and Petitbon for 2 earned a first down on the Trojan 20. Lattner cracked over right guard for 8 yards, Petitbon added a yard, and Lattner powered behind his left guard for a first down on the 7. The crumbling Trojan wall braced for another charge inside the tackles, but Guglielmi sent Petitbone wide around right end for the touchdown. Joseph's point-after kick ended the scoring.

The final score was Notre Dame 19, U.S.C. 12.

31

Notre Dame vs. Pennsylvania

SEPTEMBER 27, 1952

PHILADELPHIA — Pennsylvania and Notre Dame played to a 7-7 tie in Franklin Field today before 74,518 spectators who were convinced no other result would have been fair to either team. It was the largest crowd that ever had seen an opening game in the past.

A Pennsylvania punt that rolled dead on the 8-yard line slowed Notre Dame's opening attack, but for most of the 30 minutes in the first half the Fighting Irish were the superior team. The situation was reversed in the last two periods.

Notre Dame's offensive line, as observers predicted, was below usual caliber. It couldn't outcharge the Penn forwards with consistency and as a consequence the fast-stepping Irish backs were held in check time after time when a few yards would have meant control of the ball.

This was the first time Notre Dame had been tied in an opening game since Wisconsin emerged with a 7-7 score in 1942. It also was the first time Pennsylvania was able to match the Irish in touchdown production. The two previous games resulted in 60-20 and 49-0 Notre Dame victories.

Despite the low score, there were stars galore, but most of them were on defensive units. George Bosseler, Noel Schmidt and George Trautman, Penn's linebacking trio, seldom let a Notre Dame runner get away for more than a few yards. Capt. Bob Evans, the Quakers' brilliant, two-platoon operator, played his heart out until he was carried off the field in the late moments with a cramped leg.

Notre Dame's Jack Whelan roamed from side to side when his team was on defense, smacking down enemy ballcarriers with tremendous vigor and accuracy. Capt. Jack Alessandrini, Sam Palumbo, Gene Carrabine, Dave Flood, Jack Lee and two-way performer Johnny Lattner were largely responsible for their team's success in holding Penn to one touchdown.

Lattner was the biggest ground-gainer of the game. He carried 16 times for 87 yards. Penn's George Varaitis, the 215-pound, tall back who hits a line with the power of a Rocky Marciano, traveled 68 yards in 14 efforts.

Penn gained two first downs after taking Notre Dame's opening kickoff, but the Irish defense braced and forced Ed Binkoski to punt. The ball took a goalward bounce after landing on the Irish 15 and rolled to the one. Irish quarterback Tom Carey and Lattner each made two yards from scrimmage after which Lattner kicked from his end zone to his 45. Bosseler returned 10 yards.

Notre Dame's Whelan held Bill Deuber to four yards and on the following play Deuber fumbled. Fred Magialardi recovered for Notre Dame on his 36. Neil Worden exchanged the courtesy on the next play and Ed Surmaik fell on the ball on the Irish 36, exactly the spot from which the offense had begun. Penn's attack went nowhere, and on fourth down Binkoski punted out of bounds on the Irish 11.

It was at this juncture Notre Dame began to look like Notre Dame. It moved 89 yards in 15 plays for a touchdown. Heap and Worden collaborated for a first down on their 25. Lattner took Carey's pitchout to the Irish 47. Heap picked up 3 and Worden 5 inside the tackles, then Lattner broke away to Penn's 23, slipping away from three tacklers.

Carey, while running from a split-T formation, which Notre Dame employed most exclusively today, got through his right tackle for 5 yards. Worden added 2 and Heap 1. Lattner banged through center for 6 yards, but Notre Dame was penalized five yards for being offside.

Ralph Guglielmi relieved Carey at quarterback and pitched to Heap for a first down on Penn's 11. Guglielmi's next pass rolled off

Lattner's fingertips in the end zone. He then lateralled to Lattner, who was forced out of bounds on the three. Two thrusts at the middle put Lattner over the goal line. Menil Mavraides, with Carey holding, kicked the extra point.

A minute or two later in the first quarter, Flood recovered Don Zimmer's fumble on the Quaker 44. Guglielmi then arched a beautiful pass to Heap for a touchdown, but the play was nullified when Notre Dame was penalized for holding.

The Irish had another scoring opportunity when Flood and Al Kohanowich collaborated in recovering a fumble by Schmidt, Penn's safety man, who let the ball get away while trying to field Lattner's high punt. Heap and Guglielmi in two rushes moved the ball to the 8-yard line as the quarter ended.

Lattner bulled his way six yards, but the Irish were penalized five yards for backfield-in-motion. Worden made only a yard at center and Guglielmi's fourth-down pass was incomplete. Penn took over on its 13. Notre Dame never again got that close to the Quaker goal.

The Quakers' Walter Hynoski quick-kicked to Notre Dame's 46 and the Irish started another upfield parade that ended ingloriously when Charles Assif of Penn recovered Guglielmi's pitchout to Heap on the Easterners' 35. Penn tried valiantly to capitalize on this break, but the Irish defense held firm on the eight. Adams passed to Deuber for a first down on the South Benders' 28 where Whelan grounded the receiver. Adams, faking a handoff, ran seven yards to the right side of the line before Palumbo dumped him. Zimmer then earned a first down on the 17.

Here Notre Dame put up its do-or-die stand. Magialardi held Deuber to two yards. Adams' pass to Ed Bell, one of Penn's offensive standouts, was incomplete. Binkoski then powered over right guard for seven before Alessandrini stopped him. Adams' fourth down pass to Deuber fell harmlessly and the Irish took over on their eight. They gained a first down in three rushes just before the half, which ended with a 7-0 count.

Penn's touchdown came with startling speed in the third quarter. Lattner had punted to the Quakers' Bosseler, who signaled a fair catch on his 35. On the next play, Adams threw a long pass over the head of Notre Dame's Dan Shannon and into the arms of Bell, who raced the remaining 26 yards to the goal line without an Irish hand touching him. Carl Sempier's extra point kick split the uprights and the score was tied, 7-7.

Notre Dame couldn't get its offense clicking again until the fading moments of the game. Binkoski's punt that soared out of bounds on the 5 kept the Irish in check for the next few minutes and Penn kept on the pressure when Schmidt intercepted a pass by Heap and returned five yards to the Irish 28. The Notre Dame defensive team again made good in a tough spot and held on the 20.

Penn then intercepted another Notre Dame pass, this one from Guglielmi at the start of the fourth period. Bosseler was the villain or hero, depending on which side of the stadium you were sitting, and he ran back eight yards to the Irish 45. Penn's next pass, which went from pole to pole, probably the longest in history, was thrown by Binkoski and caught by Hynoski on the 30. Bosseler bowled down the middle on the next play to the 15, where Whelan downed him. Notre Dame's Kohanovich pulled his teammates out of this embarrassment by recovering Zimmer's fumble on the the Irish 13.

Notre Dame made a first down by rushing and Carey completed a screen pass to Don Penza for 14 yards, but a 15-yard penalty nullified the gain and Lattner punted to Bosseler, who made a fair catch on Penn's 35. On the first play of the drive, Binkoski's long pass was intercepted by Whelan, who legged it back 13 yards to the Quakers' 45. The Irish were set back 15 yards for clipping on the runback.

Penn's substitute tailback, George Varaitis, shattered the Irish line for three first downs, but then Notre Dame, as usual, held in the pinch, and after an exchange of punts the South Bend unit got the ball on its 19 with less than two minutes to play.

Guglielmi passed to Lattner, who was knocked out of bounds on his 41. His next heave to Heap was good for 7 yards and he then hit O'Neil for a first down on Penn's 37. Next he clicked to Lattner on the 26, but Bell of the Quakers knocked the ball out of his arms and his teammate, Schmidt, recovered it in the air. The Quakers then proceeded to churn it out by running it up the middle of the Irish line to consume the remaining seconds.

Guglielmi completed eight of his 16 passes for 80 yards. He had one interception. Carey connected on two out of four for 17. Penn's Adams made good on seven out of 17 yards for 171 yards.

32

Notre Dame vs. Texas

OCTOBER 4, 1952

AUSTIN, Tex. — Notre Dame today spotted the University of Texas, the nation's fifth-ranking football team, a field goal in the first half and then came back with an offensive punch that earned a 14-3 victory in one of the early season's major upsets.

The crowd of 67,660, largest in the history of the home forces, was stunned by the sudden spurt of the Fighting Irish. The South Benders were under constant pressure in the first two quarters, partially due to their loose handling of the ball, but they reversed the situation completely in the last two periods.

Texas, victorious over Louisiana State and North Carolina by top heavy scores, was supposed to have the edge in every department, but when the showdown came it was Notre Dame that had the better line, the stouter defense and the more alert backs. It was Notre Dame that rolled up 218 yards by rushing to the Longhorns' 133. It was Notre Dame's Johnny Lattner who was the biggest gainer of the game.

It was Notre Dame that invariably had an operative in place when the breaks came along and, more often than not, it was Irish linebacker Dan Shannon, who broke the heart of Texas. This was the first time in its last 57 games that Texas had failed to score a touchdown.

It wasn't the case of a good team looking bad and a bad team looking good. Texas never looked bad. It played its hardest and fightingest football and the crowd stayed with it all the way until Shannon intercepted Jim Jones' pass in the last minute.

Notre Dame, despite 90 degree heat, grew stronger and fresher as the contest progressed. The Irish in the last two quarters not only played inspired football, but seemed to find themselves in a space of 30 minutes making up for the misfortunes that had dogged them against Pennsylvania and in the first half this afternoon.

No little credit for Notre Dame's whirlwind offense in the last half goes to Capt. Jack Alessandrini, who was shifted in the third quarter from linebacker to offensive right guard. Coach Frank Leahy told him during the intermission to get out there and show the life a Notre Dame leader is supposed to display. His spirit was reflected in the play of tackles Joe Bush and Fred Poehler, who began to open big holes in the Texas line.

The improved work of the offensive forwards gave Joe Heap, Neil Worden and Lattner, a potent trio of running backs, opportunity denied them at Pennsylvania and in the first two periods today.

Lattner had one of his most brilliant days in a Notre Dame uniform. His eight punts averaged 38 yards and they were so high that Notre Dame ends and tackles usually were under them to nail the receiver on the spot. The former Fenwick High School star carried 15 times for 89 yards. He caught two passes for 39 more.

Worden gained 52 yards in 11 carries and Heap 29 in eight. Heap, a twisting, driving runner, also caught two passes for 26. Ralph Guglielmi, who quarterbacked the team most of the way, proved a dangerous runner from the split-T formation, Notre Dame's basic offensive style. He carried 11 times for 53 yards.

Texas' leading ground gainer was fullback Richard Ochoa, who moved 46 yards in 12 tries. Jimmy Dan Pace and Gib Dawson, who ran wild against the Longhorns' earlier opponents, averaged less than 3 yards per carry.

Notre Dame, after a lively beginning, got in trouble two minutes after the opening kickoff when Jack Barton of Texas recovered a fumble by Heap on the Irish 43. The Longhorns traveled to the 27, where they were held for three downs and Bob Raley was sent in to kick. The punt, aimed at the coffin corner, took a backward bounce and rolled dead on the Irish 17.

The second calamitous development struck the Irish a few seconds later when Dawson of Texas recovered Guglielmi's fumble on the Irish 22. Texas advanced 9 yards in three plays, then lost the scoring opportunity when an Irishman named Al Kohanowich fell on Jones' fumble on Notre Dame's 15.

Lattner quick-kicked on third down to the Texas 49. The Longhorns moved to the Irish 39 on Jones' pass to Gilmer Spring. Sam Palumbo and Gene Carrabine held Ochoa and Pace to a total of 4 yards in two downs, but on the next play Jones whipped a pass to Stolhandske for a first down on the 18.

Jones then clicked to Dawson on the 5, where Shannon brought him down. Ochoa moved to the 2 behind center. Disaster again hit Texas within sight of pay dirt when Dawson fumbled and Carrabine recovered for Notre Dame on the 7.

Lattner nibbled at center for two yards as the first quarter ended in a scoreless tie. The Irish went nowhere and Lattner punted from his end zone to Raley of Texas, who sped back 13 yards to the Irish 37.

Ochoa's pass to Dawson earned Texas a first down on the 20 and again the Longhorns were headed for a touchdown. Two plunges by Pace and another by Ochoa moved the ball to the Irish 9. After Dawson picked up 2 yards at left guard, Carrabine broke up Dawson's pass to Stolhandske. Jones' next shot to Stolhandske was completed on the 3. On fourth down, Dawson kicked a field goal from the 10 and Texas led, 3-0.

Neither team threatened the other's goal the rest of the first half. Notre Dame never advanced to Texas' side of the 50-yard line and the Longhorns crossed midfield only once. That was on the last play of the second quarter, which wound up on the Irish 42.

The between halves ceremony was dedicated to the memory of Jack Chevigny, the former Notre Dame star who was head coach at Texas for three years. Chevigny was killed in action on Iwo Jima during World War II.

It was a new Notre Dame team that resumed play in the third quarter, not new in personnel but a unit with the old-fashioned Notre Dame spirit.

Ken Anglin of Texas kicked off to Worden, who returned to the Irish 26. Heap carried twice for five yards, then four, but the latter gain was nullified by a 15-yard penalty. Worden got back the lost yardage on a trap play that sent him over center for 15. Guglielmi then passed to Art Hunter for nine yards.

Heap banged behind his left guard for seven yards and Lattner powered over center to the Texas 44. This spurt moved the Irish from the gloom of their side of the field to the brighter plateaus of the Longhorns. Lattner, deploying behind the vastly improved Notre Dame line, twisted his way to the 31. Guglielmi, faking a handoff, picked up 6 yards around right end. Heap got through left tackle to the Texas 15, but the Irish were set back 15 yards for holding.

Then came the key play of the first touchdown drive. Guglielmi pitched out to Heap, who faded back and passed to Lattner on the 1-yard line. The Irish lined up on a tight T for the scoring smash and Lattner went over with 3 yards to spare. Menil Mavraides kicked the extra point and Notre Dame was ahead, 7-3.

Notre Dame kept up the pressure the rest of the third period but the closest it got to the Texas goal was the 30-yard line. Shannon's alertness and aggressiveness were responsible for Notre Dame's second touchdown, which came midway in the last quarter.

The Irish marched from their 15 to the Longhorn 28 on fancy stepping by Lattner and Guglielmi. Here they were slowed by a penalty and two incomplete passes. On fourth down, Paul Reynolds punted to Raley of Texas, who let the ball fall out of his hands.

Shannon rushed in with such force Raley was unable to retrieve the ball. It was Shannon who came up with it on the Longhorn 2. Heap crashed over center for the touchdown and Mavraides again kicked the extra point to wind up the scoring.

Texas tried desperately as the minutes clicked away to make a comeback by forward passing, but Notre Dame's secondary was too alert. Jack Whelan intercepted a pass from Jones on the Irish 22 to end the first threat and Shannon dashed Texas' hope for good by picking off another pass from Jones and returning 15 yards to his 41 with only 30 seconds on the clock.

Coach Ed Price of Texas after the game said Guglielmi and Lattner were the Notre Dame backs who did most of the offensive damage to his team. He agreed that the Irish continued to get stronger as time passed.

33

Notre Dame vs. Purdue

OCTOBER 18, 1952

LAFAYETTE, Ind. — Elementary football instruction advises a player to hold the ball and, if he can't hold it, fall on it.

Purdue and Notre Dame compiled an amazing record of 21 fumbles this afternoon in Ross-Ade Stadium. The Irish recovered the first eight of Purdue's 11 fumbles. They also recovered the ball after seven of their own 10 mistakes.

While Notre Dame's 26-14 victory was not based entirely on this statistic, few in the near-capacity crowd of 49,000 will deny that the Boilermakers consistently shackled their own attack long before a discouraged defense yielded a fourth touchdown to Notre Dame in the closing minutes. That touchdown definitely gave the decision in the 24th meeting between the two teams to the green-jerseyed invaders.

The lost fumbles statistics gave two each to kickoff receiver Rex Brock, quarterback Dale Samuels and to fullback Max Schmaling. Phil Mateja and substitute quarterback Roy Evans got one debit each. However, Evans' error, which snuffed out a Purdue drive in the fourth period on the Irish 11-yard line, was dictated by Irish lineman Jack Lee who prevented the handoff by Evans to Schmaling.

Brock's initial misplay on the opening kickoff cost possession on Purdue's 24-yard line and Notre Dame scored in four scrimmage plays. Brock repeated his error on the opening kickoff of the second half, but the Irish failed to benefit when Menil Mavraides missed an attempted field goal with the ball on the Boilermaker 8.

While Purdue recovered three of the Irish fumbles and the Boilermakers also intercepted four Irish passes, Notre Dame easily was the better following the ball. The season record attests Notre Dame's ability in this department. In four games, the Irish now have recovered 16 of their opponents' fumbles. In the last three games, Purdue has lost possession after 17 of its 20 mistakes.

After Notre Dame's first touchdown, Purdue counter-attacked in the first period to cover 46 yards in 10 plays and tied the score, 7-7. Samuels kicked the extra point.

Notre Dame led, 14-7, at the first quarter by putting together five first downs in a 68 yard drive. And the Irish rested at intermission with a 20-7 advantage when Ralph Guglielmi passed 37 yards to John Lattner with two seconds to play in the half.

Purdue cut its deficit to 20-14 with 7:33 left to play in the fourth period on a 32-yard pass by Evans to Bernie Flowers. This touchdown pass — Flowers' second of the game — had inception in a fumble by Irish quarterback Tom Carey that was recovered by Boilermaker defensive back Ed Zembal.

If Purdue fans questioned Notre Dame's superiority, they got a quick answer. The Irish took the subsequent kickoff and, in four first downs, marched to the Boilermaker goal line on 11 plays.

Thus, Notre Dame's two long scoring drives required nine of its total of 16 first downs and largely accounted for a net gain on the ground of 195 yards as compared to the 63 yards gained by all the Boilermaker backs.

Fundamentally, the battle was defensive with Notre Dame's linemen checking Purdue's runners consistently. John Lattner was the best back on the field, because of his power and speed at the defensive flanks on deep lateral pass plays. Irish left halfback Joe Heap had a better average, however, largely because of his skill at running around end when Lattner was a stationary wingback on the opposite flank.

Eighteen penalties were called, 10 on Notre Dame, and one-third as many were declined. Purdue was assessed five times for being offside in its ragged first period, and in the same quarter was assessed 15 yards for unnecessary roughness and lost the services of

Fred Preslosio, a 248-pound sophomore, who played the middle position on defense in Purdue's five-man line.

Purdue's defeat does not affect its position in the Big Ten race. By victories over Ohio State and Iowa, the Boilermakers are still tied for first place with Minnesota and Michigan. For Notre Dame it was their second victory in this campaign. The Irish have been tied by Pennsylvania and defeated by Pittsburgh. Today marked Purdue's initial loss since Notre Dame won last year's game, 30-9, in Notre Dame Stadium.

Notre Dame permitted Purdue to choose to receive to start the game when the Irish asked to defend the north goal after Capt. Jack Alessandrini correctly called the toss of the coin. Al Kohanowich kicked off and Brock returned 5 yards before he fumbled under the impact of Tom Seaman's tackle. Lee recovered for the Irish on Purdue's 24.

Heap was thrown for a 2-yard loss while attempting to run off left end. With right half Lattner in position as wingback on the other side of the line, Heap then ran left end to Purdue's 14-yard line.

Lattner turned Purdue's right end for 7 yards. In the next play, Heap shot into the line, fumbled and Irish tackle Joe Bush fell on the ball for a touchdown, just inside the goal line. It was the most successful ball-hawking of the game and was followed by Mavraides' successful extra point kick.

Purdue got possession three minutes later when Carey's pass to Bob O'Neil bounded from the end's hands and was intercepted by Mateja on Notre Dame's 46-yard line. Klezek turned Notre Dame's left end for 8 yards and Schmaling's second drive put the ball on the Irish 35.

Despite a 5-yard loss by Samuels, while trying to pass, and an offside penalty, Samuels passed to Jerry Thorpe on the Irish 29 and Schmaling made the first down on the Irish 23. Purdue again was offside.

On a repeat of the first down play, Samuels passed to Flowers, who was behind the defensive right half, and Flowers then ran over Irish safety Gene Carrabine to score. Carrabine suffered an injured leg muscle and left the game. Samuels' extra point kick tied the score, 7-7.

Heap took the Boilermaker kickoff and, while he fumbled out of bounds, it was Notre Dame's ball on the 32. Purdue held, but on Lattner's fourth-down punt Preziosio was called for unnecessary roughness and Notre Dame had a first down on the Boilermaker 49.

Lattner's quick thrust from regular T-formation was good for 4 yards and the right half then turned right end for a first down against a seven-man Boilermaker line. Carey's pass to Neil Worden made it first down on the Purdue 27.

Lattner was stopped, but Heap hit for 8 yards and then he went to the Boilermaker 14. Worden plunged over right guard for 7 yards. Then for the first time, Notre Dame used a backfield shift and Purdue was drawn offside. It was first down on the Boilermaker 2.

Carey failed on a sneak. Lattner then scored but Notre Dame was called for being offside. On the replay of the second down, Notre Dame's shift caught Purdue offside and the ball went to the Boilermaker 1-yard line. Worden then plunged for the touchdown and Mavraides added the point. Notre Dame now led, 14-7.

With 33 seconds to play in the second quarter, Notre Dame took Norm Montgomery's 12-yard punt, which was checked by Lee's partial block, on the Boilermaker 47-yard line. Guglielmi, who had entered the game for the first time eight plays before, passed, but Mateja intercepted for Purdue. Mateja fumbled, however, when tackled and Seaman recovered on the Boilermaker 37.

On the first play, Guglielmi ran to his right and passed to Lattner, who had escaped Purdue's defensive back and Mateja at safety. Mateja fell while trying to recover as Lattner scored. Mavraides kicked the extra point, but he had to try again when the Irish held on the play. He then missed from Purdue's 17-yard line.

A short kickoff recovered by Purdue ended the half.

In the third period, Purdue lost the ball on the Irish 25-yard line when Schmaling fumbled and Jack Whelan recovered for the Irish. Later, Samuels ran on a second-down pass play and fumbled. Notre Dame linebacker Dave Flood grabbed the ball on his 38-yard line.

Purdue lost possession for a third time when Schmaling turned the Irish left end for a first down, then fumbled and Lee recovered on the Irish 14.

The Boilermakers began the first play of the fourth quarter when Montgomery intercepted Carey's pass on the Irish 41-yard line. Evans' hook pass to Tom Redinger made the first down on the 29.

The play was repeated on third down to carry to the Irish 19.

Paul Reynolds of Notre Dame was called for interfering with Flowers on a pass at the Irish 11. It still was third down, but Schmaling missed a first down by inches. On the last attempt, Lee broke through to stop Evans' handoff to Schmaling and Sam Palumbo recovered for the Irish on their 11.

Evans' 32-yard touchdown pass to Flowers, which followed Carey's fumble and Zembal's recovery, have been noted. Notre Dame then rallied to control the ball for five minutes in its touchdown drive of 74 yards.

34

Notre Dame vs. Oklahoma

NOVEMBER 8, 1952

NOTRE DAME, Ind. — They shook down the thunder from the sky at Notre Dame today in a tumultuous requiem for Oklahoma.

Underestimated by some of their staunchest supporters, an embattled Irish eleven survived the heartbreak of early frustration, came from behind three times to tie the score and, with a mighty fourth-period thrust, dumped the Sooners from the ranks of the unbeaten, 27-21.

It was one of the historic upsets of modern times and it was conclusive. Oklahoma could put together only one sustained drive and that one, coming in the fourth quarter, crumpled before an inspired Irish defense after ranging 66 yards. Without halfback Billy Vessels, a truly legitimate claimant to all-America honors, it would have been a rout.

Vessels scored all three of Oklahoma's touchdowns. He put them in the lead three times; 7-0, in the first quarter on a 20-yard run after an 8-yard pass from quarterback Eddie Crowder; 14-7 at the half on a sensational 62-yard spring through Notre Dame's eight-man line; and 21-14 on a 47-yard jaunt with a pitchout in the third quarter.

But each time, Notre Dame came roaring back. It tied the score midway in the second period on a 59-yard advance set up by one of Oklahoma's nine fumbles and climaxed by Irish quarterback Ralph Guglielmi's 16-yard pass to Joe Heap. It tied the score again in the third period on a one-yard plunge by fullback Neil Worden after an interception by Johnny Lattner. It tied the score a third time with a 76-yard march that started from a kickoff in the third period and ended in the fourth when Worden smashed inside tackle for 3 yards.

Minute by minute, as the game wore on, it was evident that the thunderous tackling of Notre Dame's defense was taking the starch out of Oklahoma's attack. The famous Oklahoma deception was dwindling away as weary Sooners pulled themselves up from an earth-rocking jolt, and the further the game went the more Notre Dame picked up momentum.

By the time Notre Dame had come back into a tie for the third time, it was evident even to 10,000 Oklahoma partisans in the sellout throng of 57,446 that the Sooners were set up for the kill.

Menil Mavraides kicked off for Notre Dame after its tying fourth-quarter touchdown and Larry Grigg gathered in the ball on Oklahoma's 6-yard line. Grigg headed up the field. Down the field came Notre Dame's sophomore fullback Dan Shannon like a runaway tank heading downhill. Shannon met Grigg on the 20-yard line. The impact shook the stadium. Shannon was knocked out and Grigg was separated from the ball. Al Kohanowich, a junior end, recovered for Notre Dame on the Sooner 24.

In four plays, the Irish were ahead for the first time and, to all intents and purposes, the ball game was over.

Lattner, reaching the end of what Coach Frank Leahy said was his greatest performance of the season, bulled his way inside Oklahoma's left tackle and ran over the secondary for 17 yards.

Tom Carey of Chicago, who was the field general during most of Notre Dame's sensational second-half rally, came off the bench for the next play. He called a shift, the first Notre Dame used all day, and it produced its designated effect. Oklahoma was pulled offside. The 5-yard penalty made it a first down on the 2-yard line.

Worden, who was called on 26 times during this history-making afternoon and responded with 75 yards, submarined under the Sooners' right tackle for 1 yard and 2 feet. Carey then sneaked it over for the score. Irish enthusiasm fell with a tremendous groan when Bob Arrix, a sophomore fullback from Teaneck, N.J., who three times had delivered under pressure to consummate the earlier ties, flubbed his kick. This could have been the deciding point should Vessels again get the slightest break. But Vessels was getting no breaks the rest of this day. Notre Dame's defense already had the situation well in hand.

Oklahoma was set to make its one sustained drive of the afternoon, that aforementioned 66-yard advance, but when it reached the Irish 34 the defense rose up and strangled it in its tracks. The invincibility of the Sooners had long since been ended.

When Lee Getschow, a sophomore halfback from Kenilworth, Ill., batted down Vessels' long desperate pass to Max Boyston on the Notre Dame goal line to end the game, the crowd poured over the restraining rails, hoisted Lattner and Worden to their shoulders and carried them off the field amid disorder the likes of which this dignified little football plant never has witnessed. Around the edge of the mob, Oklahoma players trudged their weary way to the locker room, convinced that there is no substitute for the spirit of Notre Dame.

The inevitable outcome was forecast in the first few minutes of the game. Notre Dame received, and in four plays punted. Oklahoma's first play was a plunge by its great fullback, Buck McPhail. He went 6 yards and fumbled. Shannon recovered on the Sooner 31-yard line.

Seven plays later, Worden and Heap, directed by Guglielmi, had moved to the Sooner 4-yard line, but in their jubilation and excitement the Notre Dame backfield jumped offside on a fourth-down play that saw Lattner advance to the Sooner 1. Arrix then missed a field goal attempt from the 16.

Oklahoma had two more opportunities to show off its widely heralded offense, but both came to naught. As a matter of fact, the Sooners had 16 chances during the day and, except for their futile fourth-quarter drive, they were able to retain the ball for more than five plays on only three occasions.

A holding penalty which moved Notre Dame back to its 1-yard line late in the first period eventually set up Oklahoma's first score. Lattner's punt bounded backward and was killed on the Irish 28. Deft faking by Crowder, McPhail and Buddy Leake attracted Notre Dame's attention to the right. Vessels, in the meantime, slipped out into the left flat, took an 8-yard pass from Crowder and ran 20 yards into the end zone. Leake made the first of his three extra points for the Sooners.

Notre Dame moved against Oklahoma's defense for the rest of the period. Crowder later fumbled in the second quarter and Notre Dame's Bob O'Neil recovered on the Irish 41. Guglielmi then passed to Heap for 15 yards. After several runs by Worden, Francis Paterra and himself on a keep it maneuver to keep the Sooner defense in its seven-man line, Guglielmi passed to Heap on the 3. Heap ran over Sam Allen and fell into the end zone for a 16-yard gain and the score.

Paul Reynolds fell on Boyston's fumble on Oklahoma's 34-yard line to give Notre Dame another opportunity on the first play after the ensuing kickoff but Oklahoma regained possession two plays later when Worden fumbled and Melvin Brown recovered.

On first down, Notre Dame went into its eight-man line, an effective, but also dangerous gamble, as Vessels proved. The Sooner speedster took a handoff from Crowder on a standard T-formation quick-opening play, shot through the line and, as Lattner came up from defensive halfback, he cut to the left, wheeled down the sideline and legged it 62 yards to the goal line.

The Irish advanced 50 yards to the Sooner 15 after receiving the kickoff but were thwarted by a backfield-in-motion penalty and an incomplete pass, and went into the half trailing, 14-7.

Notre Dame recovered again at the start of the second half and, under the flawless direction of Carey, put together six first downs in an advance of 67 yards to the Sooner 6 before Lattner, while smashing off-tackle, fumbled. Kay Keller recovered for Oklahoma on the 14.

The Irish were back knocking at the door in five plays, however, when Lattner intercepted Crowder's pass and returned 28 yards to the Sooner 8. A 5-yard offside penalty against Oklahoma moved it to the 3 and Worden went over for the touchdown on third down from the 1. The score was now even, 14-14.

Two plays after the kickoff, Vessels took Crowder's pitchout, wheeled wide around Notre Dame's right end, and threaded his way through the onrushing secondary for 47 yards and a touchdown.

Except for the kickoff play on which Shannon made Grigg fumble to set up the deciding touchdown, Oklahoma did not have the ball again until Notre Dame had decided the issue.

Paterra took the kickoff in the end zone, came back 25 yards and the Irish set sail goalward under direction of Carey. Four plays netted 16 yards, then Guglielmi rushed in from the bench to lateral to Heap who forward passed to Lattner for 36 yards to the 27. A 5-yard penalty against Oklahoma for calling too many time-outs moved it to the 22. Carey then came back in and sent Worden into the line seven times. The big fullback finally scored from the 3. Arrix's extra point kick brought the score to 21-21 and set the stage for Shannon's climactic collision with Grigg.

35

Notre Dame vs. Michigan State

NOVEMBER 15, 1952

EAST LANSING, Mich. — Michigan State's mighty men won their 23rd consecutive football game this afternoon before a record crowd of 52,472 in Macklin Field. And the Irish of Notre Dame, beaten 21-3, now appear three times in the Spartans' victory list, which is the nation's best.

Today's battle, fought in Indian summer weather under a cloudless sky, was a test of strength and endurance. Neither team had an advantage in the scoreless first half. The Irish, checked in the third period, went ahead, 3-0, on 6-yard field goal by Bob Arrix.

Then, with less than six minutes remaining of the third period, the Spartans parlayed an Irish fumble and a penalty into a touchdown. The unusual combination produced a second touchdown five minutes later and, with this 14-3 score as a fulcrum, Michigan State completed the victory tabulation when Spartan fullback Evan Slonac raced 24 yards through dispirited Irish defenders shortly before the inevitable conclusion.

Seldom has any college game offered so thorough a demonstration of fundamentals. For 30 minutes, each team relied almost entirely on ground attack. In this game, the Irish had a statistical advantage but could not score. In fact, neither team could put together an attack of more than two-consecutive first downs. On offense, blocking was overbalanced by smashing tackles and defense produced a total of 12 fumbles.

The Irish committed seven fumbles, including four in the third period, and lost possession on all. This mark is exceeded this season only by Purdue's play against Notre Dame last month when the defeated Boilermakers, fumbling 11 times, lost the ball on their first eight errors.

Until today, Notre Dame had fumbled 42 times in seven games and lost possession 19 times. This included 10 fumbles against Purdue, with the ball lost three times. Notre Dame's record now is 49 fumbles, an average of six a game, and the Irish have lost the ball 26 times.

Michigan State likewise had its trouble in holding the ball but the Spartans by better position and agility, grabbed four of their five fumbles.

Spartan linebacker Dick Tamburo recovered three Notre Dame fumbles and, while none was involved in the touchdown marches, Tamburo was awarded the game football by his teammates in the weekly post-game presentation.

Other Spartan recoveries were made by linebacker Doug Weaver and guards Gordon Serr and Henry Bullough. Another recovery was credited to Ray Vogt and Don Dohoney. This actually was the most important, for from this recovered fumble on the Irish 13-yard line the Spartans started for their initial touchdown.

Today's record crowd was a record only because authorities found a few more locations. When the enlarged stadium was dedicated in 1948, 51,526 saw Michigan play here. Nine hundred more spectators got into the stadium today. Although the result apparently was placed beyond Notre Dame's ability by Michigan State's second touchdown, the spectators stayed to the end.

Johnny Lattner's 37-yard run for the Irish in the fourth quarter was backed up by his own pass to Joe Heap for 23 yards and the best sustained attack of the day. Heap's reception on the Spartan 11-yard line also set up the Spartan's most brilliant defense in a battle featuring defense. In four plays, Notre Dame was stopped inches short of a first down and more than a yard from the Spartan goal line.

Vogt and Dohoney gave Michigan State its touchdown opportunity by recovering the fifth Irish fumble of the game and the second of the third quarter on the Irish 13. Don McAuliffe, the

Spartan captain and left half, smashed Notre Dame's left tackle for 3 yards. Billy Wells, whose 15 carries matched McAuliffe's work today, picked up a yard at the other side of the Irish line. On third down, substitute quarterback Willie Thrower passed beyond the Spartan receiver in the end zone.

On this play, however, Notre Dame was penalized and the ball was placed on the Irish 1-yard line. On the next play, McAuliffe took a direct pass from center in the Spartans' single-wing formation and ripped over guard for the touchdown. Slonac kicked the first of three points and the Spartans' led, 7-3.

After McAuliffe's touchdown, 5:37 remained to play in the third period. Michigan State scored again before the teams changed goals.

Lattner's fumble on a quick-opening play was recovered by Michigan State on the Irish 15 but a subsequent penalty for holding stopped the attack. The Irish took the ball on their 18.

On the first play, Francis Paterra fumbled in a smash into the line and Bullough recovered on the Irish 21. McAuliffe led off for Michigan State with a slashing drive for 5 yards and followed with another plunge to the Irish 13. Wells then swept around right end for a first down just inside the Irish 10-yard line. Notre Dame linebacker Dave Flood made the tackle but was sidelined with a broken collar bone, the only major casualty of the battle.

Slonac continued Michigan State's attack with a smash over guard for 5 yards. Notre Dame now employed nine linemen and two linebackers and McAuliffe was tripped up by defensive tackle Sam Palumbo and the Spartan captain lost a yard. It was now third down and goal to go on the Irish 5.

Again the Irish were in a nine-man line when Spartan quarterback Tom Yewcic attempted a jump pass after taking the ball from under center. Yewcic threw but no receiver was in position over the line of scrimmage.

Notre Dame, however, was called for holding an eligible receiver and the ball was spotted on the Irish 1. McAuliffe then plunged for the touchdown.

Notre Dame's 68-yard drive immediately followed but it was turned back when Ralph Guglielmi's quarterback sneak failed on fourth down at the Michigan State goal line.

This was the high tide of Irish play. Yewcic's punting — he averaged better than 45 yards — kept Notre Dame in check the remainder of the afternoon.

State's last score was touched off by Jim Ellis' interception of Guglielmi's pass which he returned to the Irish 24. The interception, the only mark against the Irish throwers, was made after Guglielmi's pass had been touched by Heap and then by Irish end Art Hunter. Ellis came in from safety to make the interception.

Thrower's pass missed on first down. Slonac then swept left end and outraced the secondary down the east sideline to the goal line.

The third period, in which Notre Dame lost the ball by fumbles four times, also saw the Irish penalized 48 yards in their total offense of 39 yards. There were four penalties for holding, one for clipping and one for offside. Two of these penalties, as described, put the ball on the Irish 1-yard line.

Michigan State might have moved to a 3-0 lead in the first quarter except for two-consecutive 5-yard penalties for delay of game. Michigan State advanced from the Irish 34-yard line, where Notre Dame committed its initial fumble, to the Irish 18. Now it was fourth down, but penalties for delay-of-game cost 10 yards and Slonac's field goal attempt, with the ball held on the Irish 35, was short and to the right.

Notre Dame's drive to its field goal early in the third period started after Michigan State's fourth fumble, the one recovery by the Irish. The Spartans, who chose to receive to start the second half, were called for holding on the Irish kickoff and put the ball in play on their 9-yard line. On the first attack by Wells at Notre Dame's right tackle, the Spartan wingback fumbled and defensive back Lattner recovered on the Spartan 11.

Heap picked up 2 yards at left tackle. On second down, quarterback Tom Carey carried on a split-T play at off-tackle. Following the play, the Irish were penalized to their 20 for holding.

Guglielmi's pass on the replay failed but he threw to Heap, who was stationed on the left flank, for 14 yards. It was now fourth down on the Spartan 6 and Arrix came into the lineup to kick the field goal.

This game also was unusual in that Notre Dame completed only one pass in 11 attempts in the first half. It gained 11 yards. Michigan

State tried 12 passes, completing three for 19 yards. These figures demonstrate the preference for rushing and high regard for both opponents' secondary defenses against passes.

Other notes show that Notre Dame lost the ball by fumble once in the first period (on Michigan State's field goal attempt), twice in the second and four times in the third when the Spartans scored two touchdowns.

Michigan State fumbled once in the first quarter, twice in the second, recovering all three. After losing the ball by fumble in the third quarter, Michigan State had one more error and recovered in the last period.

Notre Dame's "so-called" trick shift was not in evidence today.

Michigan State finishes its season next Saturday against Marquette University. The Irish, now with two defeats (Pittsburgh and Michigan State) and a tie (Pennsylvania), face Iowa this week and a concluding game with Southern California on Nov. 29.

The Spartans have not been defeated since Maryland turned the trick in 1950. It is likely that they will be voted the nation's best in the annual poll and that their coach, Biggie Munn, will be rated the Coach of the Year by his associates.

36

Notre Dame vs. U.S.C.

NOVEMBER 29, 1952

NOTRE DAME, Ind. — Notre Dame scattered magnificent Pacific Coast Conference statistics, assorted sectional titles and Pasadena rosebuds all over the football world today by beating Southern California's proud and previously confident and unbeaten Trojans, 9-0.

The game was played before 58,394, less than 1,000 under the Notre Dame Stadium record set in 1948. The rugged battle was fought in temperature which never rose above freezing.

In beating Southern California, the relentless Irish carried on the magnificent Notre Dame competitive tradition. There was no Rose Bowl bait, no national ribbons, no conference titles, only a consuming enthusiasm for conquest.

Notre Dame added the fourth sectional champion to its list of 1952 victims. There were Oklahoma, champion of the Big Seven; Texas, winner of the Southwest title; and Purdue, which shared the Big Ten crown. The Irish tied Penn, the Ivy league king.

Now Southern California is a disillusioned team with the dream statistics that must meet Wisconsin in the Rose Bowl on New Year's afternoon in Pasadena. The Badgers' entire coaching staff was here to see how the Irish did it.

Notre Dame scored a touchdown in the second period. John Lattner of Chicago and Fenwick High School went over from the 1-foot line in the seventh minute of the period. Lattner played 59 minutes, as he did in last year's victory over Southern California.

Bob Arrix, who failed to kick the extra point after Lattner's touchdown, supplied the comfort points in the sixth minute of the third period when he kicked a field goal from the 17-yard line with Bob Joseph holding.

Fancy statistics, disseminated in abundance, had indicated the game would resolve into a test of defensive strength rather than offensive up-and-git. It was just that. But it was not a dull game because of the scoreless spans. There were fireworks in which Notre Dame got the points essential to victory by alert on following up of breaks.

On the much heralded Irish defense, Capt. Jack Alessandrini, Dan Shannon, Sam Palumbo, Jack Lee, Paul Reynolds, Jach Whelan, Menil Mavraides and all the other gents were terrific. The Trojans took lessons in defensive technique after coming to town as vaunted masters in this phase of play.

The buildup for the touchdown was negotiated on defensive alertness. The losers' biggest threat ended when the Irish held and took over on the Notre Dame 1-inch line.

The Trojans, in the course of nine-straight victories they accomplished between losses to Notre Dame, had intercepted 29 passes and returned seven for touchdowns. Today they saw Lattner, Reynolds, Whelan, Shannon and Alessandrini intercept passes with defensive play that completely befuddled Southern California.

However, the Irish failed to intercept one important pass. That was a 50-yard, fourth-period Jim Sears pitch to Jim Hayes, who caught the ball on the Irish 25 for the longest gain of the day.

The Trojans made only five first downs and gained only 87 yards from rushing and 82 from passing, which was testimonial enough for the Irish defense. Furthermore, it was one of the three Irish fumble recoveries that grew into the touchdown.

Notre Dame had taken over on its 40, a third of the way through the second period, after Trojan fullback Leon Sellers had tried for 2 yards on fourth down and couldn't make it. This break did not immediately jell and a bit later Lattner punted but Notre Dame was ruled offside.

Lattner booted again, from his 31, and did a much better job.

Sears received and attempted to lateral to another of the galaxy of Trojan stars, Al Carmichael. But Carmichael wasn't where Sears thought he was. The ball plopped to earth and Notre Dame's Mavraides fell on it on the Trojan 19.

Lattner made 2 yards. Guglielmi, who tossed the only complete Irish pass of the game, this time faked a pass and ran 5 yards. Lattner plunged for 3 yards and it was first down on the Trojan 9.

The Trojans drew a 5-yard setback for being offside, after which Lattner drove to the 2. Neil Worden plunged to within inches of the goal line. Lattner then was stopped but carried over for the score on fourth down.

Before Arrix's field goal, Notre Dame had marched from the Trojan 46 to the 10 in six plays, with Joe Heap carrying for three successive gains and Worden contributing a 15-yard romp. Notre Dame drew an offside penalty and Lattner threaded forward for 8 yards. A pass was incomplete, and on fourth down Arrix made his comfort kick from the 17. The Irish now led, 9-0.

Contrasted with the Trojans' meager total of five first downs were a dozen by the Irish. Notre Dame made 194 yards rushing and a Guglielmi pass to Don Penza was good for 10 yards. It was effected in the scoreless first period.

Worden was the top Irish overland gainer with 73 yards. Lattner accounted for 66 yards and Frank Paterra had 42 yards on five carries for the best average of the day.

Sellers gained 66 yards for the losers. Sears, with a national reputation as a punt returner, brought back two kicks for a meager 18 yards. This, however, enabled him to tie the Pacific Coast Conference record, which somehow was lost in the shuffle in the light of the afternoon's more significant events.

37

Notre Dame vs. Oklahoma

SEPTEMBER 26, 1953

NORMAN, Okla.—Notre Dame's Fighting Irish, a standup bunch of football opportunists, today had to prove their right to their nickname in winning a thrill-packed 28-21 game from a fighting Oklahoma team which didn't seem to know when it was beaten.

This was a true Notre Dame victory. Every man on the Irish team pitched in to bring about the triumph before 57,935 on Owen Field in 94 degree temperatures. You could name a dozen heroes for both teams.

In the steaming heat of this sultry Sooner afternoon it would be hard, however, to overlook Notre Dame's John Lattner, Ralph Guglielmi, Joe Heap, Neil Worden and Don Penza, and Oklahoma's Merrill Green, Larry Grigg and Buddy Leake.

This was the football game it had been advertised to be when it was set up last year, after the Irish fought back from an underdog role to upset the Sooners. Today, the Oklahomans, who had lost all of their ball-carrying talent and figured to be three touchdown underdogs, almost brought off an upset of their own against the team already nominated for the national title.

The Sooners took a 7-0 lead within the first five minutes of play, forced the Irish to tie them, then went ahead, 14-7, and made the visitors deadlock them again. Notre Dame made two touchdowns in the third quarter, then the Sooners cooked up a quick, fourth-quarter touchdown with five minutes still remaining. Thereafter, they couldn't cope with the Irish defense.

This smashing contest wound up almost even in a statistical comparison, with Notre Dame making 11 first downs to Oklahoma's 11 in the course of handing the Sooners their first home defeat in 25 games. The Oklahomans outdistanced the Irish in rushing 128 to 120, but the winners led in aerial arithmetic, 104 to 79.

Notre Dame fullback Worden headed the day's ballcarriers with a net of 78 yards in 12 tries, while Green, who rushed back a 60-yard return of a Notre Dame punt for Oklahoma's third touchdown, was best of all the Sooners.

Guglielmi, the 20-year-old Ohioan who distinguished himself in all-around style as the Irish quarterback, connected on five of 8 passes for 88 yards, including two for touchdowns to the speedy Heap. Leake wasn't as accurate. He hit on only two of seven pitches for 79 yards.

Lattner started and finished the game in the spectacular fashion which has him tabbed for the player of the year. The former Fenwick prep star juggled the opening kickoff on the Irish 2 to put his team in the hole that led to Oklahoma's first touchdown. Then he made his exit with a pass interception and a key tackle in the fourth quarter, which cost him a swollen right ankle.

In between all of this, the lanky Westsider fielded three passes for a total gain of 47 yards, toted the ball 13 times for an overall gain of 22 yards and punted six times for an average of 39 yards.

After Lattner's bobble of the opening kickoff, Notre Dame worked its way out to the 23, where Worden's fumble was recovered by Sooner tackle Dick Bowman. Jack Ging, the Sooner left halfback, did most of the work in accomplishing the first Oklahoma touchdown, with Leake supplying the extra point that gave the home boys a 7-0 lead with 10 minutes and 18 seconds left to play.

Notre Dame center Jim Schrader recovered a fumble by Max Boydston on the Sooner 15, and Guglielmi promptly pitched to Lattner. Worden was stopped twice, then Guglielmi passed to Heap in the end zone for the touchdown. Menil Mavraides came in to contribute the first of his four extra points.

Don Penza, Notre Dame's captain, made two tackles costly to the Oklahoma progress in the second quarter, and a recovery which led to field goal opportunity for Mavraides, whose boot from the Sooner 29 fell shy late in the first quarter.

Oklahoma took the ball on its 20, after Lattner had punted into the end zone. On the first play, Leake passed to Carl Allison, who was away and running for 62 yards before Heap detained him. Irish tackle Sam Palumbo thwarted Ging on the next play. Ging busted loose over right guard for a first down on the Irish 7. Leake picked up 2 on a quarterback sneak, then Ging went over center for a touchdown. Leake's extra point kick made it 14-7.

With 4 minutes to go in the second quarter, both coaches began to take advantage of the substitution rule. Penza smashed down one Oklahoma pass, then blocked a punt and recovered the ball on the Sooner 9, while injuring himself in the process. Less than 2 minutes of the half remained. Guglielmi tried a sweep around right end, then faked a pitchout and took the ball over himself for the touchdown. Mavraides' point-after kick tied the score at 14-14.

Lattner and Penza collaborated in thwarting a third quarter drive by Oklahoma, then Guglielmi set up Notre Dame's third touchdown when he intercepted a pass by Leake. Guglielmi didn't waste much time on consummating the deal. On first down, he pitched a 36-yard pass to Heap in the end zone and the Irish were ahead for the first time and to stay.

On the ensuing kickoff to Oklahoma, Grigg returned 27 yards to his own 43. Boydston recovered his own fumble on the first play, but Leake's subsequent error was picked up by Penza on the Sooner 47. Guglielmi then pitched to Heap for 15 yards. Worden drove to the Sooner 15, and joined with Heap in making it a first down on the 9. Worden crashed over the defensive right tackle and Mavraides added the extra point to give the Irish a 28-14 lead.

The fourth quarter found the Oklahomans in there pitching to the final minutes. They scored for the third time with less than six minutes left. They had pushed the Irish back after a series of fumbles, and Lattner finally had to punt.

Green, a 180-pound senior halfback from Chickasha, Okla., took the ball on the fly and, with the aid of two blocks by Leake and Grigg, was able to crash the Notre Dame secondary and score the touchdown that aroused the local faithful into thinking their lads might do what Notre Dame did to them last year — come from behind to win. The Sooners tried hard, but Lattner and Heap and Guglielmi tried just a little harder.

38

Notre Dame vs. Georgia Tech

OCTOBER 24, 1953

NOTRE DAME, Ind. — Notre Dame's rugged, powerful varsity smashed Georgia Tech's ground defenses this afternoon to whip the Engineers, 27-14, and to end their list of football games without defeat at 31. The Irish scored after receiving the opening kickoff, matched that assault under pressure following Tech's tying touchdown in the third period, and went on to victory, which a valiant opponent could not deny.

A capacity throng of 58,254, gathered in the buff brick stadium under gray, chill skies, were thrilled to view Georgia Tech's battle against overwhelming strength. The Engineers put together a brilliant drive of five first downs to tie the score in the third period and subsequently came through with a touchdown to trail it 21-14, by completion of a first down scoring pass of 35 yards.

Thereafter, the Irish had complete control and held Tech to two first downs by penalty in the last quarter. It was their fourth victory of this campaign and the sixth in succession.

Notre Dame's power rolled up 323 yards on the ground in 17 first downs. Five additional first downs were recorded by a complementary air attack, which was strategically employed by Irish quarterback Ralph Guglielmi who completed seven of 16 passes.

Guglielmi's passes added 88 yards to Notre Dame's yardage for a total of 411. The Irish also had penalties of 88 yards which were caused by nine infractions.

Notre Dame played the second half under direction of assistant coaches Joe McArdle and Bill Earley, after Coach Frank Leahy suffered a collapse at intermission and was taken to St. Joseph's Hospital in South Bend.

Georgia Tech, impotent on defense against straight power, as demonstrated by Notre Dame's Johnny Lattner and Neil Worden, swept through the same opponents for 69 yards to tie the game. The subsequent scoring pass against the Irish second team early in the final quarter added 53 yards. Thus, the two scores accounted for 122 yards of the total of 208 credited to the Engineers.

Notre Dame would not have been tied and Georgia Tech would not have come within seven points later, except for the decision to employ a second Irish eleven as a relief unit. This team, which led the rally to defeat Pittsburgh last week, deserved the opportunity. But the substitutes, taking over at the start of the second quarter with a 7-0 lead, fumbled away a scoring opportunity on Tech's 7.

This same unit also permitted Tech to score its second touchdown on Wade Mitchell's pass to Bill Teas.

Georgia Tech had a superior backfield if measured by speed. In Dave Davis, it offered one of the finest kickers in college football. But those assets were discounted by Notre Dame's line, which outcharged the Engineers on offense and defense. This was the inescapable factor on which the Irish built their victory.

Tech's 31 games without defeat started with a victory over Davidson, 54-19, on Nov. 18, 1950. Duke tied the Engineers, 14-14, in 1951, and Florida played a scoreless tie with Tech this fall under handicap of rain and wind.

Notre Dame's victory was the 15th in seventeen games in a rivalry started in 1922.

Worden and Lattner were the ballcarriers who ripped Tech's eight-man line throughout the contest. They carried for 41 of Notre Dame's 65 rushes and gained 107 yards. Each averaged approximately 5 yards.

Lattner, in particular, was the man Notre Dame asked for yardage when pressured and the Chicago lad celebrated his 21st birthday with one of his finest performances. Lattner scored the fourth Irish touchdown from Tech's 1-yard line to place the result beyond dispute.

Notre Dame, winning the toss, chose to receive to start the game and at once showed its power. Glenn Turner's kickoff, boosted by the north wind, rolled out of the Irish end zone and Notre Dame went to work from its own 20-yard line. Ten plays later Notre Dame led, 7-0.

Lattner's sharp thrust gained 6 yards when he was stopped by Larry Morris and Turner. With a flanking back on the left, Lattner got 3 yards and Guglielmi followed center for a first down on his 31.

Joe Heap's plunge on a handoff got a yard and then Heap, the fastest of the Irish backs, swept right end for a first down on Tech's 34. Lattner ripped over guard for another first down on the Engineers' 19.

Guglielmi carried for 5 yards. Worden quickly hit the same spot for 4 and then was grounded on Tech's 7-yard line by Morris, a great defensive player. Worden smashed left tackle on a power play for the touchdown with the Engineers spread to cover a flanking right end and Heap at a wingback. Menil Mavraides kicked the extra point for Notre Dame's 7-0 lead with 3:56 played.

This attack required four first downs and while Notre Dame got five more of these statistical marks in the first period, four were linked together in progress from the Irish 20 to Tech's 12 as the quarter ended.

Worden made it first down with a 12-yard smash after a fake to Lattner. The Irish second team then took over. Dick Washington, a substitute for Lattner, plunged for a yard. Dick Fitzgerald took Tom Carey's handoff for 4 yards. On third down, fullback Tom McHugh fumbled and Tech tackle Bob Sherman recovered on his 7-yard line.

This failure led to the return of Notre Dame's varsity after 4:46 of the second quarter and Lattner punted to Wade Mitchell, who made a fair catch on Tech's 22. Tech declined to run with Irish kicks until the last period.

The teams played out the second quarter with Guglielmi intercepting Mitchell's pass on the Irish 7-yard line as time expired.

Tech chose to receive to resume play in the second half. Lattner intercepted Bill Brigman's pass on the sixth consecutive play and returned 4 yards to Tech's 40.

Guglielmi then threw to his left end Paul Matz, but Matz dropped the ball when tackled. The play, never fully reported, was either recovery of a fumble or interception before the ball touched the ground. In any event, Tech then started from its 31-yard line.

For the only time in the game, the Yellow Jackets consistently outran the Irish defense. Bill Teas turned defensive right end for 12 yards, Leon Hardeman and Tech quarterback Ward Mitchell gained 8 yards. Turner smashed to the Irish 46.

Mitchell then passed to Henry Hair for 15 yards and Teas took a deep lateral around right end to the Irish 20. Hardeman lunged for 5, and Turner, after a fake to a halfback, was dropped on Notre Dame's 7-yard line. On fourth down, Mitchell sneaked over from one yard out against a massed defense and Mitchell's kick tied the score at 7-7.

Actually this was the peak of Georgia Tech's play and 8:05 remained in the third period. Notre Dame received the kickoff and Heap returned 35 yards to his 44 to start Notre Dame's drive for the touchdown that again proved Irish ground power.

Worden and Lattner advanced to Tech's 45. Worden and Lattner advanced to Tech's 45. Worden hit off-tackle, a soft spot in the invaders' line all afternoon, for 8 yards. Another drive at the same position went to Tech's 37.

Lattner ripped through with a handoff for 6 yards. Worden got 3 and then the Irish fullback made the first down by inches. Guglielmi suddenly lifted his sights and he passed to Matz for a first down on Tech's 9.

Worden failed to gain, but Guglielmi threw to Heap in the end zone for the touchdown — the first score by air against the Yellow Jackets in 22 consecutive games. Mavriades kicked the extra point. Notre Dame now led, 14-7, with 4:05 left in the third period.

Notre Dame then capitalized on Georgia Tech's major failure, a terrifically bad pass from center on a punt, although the play had been called on third down as a protection. Tech had possession on its 18 when substitute punter Jim Carlen went back for the kick.

Jimmy Morris, a replacement for Larry Morris at center, made a gigantic pass back that could not be caught. Carlen pursued the deflected ball into his end zone and twice missed at recovery. He slipped and fell and watched Irish tackle Art Hunter fall on the ball for a touchdown.

Mavriades' extra point kick gave Notre Dame a 21-7 lead.

Nine plays later, the period ended and Notre Dame once more substituted its second eleven. Teas took Tom McHugh's punt and Tech had the ball on its 47-yard line.

On the first scrimmage, Mitchell shot a long pass down the west sideline to Teas, who ran behind McHugh to catch the ball and dance into the end zone. Mitchell kicked the extra point. Notre Dame again was vulnerable to a tie at 21-14 with but 1:25 played in the last period.

Notre Dame was stopped on Tech's 27, but Heap later set up the final score when he returned Davis' 50-yard punt 28 yards to the Tech 40. Heap twice changed direction in this return.

Lattner hit the vulnerable left tackle and lateraled to Worden who completed a 19-yard gain. Despite an offside penalty, the Irish moved to the Tech 11 on Guglielmi's fourth down sneak for 2 yards, and Worden and Lattner again got the first down in three plays at 1.

Lattner smashed through untouched for his birthday touchdown, but Mavriades failed to add the extra point.

39

Notre Dame vs. U.S.C.

NOVEMBER 28, 1953

LOS ANGELES—Johnny Lattner scored four touchdowns today to show Pacific coast football fans why he is an all-America football player for a second consecutive year. And the Irish of Notre Dame, by their 48-14 victory, showed the Trojans of Southern California how to play football.

Lattner ran as few college halfbacks ever have run before. He averaged 9.25 yards for each of the 17 times he carried the ball. Lattner's fourth touchdown was a 50-yard sprint early in the last period that demonstrated beyond rebuttal his superb skill as a smashing runner, who is protected by defensive stiff arm and an amazing change of pace.

The near capacity crowd of 97,952, many hopeful that the Trojans could turn a gridiron miracle, were stunned by the perfection of the Irish ground attack for which Southern California had no adequate defense.

Notre Dame's mastery of the Trojans' defenses, perhaps inspired by last week's tie with Iowa that ended a 1953 victory march of seven triumphs, was unbelievable. The Irish piled up 336 yards by rushing (attempting only seven passes which gained 41 yards) to burst through any line formation.

Although three regulars did not play in the second half because of injury and all of the squad of 38 players saw action, Notre Dame's seven touchdowns set a record in the Silver Anniversary of this intersectional rivalry. It was 6 years ago that Notre Dame defeated Southern California, 38-7, on this gridiron. Today's winning mark of 48 points broke all marks for the series.

Not since Notre Dame whipped Indiana, 48-6, in 1951 have the Irish so completely dominated an adversary. Lattner now has become the first player ever to score four touchdowns against a Trojan eleven.

Lattner was the scoring leader. He was the main reliance of the Irish attack. But Lattner was great today because he had Neil Worden for a fullback, Joe Heap as a running mate at left half, and because Ralph Guglielmi is a master of the T-formation.

Guglielmi's direction cannot be overemphasized. He looked over Trojan ground defenses and called quick thrusts or optional laterals that confounded his opponents.

Heap gave Notre Dame its first touchdown with a record 94-yard return of Aramis Dandoy's punt that stunned the Trojans beyond recovery. But Heap had to yield when he suffered injury to his right knee. Worden was in the battle all the way to furnish the Irish with a keen two-edged assault.

Irish ballcarriers were spotlighted but Irish linemen were the workmen who blocked out Trojan defenders for the sharp smashes by Lattner and Worden. Irish linemen, always quickly forming a cordon to convoy any runner, were a barrier in Southern California's secondary.

It is impossible to give the list of those whose work was as efficient as the running by Lattner and Worden. There was no greater player, however, than sophomore guard Ray Lemek, whose speed made him remarkably effective and helped in preventing a touchdown to add to Southern California's confusion.

Art Hunter, the right tackle, who has served as center and end in preceding seasons, was a bulwark. Jack Lee, replacing Menil Mavraides in the center of a five-man line, starred until his shoulder was re-injured. Jim Schrader, an offensive center and linebacker, was invaluable.

But no one can forget the work of the Irish ends. Dan Shannon and Capt. Don Penza, who started; Paul Matz, a replacement for Shannon, and Pat Bisceglia, who took over for Penza. They blocked almost without error. They defended with surprising skill.

Southern California had men who refused to accept defeat which many realized had to be accepted after Heap scored the first touchdown. Dandoy tried on his off-tackle carries. Trojan halfback Lindon Crow, however, caused the Irish the most trouble. Crow carried Southern California's first touchdown attack that went from the Trojan 23 to the Irish 13 in twelve plays.

Crow was a terrific ballcarrier. In nine rushes he averaged more than 5 yards to top his team except for spot work by fullback Leon Sellers. Southern California, however, labored under the difficulty of starting its ground attack from a buck-lateral series. The Trojans preferred this combination. It was a delayed attack which was often under pressure of position too far within Southern California territory.

In final analysis, Notre Dame was too fast, too sharp and, above all, worked with flaming desire to prove that it is a great team.

The Trojans' failures are best indicated by their record of six first downs by rushing. Three were made in their initial attack that failed. The other three first downs by rushing were spaced through the following 45 minutes.

Southern California was a determined team. This could be questioned on basis of the final score except that those who watched this battle know that the Trojans refused to quit long after they realized they had no chance for victory.

Notre Dame raced to a 13-0 lead in the first period, getting the second touchdown on the last play of the quarter. The Trojans, however, bounced back when Des Koch's 43-yard punt return set up a touchdown in eight plays from the Irish 31. After Sam Tsagalakis kicked the extra point, Southern California trailed, 13-7. It didn't matter, of course, because the Irish came back with a 68-yard attack to accomplish a 20-7 lead at the intermission.

Notre Dame ripped through the Trojans for three touchdowns in the third period to place the game beyond reach. The Irish then led, 41-14, and the final touchdown possibly was based on a decision to leave the second Irish team in the game for the final quarter.

Southern California had the ball at the start of the last period. When the Trojans threatened with a first down on Notre Dame's 24, the varsity was sent back into action. The Irish regulars stopped this assault and immediately scored in four plays with Lattner making his climactic 50-yard run. Thereafter, Notre Dame was content to defend.

Heap's touchdown dash of 94 yards for the opening score set the pattern and it was the longest Irish run of the year. Earlier in the season, Lattner ran 92 yards against Pennsylvania.

Heap's record run was the product of the Lattner-to-Heap reception pattern on Dandoy's fourth-down punt. Heap kept possession, came full speed down the north sideline and he was in the clear with 35 yards to go. Guglielmi's extra point kick was wide. Notre Dame led, 6-0.

The Irish tallied again on the next time they had the ball. The attack carried from the Irish 39, where Heap was held to a 4-yard gain after a handoff from Lattner on Jim Contratto's punt.

Quick thrusts, with Guglielmi handling the ball, were the weapons. Heap got 4 yards against a six-man line and Lattner, who was then seldom stopped on any play, picked up 5 more. Worden then smashed defensive right tackle for 8 yards.

With a wingback to the right (Lattner), Heap took a Guglielmi lateral after a 4-yard gain to continue 6 yards. It was first down and Worden started the quick line-smashing all over with 3 yards. Heap added 3 on a handoff. Then, Guglielmi threw a hook pass to Penza for first down on the Trojan 14.

Lattner drove for 5 yards over guard. With a delay to look over the Trojan's eight-man line, Guglielmi then sent Lattner around right end with a lateral and he tore through the grasp of Trojan defensive back Bob Buckley to cross the goal line.

U.S.C. defensive end Al Hadock was taken out of the play. Guglielmi then kicked the extra point for Notre Dame's 13-0 lead as the quarter ended.

Notre Dame's second team, with Don Schaefer at quarterback, took over. Schaefer was the punter and he got away a fine kick that was grounded on the Trojan 18 but a penalty for illegal motion required him to punt again. His second kick was taken by Koch who returned the ball 43 yards before Dick Simmons tackled him on the Irish 31.

With this inspiration, the Trojans drove to the Irish goal line in eight plays. On third down, Koch made the touchdown from 5 yards out on a lateral.

Tsagalakis kicked the first of his two points-after-touchdowns. Notre Dame now led, 13-7.

If anyone now believed Southern California could win, the Irish gave a proper answer when they came back 48 yards in four plays to make it 20-7.

Heap returned the kickoff 11 yards. Lattner got 9 yards on a thrust at guard from his right halfback T-formation spot. The same play made first down. With Lattner at right wingback, Worden roared through the line 55 yards and was stopped on the Trojan 2 by Leon Clarke.

Worden was given the touchdown chance and made good on a quick-opener. Guglielmi kicked the extra point.

The bottom dropped out of the game in the third period. Notre Dame's first attack was stopped and U.S.C. had the ball on its 5-yard line where Lattner's punt was downed.

On the first play, Trojan fullback Addison Hawthorne plunged 10 yards. He was met by Guglielmi who ripped the ball from his arms and Paul Matz recovered for the Irish on the Trojan 15.

Lattner hit for 5 yards and then scored with a deep lateral from Guglielmi on which he escaped the right flank defenders. Guglielmi kicked the extra point for the 27-7 advantage.

Southern California got its second and last touchdown with a 64-yard attack with the subsequent kickoff. Dandoy, on a lateral, covered the final 12 yards.

Notre Dame countered. This time Dick Fitzgerald, who was subbing for Heap, started the drive with 8 yards. Worden and Lattner followed and, on the eighth play of the series, the Irish finished a 61-yard assault with Lattner scoring from 2 yards out.

Guglielmi booted the point for the 34-14 score and 11:09 minutes had been played in the third period.

The Trojans now were completely befuddled. After Jack Lee's kickoff, which rolled into the end zone, Crow returned to his 15. Contratto then lost 4 yards trying to pass. On the next play, Dandoy took a pitchout, ran to his left and was cornered. He turned and passed to Contratto in the end zone — a lateral — and Contratto fumbled the ball.

Pat Bisceglia recovered the ball for an Irish touchdown despite argument that the throw was a forward one and thus an incomplete pass. After the point-after kick, the Irish now led, 41-14.

Contratto's fumble, which was recovered by Matz on the Irish 35, set up the last touchdown.

Worden plunged for 9 yards but Guglielmi's surprise pass failed on second down. Guglielmi then carried behind center to midfield.

Lattner then hit through the line, veered to his right and raced down the south sideline avoiding Clarke at the goal line for his fourth touchdown.

40

Notre Dame vs. S.M.U.

DECEMBER 5, 1953

NOTRE DAME, Ind. — Notre Dame scored with its first four scrimmage plays this afternoon. The Irish then added two touchdowns in the second quarter and doubled their points in the third to whip Southern Methodist, 40-14.

This victory, the ninth in an undefeated season which included a tie with Iowa, Notre Dame proved to a crowd of 55,522 and millions of television viewers that it has one of the great offensive football teams in collegiate history. At no time was there a question of the result of this intersectional game.

The Irish continued at the pace set last week in Los Angeles against Southern California when the Trojans were beaten, 48-14. They had power, speed and passing, and were accurately directed and dictated by Notre Dame quarterback Ralph Guglielmi.

Guglielmi may not have been the most important player in the Irish assault, which now has recorded 317 points in 10 games, but the field general, by his acumen as much as physical skill, ordered the attack accurately.

Guglielmi called the game to beat Southern Methodist and he had Johnny Lattner, an all-America back for two years; Neil Worden, a superlative fullback; Joe Heap and Don Schaefer for his ball-carriers.

These stars worked behind a line that consistently outcharged the

Mustangs' varied defensive alignments. It gave each play the maximum of effort. The result of this attack, which included a new mark for effective passing in one game this season — 178 yards for six completions in 12 attempts — was the most one-sided contest in the five played with Southern Methodist. This rivalry started here in 1930 when Notre Dame won, 20-14. Until this afternoon, no game had been decided by more than one touchdown.

The Irish now lead this series, 4-1, and they also recorded the sixth unbeaten campaign under the direction of Frank Leahy.

Leahy's teams since he took charge at his alma mater in 1941, were undefeated in 1941, 1946 to 1949, inclusively, and this season. The present record without loss is 12 games, starting with the 21-3 defeat last season at Michigan State.

At the end of today's game, in which all the seniors on the Irish squad participated, students and other spectators joined in spontaneous praise of Leahy and his staff.

In the principal statistical items, today's game followed the pattern of offense the Irish established when they ran up 37 points against Purdue in the second game of the year. This attack was duplicated under pressure when Notre Dame beat Georgia Tech, 27-24, to end the Yellow Jackets' string of 31 games without defeat.

Last week, the Trojans were stunned by Irish speed and power. Today's game was a carryover without diminution of desire.

Under gray skies, with a 40-degree chill and on a soft, slippery turf, Notre Dame came up with a thrilling finale for a splendid season.

Lattner and Worden each averaged 5 yards for a total of 30 rushes. Lattner carried 16 times; Worden was given the ball 14 times. In all, 11 backs had the unusual total of 73 rushes.

By contrast, Southern Methodist had only 29 rushes and thus had to rely on passing. The Mustangs were limited to four first downs by rushing in their total of 12. They were stopped with 23 yards on the ground and were denied a first down by rushing in the second half.

Worden got three touchdowns today in his farewell performance. In three years his total is 29 touchdowns, an all-time record for Irish football.

Notre Dame started its initial touchdown attack from its 39-yard line where Jerry Norton, a Mustang halfback, had punted out of bounds on fourth down following reception of the opening kickoff.

Norton's kick covered 34 yards.

With Worden as a wingback on the left, Guglielmi ran for two yards. Lattner then took Guglielmi's lateral and raced to his left. As Southern Methodist massed to stop him, he threw to Dan Shannon who took the pass behind Duane Nutt and Norton and was dropped on the Mustang 4-yard line. It was Lattner's second forward pass of record in 10 games.

The Mustangs were offside on the next play. The penalty put the ball on Southern Methodist's 1-yard line and Worden then smashed over right guard against an eight-man line for his first touchdown. Menil Mavriades kicked the extra point for Notre Dame's 7-0 lead after 3 minutes and 10 seconds had been played.

Southern Methodist came back with a drive built around a 27-yard gain by fullback Don Miller on a delay plunge with threat of a quarterback pass. This put the ball on the Irish 36-yard line.

Norton, Nutt and Miller went to the Irish 24. Then Hal O'Brien, a left-handed passer, flipped a running pass to Doyle Nex, his left end, for a first down on the Irish 12. Miller lost 2 yards and Paul Matz replaced Shannon at defensive left end for the Irish.

Nutt gave the ball to Norton and when Lattner missed the tackle, linebacker Ray Lemek made the stop on the Irish 9.

Don McIlhenny replaced Norton and he was thrown down by Heap on the Irish 15. Nutt's incomplete pass to O'Brien ended the series. This was the Mustangs' best drive, despite failure to score.

From this point, Notre Dame had 18 consecutive plays and a first down on Southern Methodist's 4-yard line before faltering under pressure. From the Mustangs' 4, Lattner took a quick handoff for 2 yards but Worden lost the same distance. Lattner, on third down, was stopped without gain by Forrest Gregg. Guglielmi's fourth-down pass missed and S.M.U. took over.

Notre Dame's determined defense broke up the counter attack three plays later. The defense undermined the Mustangs' morale and made certain the victory.

It was a third down play on Notre Dame's 10-yard line with 5 yards required for distance. Nutt intended to pass, but he was rushed by Matz who hit him, and the ball was recovered by Frank Varrichione in the end zone for a touchdown. Mavraides missed the extra point kick, and Notre Dame led, 13-0.

Notre Dame's third touchdown was the product of five plays that covered 68 yards in the second period. From his 32-yard line, where Dick Fitzgerald had been downed on Nutt's punt, Lattner turned right end for 11 yards with a lateral from Guglielmi. Worden busted a seven-man line for 8 yards. Guglielmi then threw to Don Penza who got a pass interference call. It was now first down on the Mustangs' 27. Fitzgerald plunged for 3 yards.

On the next play, Matz went deep downfield. Lattner trailed and cut to his right to take Guglielmi's pass in the end zone for the touchdown. Mavraides' extra point kick established the 20-0 score for the intermission.

Notre Dame, having lost the flip of the coin to start the game, chose to receive to open the second half. From their 39-yard line the Irish traveled 61 yards to the goal line.

Lattner turned right end for 12 yards. Worden's 5-yard plunge was matched by 11 more yards by the burly fullback. Lattner made it first down on the Mustang 22. Fitzgerald swung around left end for 6 yards and then Worden's fumble, on a lateral from the quarterback, was grabbed by Lattner on the Mustangs' 12.

On the fourth and final play of the series, Lattner scored around defensive right end by aid of a perfect block by Worden. Mavraides' extra point sent Notre Dame ahead, 27-0, after 3:43 of the period.

A fumbled lateral to Worden which was recovered by O'Brien of S.M.U. on the Irish 44 was opportunity for the Mustangs' first touchdown. Nutt's first-down pass missed but he then threw to Nix for the touchdown. Ed Berret kicked the extra point.

Notre Dame received the subsequent kickoff and scored in five plays that covered 64 yards. The principal gain was a 42-yard pass on first down by Guglielmi to a fleet-footed Schaefer who was tackled by Miller on the Mustangs' 9.

Worden got the touchdown on the third down play and Mavraides' kick made it 34-7. Almost five minutes remained in the third period.

Two plays after the kickoff, Lemek intercepted Nutt's pass and returned 9 yards to the Mustangs' 35. Guglielmi passed to Shannon for 31 yards. Schaefer plunged for a yard and then Guglielmi handed to Worden who hit left tackle for the score. Art Hunter (Mavraides could not be substituted) tried the extra point kick and missed.

In the last quarter, Southern Methodist tallied a second touchdown against the Irish second team. Sam Stollenwerck set it up with a 41-yard completion to end Alex Litowkin on the Irish 14-yard line. Ray Berry took the touchdown pass in the end zone over the head of Irish defensive back Dick Keller. Stollenwerck kicked the final point of the game.

Afterword

SOUTH BEND, Ind. — Frank Leahy, head football coach of the University of Notre Dame, resigned today.

Acting upon the advice of his doctors, the 45-year-old mentor of the Fighting Irish abruptly ended a coaching career here of eleven years. His Notre Dame teams won eighty-seven games, lost eleven and tied nine. His record as a coach was second only to that of the late Knute Rockne.

Rockne in thirteen seasons at Notre Dame as head football coach produced 105 victories, twelve losses and three ties.

Leahy suffered a severe pancreatic attack during the Notre Dame-Georgia Tech game last Oct. 24. According to his physicians, he never fully recovered.

Today Leahy issued this statement: "The doctors advised me after my experience between the halves of the Georgia Tech game to give up coaching. Before making up my mind, I wanted to get some rest and think over the move very seriously. Notre Dame means more to me than I can ever express, not only because of the opportunities it gave to me as a student and later on as athletic director and coach, but because of all that the university stands for.

"I want to express my deep and lasting gratitude to Father (Theodore M.) Hesburgh, Father (Edward P.) Joyce and Ed Krause, the athletic director, for the very kind consideration they are now showing to me. Among the happiest memories I take away from this coaching position are of their support and the loyalty of all of the assistant coaches, students and alumni over the years.

"It will be my privilege in the days and years to come to do all within my power to assist Notre Dame and try to exemplify her teaching."

Commenting on Leahy's decision to quit, Father Hesburgh, the president of Notre Dame, declared:

"The University of Notre Dame regretfully announces the resignation of Mr. Frank Leahy for reasons of health. Mr. Leahy has rendered valiant service to the University since 1941 as head football coach, and for a while, also as director of athletics. Coach Leahy's record during his eleven-year tenure rivals even that of the immortal Knute Rockne.

"More important, he has distinguished himself as a fine Christian gentleman who represented Notre Dame's ideals to millions of Americans, young and old.

"The University is proud of Coach Leahy and his record. We are grateful for his devoted years of service and will cherish a continuing association with him through the Notre Dame Foundation, which he has volunteered to serve. In recognition of his long and fruitful service, the University is granting scholarships to each of his five sons, so that they, too, may be Notre Dame men like their father.

"We regret the illness that has occasioned his resignation as head football coach, but fully agree with the medical advice that recommends a less strenuous occupation for his future. Together with thousands of our alumni, we wish him every blessing and the enjoyment of the acclaim that is rightfully his as one of the greatest of those who have distinguished themselves in the service of Notre Dame."

University officials gave no hint today as to their choice of a successor to Leahy. His replacement, it was learned here, would be selected from the coaching staff.

Appendix

THE FRANK LEAHY RECORD

BOSTON COLLEGE ERA

1939
(9-2-0)
Captain: Ernie Schwotzer

September	30	W	Lebanon Valley	45-0	H
October	6	W	St. Joseph's	20-6	H
October	12	L	Florida	0-7	H
October	21	W	Temple	19-0	H
October	28	W	St. Anselm's	28-0	H
November	4	W	Auburn	13-7	H
November	11	W	Detroit	20-13	A
November	18	W	Boston University	19-0	H
November	25	W	Kansas State	38-7	H
December	2	W	Holy Cross	14-0	H
				216-40	

COTTON BOWL

| January | 1 | L | Clemson | 3-6 | N |

N — at Dallas

1940
(11-0-0)
Captain: Hank Toczylowski

September	21	W	Centre College	40-0	H
September	28	W	Tulane	27-7	A
October	12	W	Temple	33-20	H
October	19	W	Idaho	60-0	H
October	26	W	St. Anselm's	55-0	H
November	2	W	Manhattan	25-0	H
November	9	W	Boston University	21-0	H
November	16	W	Georgetown	19-18	H
November	23	W	Auburn	33-7	H
November	30	W	Holy Cross	7-0	H
				320-52	

SUGAR BOWL

| January | 1 | W | Tennessee | 19-13 | N |

N — at New Orleans

NOTRE DAME ERA

1941
(8-0-1)
Captain: Paul Lillis

September	27	W	Arizona	38-7	H		19,567
October	4	W	Indiana	19-6	H		34,713
October	11	W	Georgia Tech	20-0	A		28,986
October	18	W	Carnegie Tech	16-0	A		17,208
October	25	W	Illinois	49-14	H		34,896
November	1	T	Army	0-0	YS		75,226
November	8	W	Navy	20-13	N		62,074
November	15	W	Northwestern	7-6	A		46,211
November	22	W	USC	20-18	H		54,967
				189-64			373,848

N — at Baltimore; YS — at Yankee Stadium

1942
(7-2-2)
Captain: George Murphy

September	26	T	Wisconsin	7-7	A		23,243
October	3	L	Georgia Tech	6-13	H		20,545
October	10	W	Stanford	27-0	H		22,374
October	17	W	Iowa Pre-Flight	28-0	H		26,800
October	24	W	Illinois	21-14	A		43,476
October	31	W	Navy	9-0	N1		66,699
November	7	W	Army	13-0	YS		74,946
November	14	L	Michigan	20-32	H		54,379
November	21	W	Northwestern	27-20	H		26,098
November	28	W	USC	13-0	A		94,519
December	5	T	Great Lakes	13-13	N2		19,225
				184-99			472,304

N1 — at Cleveland; N2 — at Soldier Field; YS — at Yankee Stadium

1943
(9-1-0)
Captain: Pat Filley

September	25	W	Pittsburgh	41-0	A		43,437
October	2	W	Georgia Tech	55-13	H		26,497
October	9	W	Michigan	35-12	A		86,408
October	16	W	Wisconsin	50-0	A		16,235
October	23	W	Illinois	47-0	H		24,676
October	30	W	Navy	33-6	N		77,900
November	6	W	Army	26-0	YS		75,121
November	13	W	Northwestern	25-6	A		49,124
November	20	W	Iowa Pre-Flight	14-13	H		39,446
November	27	L	Great Lakes	14-19	A		23,000
				340-69			461,844

N — at Cleveland; YS — at Yankee Stadium

1946
(8-0-1)
Individual Game Captains

September	28	W	.... Illinois	26-6	A	....	75,119
October	5	W	.... Pittsburgh	33-0	H	....	50,350
October	12	W	.... Purdue.................	49-6	H	....	55,452
October	26	W	.... Iowa...................	41-6	A	....	52,311
November	2	W	.... Navy	28-0	N	....	63,909
November	9	T	..... Army..................	0-0	YS	...	74,121
November	16	W	.... Northwestern	27-0	H	....	56,000
November	23	W	.... Tulane	41-0	A	....	65,841
November	30	W	.... USC...................	26-6	H	....	55,298
				271-24			548,401

N — at Baltimore; YS — Yankee Stadium

1947
(9-0-0)
Captain: George Connor

October	4	W	.... Pittsburgh	40-6	A	....	64,333
October	11	W	.... Purdue.................	22-7	A	....	42,000
October	18	W	.... Nebraska..............	31-0	H	....	56,000
October	25	W	.... Iowa...................	21-0	H	....	56,000
November	1	W	.... Navy	27-0	N	....	84,070
November	8	W	.... Army..................	27-7	H	....	59,171
November	15	W	.... Northwestern	26-19	A	....	48,000
November	22	W	.... Tulane	59-6	H	....	57,000
December	6	W	.... USC...................	38-7	A	....	104,953
				291-52			571,527

N — at Cleveland

1948
(9-0-1)
Captain: Bill Fischer

September	25	W	.... Purdue.................	28-27	H	....	59,343
October	2	W	.... Pittsburgh	40-0	A	....	64,000
October	9	W	.... Michigan State	26-7	H	....	58,126
October	16	W	.... Nebraska..............	44-13	A	....	38,000
October	23	W	.... Iowa...................	27-12	A	....	53,000
October	30	W	.... Navy	41-7	N	....	63,314
November	6	W	.... Indiana	42-6	A	....	34,000
November	13	W	.... Northwestern	12-7	H	....	59,305
November	27	W	.... Washington............	46-0	H	....	50,609
December	4	T	..... USC...................	14-14	A	....	100,571
				320-93			580,268

N — at Baltimore

1949
(10-0-0)
Co-Captains: Leon Hart and Jim Martin

September	24	W	Indiana	49-6	H	53,844
October	1	W	Washington	27-7	A	41,500
October	8	W	Purdue	35-12	A	52,000
October	15	W	Tulane	46-7	H	58,196
October	29	W	Navy	40-0	N	62,000
November	5	W	Michigan State	34-21	A	51,277
November	12	W	North Carolina	42-6	YS	67,000
November	19	W	Iowa	28-7	H	56,790
November	26	W	USC	32-0	H	57,214
December	3	W	SMU	27-20	A	75,457
				360-86		575,278

N — at Baltimore; YS — Yankee Stadium

1950
(4-4-1)
Captain: Jerry Groom

September	30	W	North Carolina	14-7	H	56,430
October	7	L	Purdue	14-28	H	56,746
October	14	W	Tulane	13-9	A	73,159
October	21	L	Indiana	7-20	A	34,000
October	28	L	Michigan State	33-36	H	57,866
November	4	W	Navy	19-10	N	71,074
November	11	W	Pittsburgh	18-7	H	56,966
November	18	T	Iowa	14-14	A	52,863
December	2	L	USC	7-9	A	70,177
				139-140		529,281

N — at Cleveland

1951
(7-2-1)
Captain: Jim Mutscheller

September	29	W	Indiana	48-6	H	55,790
October	5	W	Detroit	40-6	N1	52,331
October	13	L	SMU	20-27	H	58,240
October	20	W	Pittsburgh	33-0	A	60,127
October	27	W	Purdue	30-9	H	57,890
November	3	W	Navy	19-0	N2	44,237
November	10	L	Michigan State	0-35	A	51,296
November	17	W	North Carolina	12-7	A	44,500
November	24	T	Iowa	20-20	H	40,685
December	1	W	USC	19-12	A	55,783
				241-122		520,879

N1 — at Briggs Stadium, Detroit; N2 — at Baltimore

1952
(7-2-1)
Captain: Jack Alessandrini

September	27	T	Pennsylvania	7-7	A	74,518
October	4	W	Texas	14-3	A	67,666
October	11	L	Pittsburgh	19-22	H	45,507
October	18	W	Purdue	26-14	A	49,000
October	25	W	North Carolina	34-14	H	54,338
November	1	W	Navy	17-6	N	61,927
November	8	W	Oklahoma	27-21	H	57,446
November	15	L	Michigan State	3-21	A	52,472
November	22	W	Iowa	27-0	A	46,600
November	29	W	USC	9-0	H	58,394
				183-108		567,868

N — at Cleveland

1953
(9-0-1)
Captain: Don Penza

September	26	W	Oklahoma	28-21	A	59,500
October	3	W	Purdue	37-7	A	49,135
October	17	W	Pittsburgh	23-14	H	57,998
October	24	W	Georgia Tech	27-14	H	58,254
October	31	W	Navy	38-7	H	58,154
November	7	W	Pennsylvania	28-20	A	74,711
November	14	W	North Carolina	34-14	A	43,000
November	21	T	Iowa	14-14	H	56,478
November	28	W	USC	48-14	A	97,952
December	5	W	SMU	40-14	H	55,522
				317-139		610,704

THE PLAYERS

Listed below are the players at Boston College and Notre Dame who earned a football monogram during the head-coaching tenure of Frank Leahy.

— A —

Adams, John	1942-43
Agrone, John	1945-46
Ananis, Vito	1939
Angsman, Elmer	1943
Arrix, Bob	1952
Asbaugh, Russell (Pete)	1941-42, 46-47

— B —

Banicki, Fred	1949
Bardash, Virgil	1950-52
Barrett, Billy	1949-51
Barry, Jack	1941
Bartlett, Jim	1949-50
Begley, Gerry	1947-49
Berelos, Hercules	1941
Berezney, Pete	1943
Bertelli, Angelo	1941-43
Bisceglia, Pat	1953
Boji, Byron	1949-51
Bolger, Matt	1941
Boudreau, Walter	1940
Brennan, Jim	1946-47
Brennan, Terry	1946-48
Brock, Tom	1941-42
Brown, Roger	1946-47
Brutz, Jim	1941
Brutz, Marty	1942, 46
Bucci, Don	1951-53
Buczkiewicz, Ted	1947-48
Burns, Paul	1949-51
Bush, Jack	1949-51
Bush, Joe	1951-53
Byrne, James	1939

— C —

Canale, Rocco	1940
Caprara, Joe	1949-50
Carey, Tom	1951-53
Carrabine, Gene	1951-52
Carter, Don	1947
Carter, Tom	1949-50
Cibula, George	1943
Ciechanowicz, Emil	1947-48
Cifelli, Gus	1946-49
Cignetti, Peter	1939
Clatt, Corwin (Cornie)	1942, 46-47
Coleman, Herb	1942-43
Connolly, Harry	1940
Connor, George	1946-47
Connor, John	1948-49
Cook, Ed	1953
Corbette, Ronald	1939-40
Cotter, Dick	1948-50
Coutre, Larry	1946-49
Cowhig, Edward	1939
Cowhig, Gerry	1942, 46
Creevey, John	1942, 46
Creevy, Dick	1941-42
Creevy, Tom	1942
Crimmins, Bernie	1941
Curley, Bob	1943
Currivan, Donald	1940
Cusick, Frank	1942
Cyterski, Len	1951
Czarobski, Zygmont	1942-43, 46-47

— D —

Dailer, Jim	1947-48
Dancewicz, Frank	1943
Daut, John	1949
Davis, Frank	1939-40
Davis, Ray	1943
Dickson, George	1949
Dove, Bob	1941-42
Dubzinski, Walter	1940

— E —

Earley, Bill	1941-42
Earley, Fred	1943, 46-47
Ebli, Ray	1941

Edmonds, Wayne	1953
Emerick, Lou	1950
Epstein, Frank	1950
Espanan, Ray	1946-49
Evans, Fred (Dippy)	1941-42

— F —

Fallon, Jack	1946, 48
Feigel, Chuck	1948-50
Filley, Pat	1941-43
Fisher, Bill	1946-48
Fitzgerald, Dick	1953
Fitzgerald, James	1939
Fiorentino, Albert	1940
Flanagan, Jim	1943
Flood, Dave	1950-52
Flynn, Bill	1948-50
Flynn, Dave	1950
Flynn, Ed	1950
Ford, Gerald	1943
Frampton, John	1947-48
Frasor, Dick	1951-53
Frawley, George	1942

— G —

Gaffney, John	1953
Galardo, Armando	1952-53
Galvani, Frank	1939-40
Gander, Del	1949-51
Ganey, Mike	1943
Gaudreau, Bill	1951
Gaul, Frank	1947-48
Gay, Bill	1947-50
Geoghegan, Terrance	1939-40
George, Don	1953
Gladchuck, Chet	1939-40
Gompers, Bill	1947-48
Goodreault, Gene	1939-40
Griffin, Bill	1939-40
Groom, Jerry	1948-50
Grothaus, Walt	1947-49
Guglielmi, Ralph	1951-54

— H —

Hamby, Jim	1949, 51
Hanlon, Bob	1943
Hargrave, Bob	1941
Harrison, Dick	1939

Hart, Leon	1946-49
Heap, Joe	1951-53
Helwig, John	1948-50
Hendricks, Dick	1953
Heywood, Bill	1946
Higgins, Bill	1948-50
Higgins, Luke	1942
Hines, Mike	1941
Hogan, Don	1941
Holovak, Mike	1940
Huber, Bill	1942
Hudak, Ed	1947-49
Hunter, Art	1951-53

— J —

Jauron, Bob	1939-40
Jeffers, Jack	1947-48
Johnson, Frank (Rodney)	1947-49
Johnson, Murray	1950
Johnston, Frank	1949-50
Jonardi, Ray	1949-50
Joseph, Bob	1951-52
Juzwik, Steve	1941

— K —

Kapish, Bob	1949-51
Kapish, Gene	1953
Katchik, Joe	1951
Keller, Dick	1953
Kelley, Bob	1943
Kelly, Bob	1950-51
Kerr, George	1939-40
Kidhardt, Louis	1939
Kiousis, Marty	1949
Kissell, Adolph	1939-40
Koch, Dave	1949
Kohanowich, Al	1951-52
Kosikowski, Frank	1946-47
Kovatch, John	1941
Krupa, Ed	1942-43
Kudlacz, Stan	1941-42
Kuffel, Ray	1943
Kuh, Dick	1948
Kulbitski, Vic	1943

— L —

Laiber, Joe	1941

Lally, Bob	1947-49
Lanahan, John	1941-42
Landry, Jack	1948-50
Lasch, Bob	1953
Lattner, Johnny	1951-53
LeCluyse, Len	1946-47
Lee, Jack	1951-53
Lemak, Ray	1953
Leonard, Bill	1947
Lesko, Al	1948
Levanitas, Steve	1939-40
Lillis, Paul	1941
Limont, Paul	1942-43, 46
Livingstone, Bob	1942, 46-47
Lucas, Carl	1940
Lucey, David	1939
Lukachik, Alex	1939-40
Lujack, Johnny	1943, 46-47
Lyden, Mike	1943

— M —

Maggioli, Achille (Chick)	1943
Mahon, Tom	1939-40
Mahoney, Jim	1948-49
Mangialardi, Fred	1951-53
Manzo, Joe	1940
Marchand, Gerry	1950
Markowski, Joe	1953
Martell, Gene	1953
Martin, Bob	1952-53
Martin, Jim	1946-49
Mastrangelo, John	1946
Matz, Paul	1951-53
Mavraides, Minil (Minnie)	1951-53
Maznicki, Frank	1939-40
Mazur, John	1949-51
McBride, Bob	1941-42, 46
McCarthy, Charles	1939
McGee, Coy	1946-48
McGehee, Ralph	1946-49
McGinnis, John	1942
McGowan, Justin	1939-40
McGurk, Jim	1946
McHugh, Tom	1951-53
McKillip, Leo	1948-50
McLaughlin, Dave	1941

McMullan, John	1953
McNeill, Chuck	1941
McNichols, Austin	1946
Mello, Jim	1942-43, 46
Mense, Jim	1953
Meschievitz, Vince	1950
Meter, Bernie (Bud)	1942-43, 46
Michaels, Bill	1947
Miezkowski, Ed	1943
Miller, Creighton	1941-43
Miller, Tom	1941-42
Modak, Dan	1949-50
Montgomery, Lou	1939-40
Moran, Tom	1940
Morrissey, Rockne	1952-53
Morro, Alfred	1939-40
Murphy, George	1941-42
Murphy, Tom	1950-52
Mutscheller, Jim	1949-51

— N —

Nash, Ralph	1940
Naumetz, Fred	1940
Neff, Bob	1941-42
Nemeth, Steve	1943
Nicula, George	1953
Nowack, Art	1953

— O —

O'Brien, Dick	1941
O'Neil, Bob	1951-52
Oracko, Steve	1947-49
O'Rourke, Charlie	1939-40
Ostrowski, Chet	1949-51

— P —

Palumbo, Sam	1951-53
Pannelli, John	1946-48
Paolone, Ralph	1950
Pasink, Adolph	1939-40
Pasquesi, Tony	1952-53
Paterra, Frank	1951-52
Patten, Paul	1941
Peasenelli, John	1942
Penza, Don	1951-53
Perko, John	1943
Perry, Art	1949-50
Petitbon, John	1949-51

Piccone, Cammille (Pic)	1942
Poehler, Fred	1951-52
Powers, Thomas	1939-40
Prokop, Joe	1941

— R —

Raich, Nick	1953
Ratterman, George	1946
Ready, Bob	1951-53
Rellas, Chris	1943
Renaud, Charles	1943
Repko, Joseph	1940
Reynolds, Paul	1951-52
Rigali, Bob	1952-53
Robst, Paul	1951, 53
Rovai, Fred	1946
Ruggerio, Frank	1943
Russell, Bill	1946
Ryan, George	1939
Rykovich, Julie	1943
Rymkus, Lou	1941-42

— S —

Saggau, Tom	1948
Schaefer, Don	1953
Schrader, Jim	1951-53
Schwotzer, Ernie	1939
Scott, Vince	1946
Shannon, Dan	1951-53
Signaigo, Joe	1943, 46-47
Simmons, Floyd	1946-47
Sitko, Emil	1946-49
Skall, Russell	1947
Skat, Al	1943
Skoglund, Bob	1946
Slovak, Emil	1946
Smith, Gene	1948-50
Smith, Lancaster	1946-48
Snyder, Jim	1943
Spaniel, Frank	1947-49
Statuto, Art	1943, 46-47
Stephens, Jack	1952
Strohmeyer, George	1946-47
Stroud, Clarke	1950
Strumski, Leo	1939-40
Sullivan, George	1943, 46-47
Sullivan, Larry	1941-42
Swenson, Ed	1939

Swistowicz, Mike	1946-49
Szymanski, Dick	1951-53
Szymanski, Frank	1943

— T —

Tassinan, Anthony	1939-40
Taylor, Bob	1951-53
Terlap, George	1943
Tharp, Jim	1943
Thomas, Deane	1948
Tobin, George	1942, 46
Todorovich, Mike	1943
Toczlowski, Hank	1939-40
Toneff, Bob	1949-51
Tripuka, Frank	1946-48
Trumper, Ed	1943

— U —

Urban, Gasper	1943, 46-47

— V —

Vangen, Willard	1946
Varrichione, Frank	1951-53

— W —

Waldron, Ronayne	1943
Wallner, Fred	1948-50
Walsh, Bill	1946-48
Walsh, Bob	1941
Walsh, Bob	1946
Warner, Jack	1941
Washington, Dick	1953
Waybright, Doug	1947-49
Weithman, Jim	1950-52
Wendell, Marty	1946-48
Whelan, Ed	1950
Whelan, Jack	1951-52
White, David	1939-40
White, Jim	1942-43
Whiteside, Bill	1949-50
Wightkin, Bill	1946-49
Williams, Bob	1948-50
Williams, Theodore	1940
Wilson, George	1953
Worden, Neil	1951-53
Woronicz, Henry	1940
Wright, Harry	1941-42

— Y —

Yauchoes, John	1939-40
Yonakor, John	1942-43
Yonto, Joe	1943

— Z —

Zabrski, Ed	1939-40
Zabrski, Joe	1939-40
Zajeski, Ben	1953
Zalejski, Ernie	1946-49
Zambroski, Tony	1949-51
Zancha, John	1949-50
Ziemba, Wally	1941-42
Zilly, Jack	1943, 46
Zmijewski, Al	1946-49

LEAHY'S ALL-AMERICANS

Listed below are the football players at Boston College and Notre Dame who earned first-team all-America status during the head-coaching tenure of Frank Leahy.

Player	Year(s) Selected
Gene Goodreault	1939-40
Chet Gladchuck	1940
George Kerr	1940
Charlie O'Rourke	1940
Hank Toczylowski	1940
Bernie Crimmins	1941
Bob Dove	1941-42
Angelo Bertelli	1942-43
Pat Filley	1943
Creighton Miller	1943
Jim White	1943
John Yonakor	1943
George Connor	1946-47
Johnny Lujack	1946-47
John Mastrangelo	1946
George Strohmeyer	1946
Ziggy Czarobski	1947
Bill Fischer	1947-48
Leon Hart	1947-49
Emil Sitko	1948-49
Marty Wendell	1948
Jim Martin	1949
Bob Williams	1949-50
Jerry Groom	1950
Bob Toneff	1951
Johnny Lattner	1952-53
Art Hunter	1953

LEAHY'S ASSISTANT COACHES

Listed below are the individuals who served as assistant football coaches at Boston College and Notre Dame during the head-coaching tenure of Frank Leahy.

Name	School	Tenure
Terry Brennan	Notre Dame	1953
Marty Brill	Notre Dame	1946
Bill Cerney	Notre Dame	1941
Bernie Crimmins	Notre Dame	1946-51
Hugh Devore	Notre Dame	1942-43
John Druze	Boston College	1939-40
	Notre Dame	1941, 46-53
Ted Galligan	Boston College	1939
Bill Earley	Notre Dame	1946-53
Jake Kline	Notre Dame	1943
Ed "Moose" Krause	Notre Dame	1942-43, 46-47
Johnny Lujack	Notre Dame	1952-53
Joe McArdle	Boston College	1939-40
	Notre Dame	1941, 46-53
Bob McBride	Notre Dame	1949-53
Ed McKeever	Boston College	1939-40
	Notre Dame	1941-43
Fred Miller	Notre Dame	1948-53
Wayne Millner	Notre Dame	1942
Bob Snyder	Notre Dame	1942
Wally Ziemba	Notre Dame	1943, 46-53

TOP 20 FINISHES

Listed below are the Associated Press final Top 20 rankings for Frank Leahy's teams at Boston College and Notre Dame.

Season	School	Record	Final Ranking
1939	Boston College	9-2-0	11th
1940	Boston College	11-0-0	5th
1941	Notre Dame	8-0-1	3rd
1942	Notre Dame	7-2-2	6th
1943	Notre Dame	9-1-0	1st
1946	Notre Dame	8-0-1	1st
1947	Notre Dame	9-0-0	1st
1948	Notre Dame	9-0-1	2nd
1949	Notre Dame	10-0-0	1st
1950	Notre Dame	4-4-1	None
1951	Notre Dame	7-2-1	None
1952	Notre Dame	7-2-1	3rd
1953	Notre Dame	9-0-1	2nd*

* In 1953, Maryland received the A.P. and U.P.I. number one ranking while Notre Dame was ranked number one in all other polls.

About the Editor

Mike Bynum is one of the South's most successful young authors. He is the author of eight previous books which are all based on football, including the highly successful *Bear Bryant's Boys of Autumn* and *Knute Rockne: His Life and Legend,* and the recently published *Vince Lombardi: Memories of a Special Time.* Adding to his list of credits, Mike served as consulting producer to the Mizlou TV special *Bear Bryant — Countdown to 315* which was produced for N.B.C.

A former student manager for Coach Bryant's Crimson Tide football team and honor student at The University of Alabama, Mike is completing a series of biographies on football's greatest coaches. Afterwards, he will be attending law school.